Contents

Norfolk Beers from English Barley A History of Steward & Patteson, 1793-1963

by

Terry Gourvish

Research by

Pam Barnes

Centre of East Anglian Studies
University of East Anglia, Norwich

British Library Cataloguing in Publication Data

Gourvish, T.R.
Norfolk beers from English barley : a history of Steward & Patteson, 1793–1963.
1. Steward & Patteson — History
2. Norwich (Norfolk) — Industries —
History
I. Title
338.7′6633′0942615 HD9397.G74S/

ISBN 0-906219-22-1

Front cover: Advertising placard of the 1930's
(Norfolk Museums Service [Bridewell Museum Norwich])

Centre of East Anglian Studies
University of East Anglia
Norwich NR4 7TJ

List of illustrations

List of figures and maps

page

Figures

Map

List of tables

Foreword

by Sir Jeremy Morse

From my childhood I heard my family talk about 'the Brewery'. When the War came, and we went to live with my grandmother on the edge of Norwich, my vague picture of it was exchanged for the reality. I went down to Pockthorpe, smelt the smell of the hops, got to know its people and buildings, and came home with long lists of pubs.

From my father and my uncle I learnt some of the history. At the end of the eighteenth century John Morse, one of our forebears, had bought a small brewery which was soon merged with another called Steward & Patteson. From these modest beginnings, the business spread in widening circles from Norwich to Norfolk to East Anglia. When it was eventually taken over by Watney Mann in 1963, it had occupied six generations of male Morses and sustained a much wider family circle.

But it is not just family feeling that has prompted the commissioning of this book. At the suggestion of Mr Michael Falcon I approached the Centre of East Anglian Studies at the University of East Anglia, and they put me in touch with Dr Terry Gourvish. Together we agreed that what he would write would be primarily a history of the business - but relating it to the local and regional scene, to the British brewing industry as a whole, and to so much of the family history as was relevant to it. All these strands he has skilfully woven together at readable length. If you leaf through the illustrations, you will find directors and draymen, breweries and pubs, barrels and bottles, horses and wherries and lorries. The text fills this out with the human stories and business figures which show that 'S and P' was always important on the regional scale, and occasionally so on the national scale.

Unlike most business histories, which are produced to mark some anniversary in a continuing existence and so suffer (to my mind) from the fact that neither the author nor the readers know how it will end, in this case the story is complete. There is no more brewing at Pockthorpe, and the buildings have been converted to other uses. Sad though it was to see the end of Steward and Patteson after 170 years of thriving existence, I hope and believe that readers will enjoy the history of an East Anglian business which those connected with it remember with pride and affection.

Preface

In 1979 Sir Jeremy Morse, son of the last chairman of Steward & Patteson, asked me to write a business history of this once leading firm of East Anglian brewers, before 'S & P' became too dim a memory. I readily agreed, although other obligations prevented me from completing the text until the summer of 1986. I should like to express my thanks to Sir Jeremy for his patience and encouragement. He generously provided funds to support the research work on which the history is based, and offered pertinent comments on successive draft chapters. I was lucky to find in Dr Pam Barnes the ideal research assistant; someone who carried out her work with considerable skill and care, and undertook even the most routine tasks with enthusiasm. Dr Richard Wilson provided an academic stimulus which was greatly appreciated. He not only offered me the benefits of his own experience as Greene King's commissioned historian, but also read the entire manuscript in draft and rescued it from a number of errors and inconsistencies. On top of this, as acting Director of the Centre of East Anglian Studies in 1986–7 he organised the publication of the book. I also benefited from conversations with the late Brigadier J.R.T. Aldous, author of a family history of the Morses; Dr Roger Ryan, who gave me the benefit of his researches into the Norwich Union and the Pattesons; Michael Riviere and the late Donald Steward, former directors of Steward & Patteson; and John Strickland, the former brewer, who unearthed a copy of the Yarmouth 'Punishment Book' quoted in Chapter Five. I owe a particular debt to Michael Ripley, Senior Public Relations Officer of the Brewers' Society, who was extremely helpful with queries about breweries and the brewing process and arranged access to the Society's invaluable library, with its fine collection of brewing journals. Jane Fiske kindly passed on some of the results of her work on the diaries of James Oakes. Finally, valuable comments emerged from a business history seminar held at the University of East Anglia in September 1984 which considered, *inter alia,* a paper on brewing profitability, written jointly with Richard Wilson and subsequently published in *Business History* in July 1985.

The main source material for the history was the collection of brewing papers of Watney Mann's predecessor companies, deposited in the Norfolk Record Office. I should like to thank the archivist, Jean

Kennedy, and the Record Office staff for their assistance. These papers were usefully supplemented by photographs and miscellaneous documents which were gathered together by the late John Stokes, former managing director of Watney Southern, with the aim of assisting the writing of a history. The staff of the Colman & Rye Library in Norwich were extremely helpful in guiding me on matters of local history. Photographs from the Library are reproduced by courtesy of Norfolk County Library. I should also like to express my thanks to David Jones of the Bridewell Museum; Sheree Thurston of the Norwich Union; the Audio Visual Centre of the University of East Anglia; and David Mew, of the School of Environmental Sciences at UEA, who drew the map. The book would not have reached the publication stage without the help of Dr Hassall Smith, Director of the Centre of East Anglian Studies; Jill Baker, who supervised the production stages in the Centre; Mavis Bithray, who put the text onto computer disc; Judy Sparks, who typed many of the tables; Jean Barriskill, who typed the pedigrees; Professor James McFarlane, who advised on the programming; and Richard Malt, who designed the cover and advised on illustrations. The staff of the Printing Unit at the University, and in particular, Richard Johnson, Les Wallace and Evelyn Mould, put the raw materials together. I am indebted to them all.

Steward & Patteson had a life of almost two centuries. As is true of many firms, the surviving records are patchy, and there is very little for the years prior to 1880. This must inevitably be reflected in the book. However, I have tried to provide an accurate record, without undue conjecture or invention, as the materials allow. My main intention was to write a *business* history. The focus is thus upon the brewery as an enterprise, and there is more about production and financial returns, for example, than about pub life and family exploits. The book is not intended to be an anecdotal account of 'beer and skittles' in the Richard Boston tradition. Nor does it have any pretence to being a substantial piece of academic writing. It tells the story of one firm, though there are references where appropriate to the regional and national contexts. It is a tale of a business competently run, which not only traded successfully from Georgian to neo-Elizabethan times but also established a reputation for quality and social responsibility.

T.R.G.
Norwich
February 1987

1

Origins: The Pattesons

The emergence of Steward & Patteson of Norwich as a major East Anglian brewery is in essence the history of four prominent families - the Pattesons, Stewards, Morses, and Finches. All were active in the business and political life of the region, and all brought important brewing interests into the expanded company that had been established by the late 1830's. But the origins of the concern are located in relatively modest circumstances. In 1793 Charles Greeves sold his small brewery in Pockthorpe, Norwich, to John Patteson (II), marking the entry of the Patteson family into the industry.[1]

John Patteson II (1755-1833)

John Patteson II was the son of Henry Sparke Patteson (III), a Norwich ironmonger, and Martha Fromanteel, daughter of an attorney and mayor of Norwich.[2] Little is known of his father, but he appears to have been one of the less successful in a family of ironmongers, merchants, and bankers which came to Norwich from Birmingham in the first half of the eighteenth century and quickly established itself as a member of the city's Anglican Tory elite.[3] His death in 1764, when John was only nine years old, was a calamity which was to prove fortuitous. John went to live in the imposing Surrey Street mansion of his uncle, John Patteson I (1727-74), a successful wool-stapler and partner in the firm of Patteson & Iselin (John Iselin was a Swiss from Basle). John I, mayor of Norwich in 1766, was clearly one of the city's leading merchants. Under his tutelage, John II was educated, first at Greenwich, by the Revd Dr Burney, and then in Leipzig (1768-71), where he received a thorough grounding in the woollen export trade and made contact with his uncle's clients. This early experience was soon put to good use. In 1774, at the age of nineteen, John inherited his uncle's business interests, together with estates at Colney and Bawburgh, and the house in Surrey Street. These resources were augmented by his marriage in 1781 to Elizabeth, daughter of the well-to-do Robert Staniforth of Manchester.[4] Patteson participated fully in the business, political, and social life of the city. As a Tory he served on the Norwich Corporation for fifty years (1781-1831), and was mayor in 1788. For a brief period he also sat in the House of Commons, representing Minehead (1802-6) and Norwich (1806-12). His reputation as a paternalist and disciplinarian seems to have been deserved. In 1797, when the threat of a French invasion was cause for anxiety in Norwich, he was instrumental in the creation of a local militia, which he subsequently commanded as Lieutenant-Colonel. In the following year he opened a subscription fund to aid the government, putting up £200 himself, and inducing his brewery employees to subscribe £42.[5] However, it was his taste for lavish entertaining that took the eye. This had been cultivated at an early age by visits to London and Bath, and a tour of Europe in 1778-9.[6] When Prince William Frederick, later the 2nd Duke of Gloucester, came to Norwich in 1797 to take command of the troops of the Eastern District, Patteson organised the civic welcome, which included a tour of his brewery.[7] The visit was followed by others. In 1801, for example, the Prince stayed with Patteson in Surrey Street, acting as a witness at the baptism of William Frederick, one of his sons.[8] Such an expensive social life, conducted at a time when the fortunes of the Norwich textile industry were declining in favour of the challenge of Yorkshire cloth, placed an undoubted strain on the family's financial resources.

At the same time Patteson began to take an active interest in brewing. The diary of one of his friends, James Oakes, the Bury St Edmunds yarn dealer, suggests that he was connected with Greeves's brewery as a partner in 1792. When Greeves decided to retire early in 1793 Patteson tried to persuade Oakes to join the firm as a partner. When this offer was rejected - Oakes went into banking instead - Patteson took over the business alone, with the aim of finding a future occupation for his eldest son, John Staniforth Patteson (1782-1832).[9] He also began to acquire public houses. The early evidence is very far from complete, but we do know that he had inherited the 'Black Horse' in St Gregory's which had been bought by his father in 1760, and he leased a public house in St Stephen's Road in October 1792, almost a year before the acquisition of Greeves.[10] The Greeves brewery was a small one. In the year ending 5 July 1793 it brewed only 1,519 barrels (barrel = 36 gallons), under 3 per cent of the total production recorded by Norwich's eight common brewers.[11] However, Patteson's entry into brewing was no half-hearted affair. He soon went on to buy two more breweries in Norwich, that of James Beevor, together with public

1. John Patteson II (1755–1833), founder of the brewery [*Castle Museum, Norwich*]

houses and two malthouses, in 1794, and the business of Jehosophat Postle, in 1795. Both had been brewing for at least a decade, and were producing over twice as much beer as Greeves in the early 1790's. Together, the three concerns brewed 9,166 barrels in 1792-3, about 15 per cent of recorded production.[12] This suggests that Patteson took over a capacity to supply about ninety public houses, a fairly substantial business for a provincial concern.[13] In addition, his interests were extended to embrace Yarmouth. In 1793 or 1794 he bought William and James Fisher's North Quay brewery. The premises, which had once belonged to William Browne, were sizeable. The rate assessment for July 1795 was £50 for the brew-house, £70 for four malthouses, £26 10*s*. [£26.50] for eight storehouses, £15 for two warehouses, £2 for a cellar, £3 for cinder-ovens, and £10 for stock valued at £200 (indicating stock of about £5,000). With a total of £176 10*s*., the assessment was second only to Lacon's in the town. Seventeen public houses were also included in the sale, with an average rateable value of £6 16*s*. 5*d*. [£6.82].[14] Patteson was first in partnership with a Mr Thompson, but in 1798 he offered a half-share to William Gould, Oakes's son-in-law, and a new partnership was drawn up.[15]

Whatever the overall size of Patteson's brewing investment, there is no doubt that the diversification it represented made sound sense to a man whose consumption was increasing while at the same time his major source of income - textiles - was becoming more uncertain. Brewing was not without its problems in the French War period, of course. Raw material costs rose sharply, and there were substantial increases in taxation. However, it was to prove a more stable investment than Patteson's other, non-textile interests, banking and insurance. Nevertheless, brewery profits were not sufficient to ward off Patteson's financial difficulties, which came to a head in the post-war slump of 1817-18. The precise facts are uncertain, but his biographer refers to 'large and unsuccessful English and foreign ventures' in textiles and the failure of a London bank. It is clear that he was forced to part with substantial assets in the course of 1818 and 1819. These included the estates at Colney and Bawburgh, the house in Surrey Street, which was sold to the Norwich Union Life Society, and over 200 paintings, which realised £2,349 at Christie's.[16] Here, the family's connection with the Norwich Union seems to have been a crucial element in its survival. Both Patteson and his son John Staniforth had been directors of the Life Society since its foundation in 1808. In 1818 the Fire Office, founded in 1797, experienced heavy losses, and the autocratic management of Thomas Bignold was called into question. Patteson agreed to act as mediator in the dispute which followed, and as president of both societies helped to oust Bignold in favour of his three sons, Samuel, John Cocksedge and Thomas, who took over the management under the supervision of a Committee of six directors. Patteson's reward was a large, face-saving loan. The exact figure is not known, but as much as £27,819 was outstanding on his death in 1833.[17]

The events of 1817-19 had an important bearing upon the future organisation of the brewery. Patteson, while retaining the presidency of the Norwich Union Life Society, withdrew from business and his interests, including the brewery, were taken over by his son, John Staniforth. More than this, however, the business was transformed by the introduction in 1820 of four members of the Steward family of Yarmouth as partners. Trading as 'Steward, Patteson & Stewards', the brewery was no longer an exclusive preserve of the Patteson family.

John Staniforth Patteson (1782-1832)

John Staniforth Patteson was closely associated with his father's business interests from an early age. Educated at Ipswich Grammar School and Trinity College Cambridge, he appears to have taken an active interest in the brewery when his father became an M.P. Unfortunately, no detailed information about his work in the business has survived. He did live quite close to the Pockthorpe site, however, in a house in Magdalen Street which had been sold to his father with Beevor's brewery. Moreover, his marriage in 1808 to Anne Elizabeth, daughter of William Tasker, a Rotterdam merchant, provided an additional connection with the industry. In the same year Anne's sister, Hannah, married George Morse, who had just entered his father's brewery, also in Norwich. This link was to be of considerable significance in the growth of Steward & Patteson, since the two families joined forces in 1831 and a new brewery partnership was made (see Chapter 2).[18] While less flamboyant than his father, John Staniforth was no less effective a figure in Norwich's economic elite. Indeed, it is quite easy to confuse father and son. Both were founder-directors of the Norwich Union Life Society in 1808 and went on to join the Fire Society Board, in 1818 and 1821 respectively. Both were active in local politics and the militia. John Staniforth acted as Sheriff in 1811, Mayor in 1823, and, like his father, commanded a Norwich regiment. There is no evidence to suggest that he was personally affected by his father's financial problems after 1817. He became a director of the Fire Society after its merger with the Norwich General Fire Assurance Company in 1821, which indicates that his own position was sound (this was a pre-requisite for membership of the reformed board).[19] Growing wealth from the 1820's is also suggested by a move of house, first to 31, King Street in 1824, and then to Cringleford, outside Norwich, in 1831. He died in 1832, a year before his father. The Patteson interest in the brewery now rested, less certainly perhaps, in the hands of his executors. His fourth son, Henry Staniforth, was aged sixteen, and prevented from participating as a partner until 1840. But by this time, of course, the concern had been transformed by a process of merger and growth.

2

Brewing in Norwich, 1793-1837

Patteson's Brewery, 1793-1820

Under John Patteson's guidance, the production of beer in the Barrack Street brewery, Pockthorpe soon expanded rapidly. In the first full year of operations, 1794-5, 7,277 barrels of strong beer were brewed, which suggests a total production of about 9,000 barrels, matching the combined total of Patteson's predecessors, Greeves, Beevor, and Postle. Five years later, production had almost trebled. Strong beer production had risen to over 20,000 barrels, and with table and small beer the brewery must have turned out over 26,000 barrels (Table 1). The growth of Patteson's business appears to have been achieved at the expense of the town's leading brewers. There is no evidence of a substantial rise in regional demand in the 1790's, and the output of the common brewers remained at a level of 60,000 barrels (50,000 of strong beer). On the other hand, two of the large firms, Tompson's and Weston's, who had popularised the local 'Norwich Nog', together lost 6,000 barrels in strong beer production between 1795 and 1800. Consequently, Patteson's 'market share' rose from under 20 per cent in 1795 to over 40 per cent in 1800. Expanding production was accompanied by the acquisition of public houses. When John Day, a prominent brewer and woolfactor, died in 1794, Patteson bought his pubs at

TABLE 1

The Strong Beer Production of Norwich Common Brewers (in Barrels), 1794–1800

Year ending 5 July	*John Patteson*	*S & T Tompson*	*Peter Finch*	*John Morse*	*Charles Weston*	*Daniel Ganning (ex-John Day)*	*William Latten*
1795	7,277	12,851	8,353	-	7,188	7,341	206
1797	16,139*	12,176	8,856	-	7,696	8,011	230
1800	20,019	8,830	7,610	6,843	5,530	-	-

Source: Norfolk Chronicle, 1795–1800, and see Appendix D, Table 1.

* Patteson's total production (with table and small beer) = 21,689 barrels.

Bawdeswell, Cawston, East Tuddenham, and Hoveton, at prices ranging from £220 to £500 each.[1] The transactions also suggest that Patteson was able to supply houses within a radius of fifteen miles from Norwich, despite the inadequacies of transport before the railway.

Patteson's Pockthorpe brewery was undoubtedly a large provincial concern as early as 1800. Its output, while small in comparison with the large-scale production of the London porter brewers, was five times the average for England and Wales. Furthermore, a considerable capital investment is indicated. If we accept contemporary estimates that about £7-£10 a barrel was invested in country brewing, including public houses, a rough estimate of at least £140,000 may be derived.[2] The number of public houses supplied in 1800 is not known, but it is not extravagant to suggest that this may have been 180. Unfortunately, detailed information on the brewery's activities has not survived, an all too common feature of businesses of this date. Production methods, materials used, prices, costs, and profits must remain a matter of conjecture. However, an 1820 plan of the brewery shows that a steam engine house had been erected alongside the horse mill adjacent to the brewhouse. We may also safely assume that Patteson's used local malt, and produced a range of beers, from the young, light beer to the longer-life, vatted 'Nog'. Some porter was also brewed, although sales were restricted by the successful penetration of the Norfolk market by London brewers shipping via Yarmouth and the river Yare. In the 1790's, for example, Whitbread's alone sent 5,000 barrels a year to Thomas Hubbard of Yarmouth, and a further 3,000 barrels to Samuel Smith of Norwich.[3]

The first two decades of the nineteenth century proved to be an extremely challenging time for the British brewing industry. The period began with a sharp increase in the levels of taxation, justified by the continuation of the war against the French. The duty on hops was raised from 15*s.* to 23*s.* 4*d.* a cwt. in 1801, that on strong beer from 8*s.* to 10*s.* a barrel in 1802, and the malt duty increased from 1*s.* 4¼*d.* a bushel to 2*s.* 5*d.* in 1802 and 4*s.* 5¾*d.* in 1804 [Hops: 75p to £1.17; beer: 40p to 50p; Malt: 6.8p to 12.1p and 22.4p]. Thus, in the period 1804-16 the duties on these items were, on average, 30, 25, and 320 per cent higher than before 1801. There was also a considerable increase in raw material costs. The price of Norfolk pale malt, for example, about 44*s.* [£2.20] a quarter in the late 1790's, averaged 81*s.* 6*d.* [£4.08] in 1804-16.[4] The effects of rising costs on local breweries are difficult to assess with the meagre evidence at our disposal. However, we can be confident

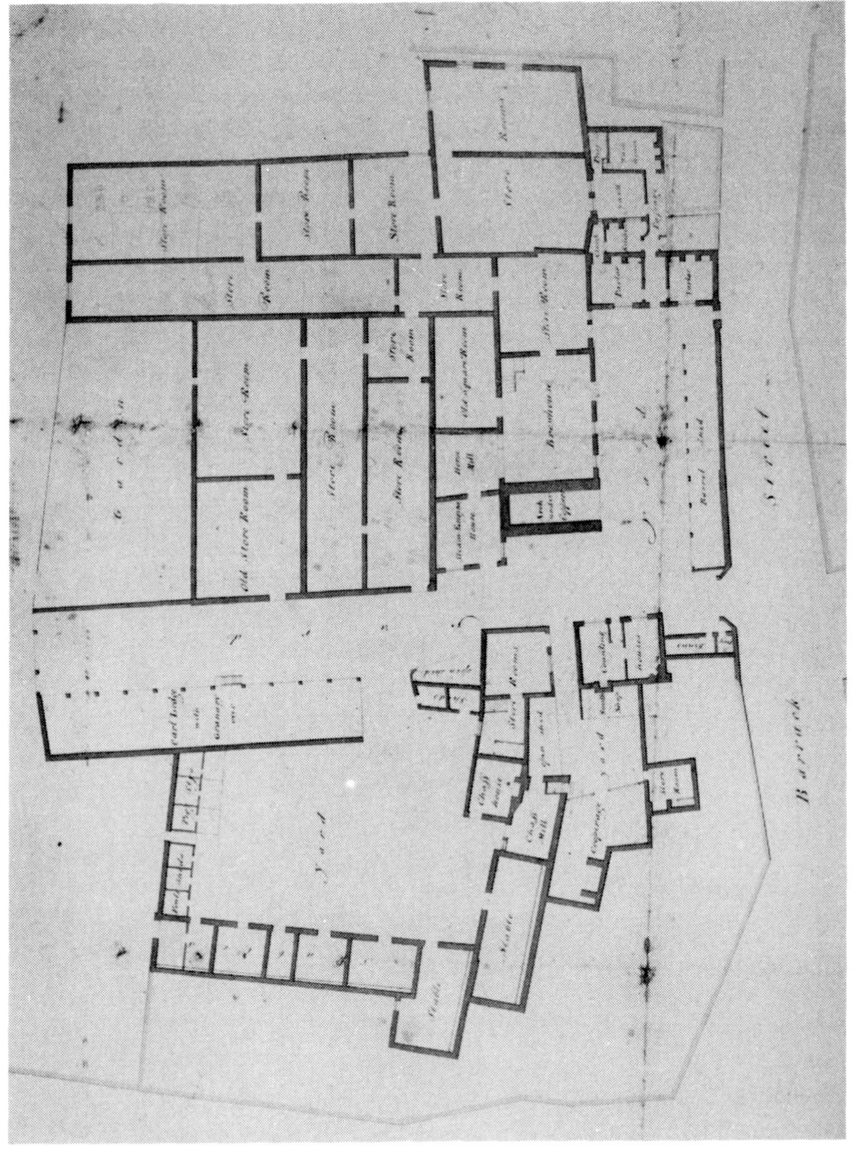

2. Plan of Pockthorpe Brewery, 1820 [*Norfolk Record Office*]

that the common brewers raised the price of their beers. In London the price of porter (charged to publicans) was 55 per cent higher in 1804-16 than before 1799,[5] and it is likely that Norfolk prices rose in like manner. There may also have been some moves to reduce costs by adulteration, although such actions were usually carried out in the public house rather than in the brewery. On the other hand, two factors helped to maintain the demand for the beer produced by common brewers. First, the decade 1811-21 saw a substantial growth in population. In Norfolk there was an increase of 18 per cent, much higher than in the preceding and succeeding decades, while in Norwich the population rose by 35 per cent to reach 50,000 in 1821. Second, there seems little doubt that the smaller-scale producers - the victuallers (brewing publicans) and home-brewers - suffered most from the escalation in costs. This tilting of the balance in favour of common brewing helped concerns such as Patteson's to maintain production in the face of rising prices.

In the absence of business records, it is difficult to measure Patteson's progress with certainty. However, the increase in duties in 1801-4 does appear to have contributed to problems with the Yarmouth business. Profits fell, and the brewery, together with its malthouses and pubs, were sold to Paget & Co. (the partners were Samuel Paget, James Adcock, and Dawson Turner) in 1804.[6] In Norwich, the situation seems to have been better. Patteson continued to tie pubs to the Pockthorpe brewery. For example, he acquired the freeholds of the 'Whip & Egg', Coslany, the 'White Lion' in Drayton, and the 'Briton's Arms', Elm Hill, Norwich in the years 1807-14, while his son bought 'The Shuttles' for £360 in 1811.[7] Outlets were also obtained on lease - the 'Jolly Maltsters' in King Street was tied in this way in 1800[8] - although this course of action was not, it seems, pursued with vigour. For Patteson's, as for other leading local brewers, such as Sir Edmund Lacon, of Yarmouth, freehold acquisition was much preferred to leasehold, a strategy which contrasted with the situation in London.[9]

With some rationalisation of their interests, the Pattesons weathered the storms of the French War period. This was scarcely surprising. Men with an acknowledged experience of trade and finance throughout East Anglia and an ability to organise men and materials should have made a comfortable living in an industry where an emphasis on the quality of raw materials, hygienic production in the brewery and a good tied house trade were the essential elements of success.[10]

Steward, Patteson & Stewards, 1820-31

In 1820, following serious financial pressures on the Patteson family, and the enforced retirement from business life of John Patteson, the brewing business was reconstituted as a co-partnership. There were five partners: John Staniforth Patteson; William Steward of Yarmouth; his brothers Ambrose Harbord Steward and Timothy Steward the elder; and the latter's son, Timothy Steward, the younger. The Stewards were a family of Yarmouth privateers and merchants. They can be traced to Nicholas Steward of Wells-next-the-Sea (died c.1520), and Timothy Steward I (1696-1769), who left Wells to settle in Yarmouth. He married Hannah, only child of Christopher Harbord, and through her inherited property in the town. Their only son, Timothy II (1733-93), was a successful privateer. His prizes included the captured Swedish vessel, the *Sophia*, acquired in 1781. He also married advantageously, gaining property through his wife, Mary, the only child of Ambrose Palmer (the eldest son of William Palmer, landowner, who died in 1771). There were three sons, William, Timothy (III), and Ambrose Harbord.[11] All were successful as merchants and enjoyed the prosperity that came to Yarmouth as a naval base during the French Wars.[12]

William Steward (1760-1841) was first and foremost a merchant, but from the turn of the century built up an extensive investment in brewing and public houses which by 1830 extended over the whole of East Anglia and as far as Kent.[13] A captain in the Yarmouth militia during the wars, he also helped to establish the town's hospital in 1838. Timothy the elder (III) (1762-1836) combined the occupations of merchant and shipowner. The Yarmouth Rate-Books give a rough indication of the standing of the Stewards. In 1790 both William and Timothy had stock valued at £50 (i.e. worth about £1,250): William owned a house rated at £10 and Timothy one rated at £8. By 1801, their houses were rated at £20 each, their stock at £100 (indicating stock worth about £2,500) each, and they were in occupation of three warehouses.[14] At the time of the brewery partnership, William had ceased to be active as a merchant: the Rate-Book for October 1820 shows him without either stock or warehouses. Timothy, on the other hand, continued to own a warehouse and a counting-house, and to hold stock valued at £100.[15] The third brother, Ambrose Harbord Steward (1770-1837), was the most successful as a Yarmouth merchant. Acting as a 'prize agent' in the Wars, he also profited greatly from naval contracts. His services to the fleet blockading the Texel won the admiration of Nelson, and this was no doubt reflected in the financial rewards obtained.[16] The scale of Ambrose's activities may, once again, be estimated by reference to the Rate-Books. In July 1800, for example, he was renting no less than twenty-five properties in the town, including six warehouses, four granaries, four fish curing-houses, three malthouses, and two storehouses, and his stock was valued at £100 (£2,500). His total rate liability amounted to £175 10*s*. The assessment for April 1801 shows him in occupation of twenty-one properties, at a cost (in rates) of £151 5*s*.[17] He certainly did well enough to retire to the country. Moving to Stoke Park, near Ipswich, he acted as High Sheriff of Suffolk in 1822.

Having made very substantial war-time profits, the Steward brothers' entry into brewing was a logical and profitable step after 1815. Their involvement, therefore, was largely that of non-participating investors. Nevertheless, Ambrose Steward was instrumental in the establishment of the Country Brewers' Society, forerunner of the Brewers' Society, in May 1822. He chaired the first meeting on 24 May, held in the Exchequer Coffee House, at which John Staniforth Patteson was also present, when brewers planned their opposition to the government's licensing bill, and was elected 'chairman of the committee' in the following month. Indeed, the Steward brothers were a dominant element in the Society for the rest of the decade. William Steward led the lobby of parliament in connection with the Beer Act of 1830.[18] A more active role in brewing itself was assumed by Timothy Steward the younger (IV) (1796-1858), who moved to Norwich and with John Staniforth Patteson took on the day-to-day management of production and distribution. When Patteson died in 1832, Timothy became the firm's managing partner. His connections with the trade were strengthened by a marriage to a brewer's daughter, Lucy, only child of John Scarlin Tuthill. Ownership of a fine house, Heigham Lodge, in the west end of the city, was clear evidence of his later importance as one of Norwich's leading businessmen. He held several directorships, including seats on the board of the East of England Bank, the Norwich Union Life (1835-58), the Norwich Union Fire (1842-58), Norwich Yarn, and Norwich Steam Power companies. His political affiliations were described as 'Old Whig', and he acted as Sheriff of Norwich in 1855.[19]

The Stewards' stake in the new business of Steward, Patteson & Stewards was a considerable one. While no partnership deeds survive before 1838, the evidence suggests that the newcomers contributed two-thirds and Patteson only one-third of the total brewery capital. The division of capital among the Stewards is unclear, but later evidence suggests that William and Ambrose Harbord held the largest stakes. The capital may have been divided as shown in Table 2. The immediate effects of the amalgamation of Steward and Patteson interests are not recorded, but we may safely assume that the market area of the brewery was extended by the public houses which the Stewards brought into the business. Expansion also proceeded by means of further acquisitions in the 1820's. In 1820, for example,

TABLE 2

Pockthorpe Brewery Partnership, 1820–31: Division of Capital (estimated)

Partner	*Share (%)*
John Staniforth Patteson	33
William Steward	27
Ambrose Harbord Steward	27
Timothy Steward, the elder & Timothy Steward, the younger	13
	100

Patteson leased the 'Mill Tavern' in Norwich, and four years later the firm took out a ninety-year lease on the 'Spread Eagle', also in the city.[20] Nationally, the picture was a gloomy one. Production in the second half of the decade fell below the level of the turn of the century, and the reduction of the duties on spirits, together with widespread complaints about poor quality beer, caused considerable problems for the common brewers.[21] However, in Norwich, Steward, Patteson & Stewards extended their control of the local market. They had tied 120 public houses through ownership and lease by the time the restrictive licensing system was relaxed with the Act of 1830, and with sales to the free trade, were probably selling as much beer as they had done in 1800.[22] Their position in the trade continued to be a dominant one. In Norwich alone they controlled eighty public houses, about 20 per cent of the total number of outlets.[23] The firm also produced about a quarter of the output - 87,000 barrels - of the public brewers in the Norwich Collection area in 1822-3.[24]

The Norwich Rate-Books provide additional evidence of the prominence of Steward, Patteson & Stewards in the city. Unfortunately, the assessments for the parish of Pockthorpe prior to 1825 have been destroyed. However, in June 1825, the firm was occupying three malthouses rated at £40, £20, and £14 respectively (the two smallest appear to have been occupied by John Staniforth Patteson in an individual capacity). The brewery premises were rated at £71 10*s*.: £46 for the 'Brewhouse', £5 10*s*. for the 'Malt-Office', and £20 for the Stock, valued at £1,000 (i.e. £25,000).[25] This suggests a scale of operations as large as any of the other leading brewers such as Tompson, Morse, Finch, Youngs, and Weston. The breweries of Charles Tompson and Morse & Son were assessed for higher sums, it is true, but both included substantial private houses on the site, with a rateable value of about £30 each (Table 3).

TABLE 3

Rate Assessment of Leading Breweries in Norwich, June 1825

Brewer	*Brewery Site*	*Additional Malthouses*	*Remarks*
Charles Tompson	£109 10*s*.	....	includes House [c.£30]
Morse & Son	£85 10*s*.	....	includes House [c.£30]
Steward Patteson & Stewards	£71 10*s*.	£74 [3]	includes Stock £1,000 [£20]
Finch	£59 10*s*.	....	includes Stock £300 [£6]
Youngs & Co.	£46	£13 [1]	excludes Stock £100 [£2]
Charles Weston	£40	£20 [1]	includes House and Stock £500 [£10]

Source: Norwich Poor Rate Book, June 1825, N/T23/1, N.R.O.

Steward, Patteson & Stewards retained their strong position in the local brewing industry in the late 1820's. The future, however, was far from certain. Continuing problems of high costs, common in all areas of the country, had been offset in large measure by raising the price of beer. While no detailed information has survived, William Steward, in his evidence to the Select Committee on the Retail Sale of Beer in 1830, claimed that the country price was 55*s*. a barrel to the publican and 6*d*. [2½p] a 'pot' (quart) in the pub.[26] If we assume that he based his statement on the prices charged by his own firm, then Stewards were charging only 20 per cent more than the current (1826-30) price of the cheaper London porter at 45*s*. a barrel or 5*d*. a pot.[27] The Norwich concern had a firm grip on its retail trade, of course, and was thus in a position to resist a shift to competitors offering lower prices. But the threat of a free trade in beer was a very real one. The Acts of 1830, while abolishing the duty on beer (10*s*. a barrel), ended the restrictive licensing system by allowing anyone to open a 'beer house' on payment of a nominal, £2 2*s*. licence fee. The intention was to reduce beer prices, and to establish a new type of drinking place outside the control of brewer and magistrate. Within two years, over 33,000 beer houses had been opened.[28] This represented a very serious potential challenge to the dominance of the tied-house system in Norfolk (and elsewhere), and promised a sharp fall in the value of the considerable capital the partners had invested in public houses. Country brewers viewed the industry's prospects with alarm. For the Pockthorpe brewery, however, a potential crisis was once again met by further consolidation and growth. In 1831, the firm amalgamated with George Morse, another of Norwich's leading brewers.

The merger with George Morse: Steward Patteson & Co., 1831-7

By an agreement dated 27 June 1831, the businesses of Steward, Patteson & Stewards and George Morse were consolidated to form 'one joint trade'. The amalgamation was to run for ten years and three months from 9 July 1831, although it was extended, in fact, by subsequent partnerships.[29] The arrangement brought together two of Norwich's leading brewers. Indeed, the interest of the Morse family in the industry was almost as old as that of the Pattesons. It began in 1797, when John Morse purchased Day's 'porter brewery' in Oak Street, Norwich, and twenty-one public houses, for the sum of £10,230.[30] Under Daniel Ganning's control as Day's executor the business was producing about 8,000 barrels a year at this time, considerably less than its output in 1791-3, when with 13,600 barrels a year (10,500 of them of strong beer) it was Norwich's largest brewery.[31] Day's had held eighty-three licences in Norwich, including thirty-three houses on freehold or long lease, and twenty-four on short lease, and supplied a further thirty houses in the county (twenty-five freehold or copyhold, five leasehold). After the death of John Day senior in 1794, some properties were disposed of prior to the sale in 1797 - John Patteson bought some of the country public houses, for example - but it seems likely that Morse acquired further public house properties in separate transactions. Certainly, the business remained a fairly large one by local standards. In 1797-8 and 1799-1800 its production of strong beer amounted to 7,649 and 6,844 barrels respectively.[32]

John Morse (1745-1837) had, like Patteson, moved into brewing during the uncertain conditions facing the local economy in the 1790's. Although his precise business interests prior to brewing have not been traced, contemporary sources refer to him as a 'manufacturer', and it is clear that he was a prominent figure in Norwich. Sheriff in 1779, he went on to act as mayor twice, in 1781 and 1803, and he lived in comfortable surroundings in Surrey Street, and, later, in St Catherine's Close [now housing the BBC]. He was twice married, first in 1775 to Elizabeth, daughter of John Boycott, a dyer, of Sprowston Hall, and then in 1781 to Sarah, daughter of Francis Twiss, a successful merchant from Rotterdam. The marriages produced four sons and four daughters.[33] It was the third son, George (1783-1852), the first son of his second marriage, who was to take on the family's brewing interest.

Under Morse's ownership the Oak Street brewery held its own in the more difficult conditions of the early nineteenth century. Further public houses were acquired, among them the 'Dolphin' in Heigham Street, once the home of Bishop Hall, which was bought in 1818.[34] The Rate-Books once again give us an indication of the size of the brewery site. The assessment was certainly a large one: £78 in December 1797, £80 10*s*. in August 1800, and £85 10*s*. three years later. However, later references make it clear that the property included a substantial private house and some malthouses in addition to the brewhouse and its associated buildings. Nevertheless, the suggested scale of the business was impressive by local standards.[35] In 1803 Morse entered into a partnership with a Mr Adams, and the brewery traded as 'Morse & Adams' until 1823 or 1824. Nothing is known about Adams, and the circumstances surrounding the partnership are unclear. However, John Morse was by no means a young man, and he may have wished to devolve some of the managerial responsibility upon his new partner. During the twenty years of the agreement, the business appears to have grown steadily, and production was probably in the region of 12-15,000 barrels a year when the name of Adams was dropped in favour of 'Morse & Son'.[36] John's son, George, had embarked first of all on an army career. He served with the 57th Regiment, attaining the rank of Captain before retirement in 1806. He then returned to Norwich, and married Hannah Tasker in 1808. As we have already noted, his wife was the sister of John Staniforth Patteson's wife Anne Elizabeth. The exact date of George's introduction to the affairs of the brewery is again not known. However, it is likely that he was given some responsibilities before he became a joint partner.

In 1829, on John Morse's retirement, George was left in sole control of the brewery, and two years later he decided to amalgamate with Steward Patteson & Stewards. The reasons for the merger have never been explained. It is tempting to assert that the uncertainties created by the legislation of 1830 persuaded George to throw in his lot with the Pockthorpe rival. On the other hand, it may have been simply that George preferred the life of sleeping partner to that of owner-entrepreneur. The evidence seems to point this way. In 1835, a year after the death of his wife Hannah, he married again - his second wife was Rebecca, daughter of William Herbert of Norwich - and purchased Catton Park, an imposing country house to the north of the city. The life of a Norfolk gentleman was more to his liking than the daily concerns of malting and brewing.[37] He was certainly no stranger to the partners of Steward Patteson & Stewards. In addition to the family connection, he was a business associate of Patteson's as a director of the Norwich Union Fire Society (1826-52, Vice-President, 1848-52).[38] One thing is clear. Steward Patteson & Stewards were interested much more in Morse's pubs than in his brewing plant and premises. Only a week after the new partnership commenced, an advertisement was placed in the *Norfolk Chronicle* offering the plant for sale, and the brewery site for sale or rent. The advertisement gives a detailed description of Morse's equipment, and is therefore reproduced in full:

'TO BE SOLD. A Complete BREWING PLANT Consisting of dome-headed Copper capable of boiling 80 barrels, Grigory's Patent Refrigerator calculated to cool 40 barrels per hour, two working Squares, capable of working 120 barrels each, two nearly new coolers, each 28 feet long by 18 feet wide, horizontal Mashing Machine, seven Store Vatts, varying in size from 110 to 230 barrels each, four smaller Vatts, three of which hold 17 barrels each and one 40 barrels, with a variety of other Utensils.'[39]

There is nothing here to suggest that Morse's plant was delapidated or antiquated when he decided to give up production himself.

The amalgamation with Morse added seventy-seven public houses

- sixty-two in Norwich, fifteen in the county – to the 121 outlets already controlled by the Pockthorpe brewery. The total of 198 tied houses was without any doubt a very large number for a provincial brewery in the early 1830's, many more than those of regional competitors such as Paget's and Lacon's of Yarmouth.[40] The partnership agreement stipulated that the public houses were to remain 'the separate property of the partners in whom they are now vested',[41] and both the capital investment and profits of each partner were determined on the basis of such ownership. With thirty-nine per cent of the public houses in 1831, George Morse came in with the largest stake in the new firm of 'Steward, Patteson & Co.'. The exact division of capital and profits has not survived, but later evidence suggests it to have been as shown in Table 4. Thus, for the second time in eleven years, a significant change in the relative shares of the partners had taken place. Managerial responsibility remained the same, however, with Patteson and Timothy Steward the younger continuing as managing partners.

TABLE 4

Pockthorpe Brewery Partnership, July 1831: Division of Capital (estimated)

Partner	*Share (%)*
George Morse	40
John Staniforth Patteson	20
William Steward	16
Ambrose Harbord Steward	16
Timothy & Timothy Steward	8
	100

Source: Steward & Patteson Partnership Deeds: Indenture, 20 November 1838, BR11/8, N.R.O.

Further changes in both ownership and management followed in quick succession. On the death of Patteson in 1832, his share was taken on by his executors, Anne Elizabeth Patteson, his wife, Revd William Frederick Patteson of St Helen's, Norwich, his brother, and Henry Francis, his attorney.[42] Timothy Steward assumed sole responsibility for the management of the brewery from this date. Four years later, he was able to increase his holdings by purchasing his father's share on his death in June 1836.[43] The conditions facing the new partnership in the 1830's are not easy to gauge. It may be assumed that the freeing of the beer trade encouraged new entrants, not only as publicans but also as common brewers and brewing publicans. Large investors obviously feared that the value of their public houses would fall. However, locally the trade does not appear to have altered very much. The directories and rate-books, while not always an accurate guide to events, show that the leading brewing firms remained much as they were between 1829 and 1837. The only significant changes were the merger of Morse's with Steward Patteson & Stewards, and the purchase of Isaac Johnson's brewery in St Stephen's Street by Richard Crawshay in 1834 (see rate assessments in Table 5).[44] Certainly, the new conditions were a spur to ambitious small producers. Thomas Massey, for example, the brewing-publican of the 'Champion' in St Stephen's, offered his beer at the reduced price of 30*s.* a barrel in October 1830, and we may presume that others followed his lead in seeking customers from the expected increase in the number of retailers.[45] Indeed, the £2 2*s.* 'beer shop' soon made its appearance in Norwich. *White's Directory* for 1836 lists sixty-nine of these in the city.[46] There was also a strong competitive challenge from outside the region. Guinness was freely available from Norfolk distributors in the 1830's, and William Burroughs of Yarmouth offered Whitbread's beer both to the trade and to retail customers, at a price, to the latter, of £1 7*s.* 6*d.* a half-barrel for porter, and £1 12*s.* 6*d.* for stout.[47]

TABLE 5

Rate Assessment of Leading Norwich Breweries, 1829–37 (June)

Brewer	*1829*	*1831*	*1833*	*1835*	*1837*
Charles Tompson*	£100	£100	£100	£100	£100
George Morse	£55 10*s.*	£55 10*s.*	£45 10*s.*[e]	£39 10*s.*[e]	....
Steward Patteson	£55	£55	£65	£65	£60
Finch*	£53 10*s.*	£53 10*s.*	£50	£50	£50
Youngs & Burt	£46	£46	£49	£49	£49
Richard Crawshay	....	....	....	£36	£36
Charles Weston*	£30	£30	£30	£30	£30

Source: Norwich Poor Rate Books, N/T23/14, 21, 27, 34, 41, N.R.O. Figures are for brewery site only and include malthouses where located on the premises.
* Includes house (Finch £10, others unspecified).
[e] Premises 'empty'.

It is difficult to estimate how well Steward, Patteson & Co. fared in these circumstances. As large-scale owners of public houses they probably viewed the 'beer shop' with considerable alarm. However, fears of a marked decline in public-house values evaporated very quickly. Only a decade after the Beer Act, the *Norfolk Chronicle* was able to state [in 1840] that 'The great increase in the value of country public-houses apparent from the enormous prices which have lately been realized for this description of property leads us to believe that the shock which the trade suffered on the passing of the Beer Bill some years since has been entirely recovered, and that country public-houses are now even of greater value than they were antecedent to the passing of that measure'.[48] This suggests that the decision to merge with Morse, whether taken for defensive reasons or not, was not necessarily accompanied by a serious contraction of the local market. At any rate, the company soon took a further step towards growth, by merging with Peter Finch's brewery in 1837.

3

Steward, Patteson, Finch & Co.: Growth and Consolidation, 1837-80

The merger with Peter Finch, 1837

Of the four families engaged in the brewing business of Steward, Patteson, Finch & Co., the Finches had the longest connection with the trade. In 1771 Peter Finch II (1726-1807), son of the Reverend Peter Finch (I), a minister at the presbyterian Octagon Chapel, acquired Nuthall's brewery in Oak Street, in the parish of St Mary's Coslany. The Rate-books suggest that the concern was a sizeable one. The property, which included a house rated at £8, was assessed at £55, while the 'Stock' assessment of £200 indicates a total value of about £5,000. In 1773 the property assessment was increased to £60, and it became £69 two years later. The Stock figure fell to £100 in 1776, but was increased to £300 (value: £7,500) in 1789.[1] The first information on production is for 1791-2, when 8,936 barrels of strong beer were made. In the following year 11,005 barrels were produced. Clearly, Finch's brewery ranked with Day, Tompson and Weston as a leading Norwich common brewer.[2] Peter Finch II, who is described in Chase's Norwich Directory of 1783 as an 'attorney and brewer', was also a magistrate and Clerk of the Peace, and a founding director in 1792 of the Norwich General Fire Assurance Company. He had intended to give up the brewery to his son, Edmund Rolfe I (1764-93), but the latter's untimely death at the age of 29, leaving two infant sons Edmund Rolfe II (born 1789) and Peter III (born 1791), precluded a formal retirement. He turned instead to his son-in-law, John Scarlin Tuthill, who assumed responsibility for the brewery's management. When Peter II himself died in 1807, at the age of 81, the concern passed into Tuthill's temporary care, until the grandsons were ready to take up their inheritance. This they did in 1812 in a partnership which lasted until the death of Edmund Rolfe II in 1831.[3] Peter III, the more active partner in the business, was also a local politician of some repute. Of 'Old Whig' persuasion, he acted as Norwich's sheriff in 1825 and served as mayor two years later. His decision to merge with Steward, Patteson, and Morse in 1837 cannot be readily explained. However, as a bachelor and with his brother dead there was no obvious heir to the brewery, and therefore no over-riding reason for retaining independence. In the absence of business records, it is difficult to assess the brewery's relative position in Norwich, of course. The Rate-books tell us that Finch's property assessment had been reduced from £69 to £53 10*s*. by 1822, and to £50 (including £10 for a house) by 1833, but it would be dangerous to infer too much from this.[4] But we can say that a merger of the 'loose association' type had obvious attractions in the competitive environment of the mid 1830's, and Finch was already closely connected with the partners in Steward, Patteson & Co. As we have seen earlier, his cousin Lucy, daughter of John Scarlin Tuthill, had married Timothy Steward the younger, the brewery's managing partner. There were also business connections. Peter and Timothy joined George Morse on the board of the Norwich Union Life Insurance Society in the same year - 1835. Indeed, the invitation to amalgamate brewing interests may have come from Steward & Patteson. The 1831 partnership had been altered considerably by the death of two of the six participants - John Staniforth Patteson (1832), and Timothy Steward the elder (1836), and it is significant that Finch was to be given an active role in the enlarged concern as a managing partner (see below).

By an agreement dated 26 September 1837 the businesses were consolidated as 'Steward, Patteson, Finch & Co.' in a twenty-one-year partnership from 1 November. The brewery capital, which included £7,800 for the Pockthorpe premises,[5] was fixed at £30,000 and divided among the partners as shown in Table 6. Finch's brewery was taken on account at its fixed plant value, and £2,000 was to be paid out of the consolidated capital in consideration of the goodwill of the independent

TABLE 6

Pockthorpe Brewery Partnership, November 1837: Division of £30,000 Capital

Partner	*Share*	*%*
George Morse	£9,000	30
Peter Finch	£7,500	25
Executors of J.S. Patteson	£4,500	15
William Steward	£3,600	12
Ambrose Harbord Steward	£3,600	12
Timothy Steward the younger	£1,800	6

Source: Steward & Patteson Partnership Deeds: Indenture, 20 November 1838, BR11/8, N.R.O.

business. However, it is not clear whether these transactions involved a reduction in the amount of the agreed capital. The public houses remained, as before, in the separate ownership of each partner or group of partners. The partners agreed to suspend their individual liability for debts for one year, and this arrangement was extended for a further year when formal articles of copartnership were drawn up on 20 November 1838. In the meantime, however, the position changed. A fortnight after the 1837 agreement was signed Ambrose Steward died, and his share was bought by his nephew and son-in-law, Charles Steward of Blundeston.[6] Shortly afterwards, Timothy Steward increased his stake by purchasing half of Peter Finch's share, and when the articles were signed the capital shares were as outlined in Table 7.

TABLE 7

Pockthorpe Brewery Partnership, November 1838: Division of Capital

Partner	*Share (%)*	*Share assuming a capital of £30,000*
George Morse	30	£9,000
Timothy Steward	18.5	£5,550
Executors of J.S. Patteson	15	£4,500
Peter Finch	12.5	£3,750
William Steward	12	£3,600
Charles Steward	12	£3,600

Source: Steward & Patteson Partnership Deeds: Indenture, 20 November 1838, BR11/8, N.R.O.

The merger with Finch brought Steward & Patteson approximately fifty-five more public houses, forty of which were in Norwich, making a total of about 250 retail establishments tied to the Pockthorpe brewery.[7] The exact number in this expanded empire is not known, but there is evidence to suggest that over 70 per cent were situated in Norwich itself. A printed census of public houses in 1845, summarised in Table 8, revealed that the company owned no less than 183 outlets, 33 per cent of the total of 558. It had thus consolidated its position as the leading common brewer in a city dominated by this type of enterprise. As Table 8 indicates, the six major concerns owned no less than 72 per cent of the public houses.[8] Steward & Patteson was also one of the most experienced firms. Only Weston's was in existence prior to John Patteson's purchase of the Greeves brewery in 1793, and two of the large brewers were newcomers. Bullard & Watts entered the trade in 1837 (Richard Bullard was a former publican-brewer), while J.B. Morgan acquired Tompson's brewery in King Street in 1845, the year

TABLE 8

Public House Ownership in Norwich, 1845

Owner	*Number of houses owned*	*% of total*
Steward Patteson Finch	183	32.8
Youngs & Burt	71	12.7
J.B. Morgan (ex-Tompson)	59	10.6
Charles Weston	32	5.7
Bullard & Watts	32	5.7
Richard Crawshay	25	4.5
Robert Seaman	22	3.9
Sundry small owners	134	24.0
Total	**558**	**(99.9)**

Source: List of Inns and Public Houses in the City of Norwich and County of the Same City (published by Robert Campling, Norwich, 1845). Note: the figures here have been corrected for errors and omissions, and thus differ from those given in P.J. Corfield, 'The Social and Economic History of Norwich, 1650–1850', London University Ph.D. Thesis, 1976, p.443. The total of 558 excludes beer shops. Cf. *Blyth's Norwich Directory* (Norwich, 1842), which has a total of 609, including 53 beer shops and 6 hotels.

of the census, although the family claimed to have been brewing since 1720.

By 1840, then, the concentration of beer production in Norwich, and the dominance of its common brewers in the ownership and control of the retail trade, were well established. Supporting evidence comes from the excise returns. In the Norwich collection district (Norwich and the northern and eastern parts of Norfolk), common brewers made nearly 90 per cent of the beer brewed in April 1822-April 1823 and in the first nine months of 1830, compared with a figure of just over 50 per cent for common brewers in the English and Welsh counties as a whole (excluding London). And in the years 1836-42 the forty or so common brewers, who together made up about a quarter of the total number of local producers, took 89 per cent of the brewing malt consumed in the region, compared with a figure of only 49 per cent for the English and Welsh counties.[9] The relative insignificance of licensed victuallers and beer-house keepers in the manufacture of Norfolk's beer certainly contrasts with the position in Yorkshire described by Sigsworth,[10] and, more particularly, with that in areas such as Barnstaple and Shropshire, where the common brewers' share of total malt consumption was as low as 2-4 per cent.[11] However, the picture in Norfolk was by no means unique. The domination of local production by common brewers can also be found outside London in the collection districts of Liverpool, Surrey, Rochester, Canterbury and Sussex, among others.[12] Since overall beer consumption both in

Norfolk and in England and Wales was probably not expanding in the 1830's and 1840's, large provincial brewers such as Steward, Patteson, Finch & Co. could only make progress by either merging with existing competitors or by extending the area of distribution.[13]

Consolidation and Growth, 1840-50

How successfully, then, did Steward & Patteson meet the challenge of competition in the relatively static market conditions of the mid-nineteenth century? The evidence suggests that their response was vigorous. This was no passive association of rentiers, with managerial decisions left to a humble brewing manager or salaried clerk. The articles of partnership of 1838 provided for the business to be run by Timothy Steward and Peter Finch as managing partners, with annual salaries of £400 and £100 respectively. In addition, Henry Staniforth Patteson, the son of John Staniforth Patteson, joined the brewery in 1832, at the age of sixteen, and soon became involved in its day-to-day affairs. The management 'team' was strengthened when he became a partner, probably in 1841. These arrangements indicate an active supervision by the partners and an organisational structure appropriate to a large provincial concern.[14]

A company letter-book covering the years 1842-7 has survived, and this gives a partial but valuable insight into brewery operations in the period. It is clear, for example, that the company was pursuing a policy of growth by expanding the area of distribution. There was a determined effort to establish a foothold in the lucrative but intensely competitive London market. Trading began some years before 1841, when in the first five months Steward, Patteson, Finch sent 333 barrels to Simon Silcock, their London agent, charging 46*s*. for their XXX and 31*s*. for their X ale (Table 9).[15] Unfortunately, Norwich lacked speedy transport facilities for such a trade in the early 1840's. The city was not connected with London by rail until 1845, when the route *via* Ely and Cambridge was opened, and the shorter route *via* Ipswich and Colchester was not available until 1849.[16] Beer had therefore to be sent by wherry along the river Yare to Yarmouth, and then trans-shipped for the journey to London by steam packet. The voyage often had deleterious effects on the condition of the beer, particularly in warm weather. This problem, together with the generally depressed state of the market in the early 1840's, caused Silcock to reduce his orders, much to the brewery's disappointment. As Table 9 shows, he cut his

TABLE 9

Steward, Patteson, Finch & Co.'s beer 'exports' to Simon Silcock of London, 1841–5

Period	*Beer sent (nos. of barrels, 36 galls)*			*Total*	*Monthly Average*	*Full barrels returned*
	XXX	*XX*	*X*			
Jan - May 1841	n.a.	n.a.	n.a.	333	66.6	n.a.
Jan - May 1842	n.a.	n.a.	n.a.	198	39.6	n.a.
Jul - Dec 1842	170	6	37	213	35.5	14
Jan - May 1843	60	20	30	110	22.0	-
Jun - Dec 1843	150	-	36	186	26.6	12
Jan - May 1844	70	-	18	88	17.6	-
Jun - Dec 1844	105	-	12	117	16.7	26
Jan - May 1845	30	-	-	30	6.0	-
Jun - Dec 1845	30	-	10	40	5.7	-

Source: Steward, Patteson, Finch & Co. Out-letter book, July 1842-April 1847: letters to Simon Silcock, BR1/44, N.R.O.

order sharply from about sixty-seven barrels a month in January-May 1841 to only twenty-two barrels in the corresponding period of 1843. Timothy Steward took the matter up with him in June 1843, only to be informed that Lacon's Yarmouth ale beat Steward & Patteson hollow.[17] In 1845 only six barrels a month were sent down to London. The renewal of brewing equipment in 1846-7 (see below) suggests that the quality of the beer was capable of improvement. However, the explanation for the adverse comparison with Lacon's went beyond a mere quality difference. Although it is true that Lacon's had already built up an impressive reputation in the capital, the company enjoyed the advantage of brewing on the coast, and were thus able to avoid some of the transport problems involved in sending beer to London before the railway network was established. There is also evidence to suggest that Silcock was mistreating Steward & Patteson's beer, regarding it as capable of being stored for long periods like London porter, when it was in fact a fast-maturing beer without keeping qualities.[18]

While Silcock's orders fell away, others expressed an interest in the Norwich ale. In February 1846 beer was sent to Mrs McKenzie, of the 'India Arms' in Broad Street, and in March Arthur and Timothy Steward corresponded with William Morgan of East Greenwich with a view to establishing a London agency. However, no permanent arrangements were made with either party.[19] The brewery also attempted to establish agencies outside London. Since the company was already taking its coal supplies from Newcastle, it was anxious to create a reverse trade in beer, and in 1843 it asked its coal agent, George Seppings, to make inquiries in the town with the aim of setting up a beer agency. In the same year, there was also an attempt to enter into an agency agreement with John Lamont of Horsleydown. However, there is nothing in the correspondence to suggest that anything came of these negotiations.

Far more important to the progress of Steward Patteson Finch & Co. was its expansion by acquisition and merger nearer home. In September 1841 the Coltishall brewery was sold with its fifty-three pubs for about £50,000, and although the buyer was not named, some of the estate appears to have been acquired by the Company.[20] The year 1845 was a significant one. In April the partners entered into a twenty-one year lease of the twenty-two public houses belonging to John Sayers Bell, the Gorleston brewer. Eight of these were in Gorleston, three in Lowestoft, two in Oulton, and the rest in villages on or near the coast. The annual rent was fixed at £625, with the lessees paying all rates, taxes and outgoings except land tax, income tax, and quit rents. The lessees also gained access to the 'Fox and Hounds' at Filby, which Bell was supplying as a yearly tenant. Also early in 1845, the partners borrowed £28,000 on mortgage to purchase the brewery, public houses, and other premises belonging to Samuel Paget & Son, the Yarmouth brewers, a property which had been owned by John Patteson forty years previously (see Chapters One and Two). The sale brought Steward & Patteson twenty-five tied houses in Yarmouth, about 15 per cent of the total number of retail outlets, representing a considerable challenge to the region's other major brewer, Lacon's, which owned thirty-eight houses (23 per cent) in the town.[21]

The acquisition of nearly fifty public houses in the Yarmouth/Gorleston area, together with extensive premises in Yarmouth, including warehouses, storehouses, a shop, and two private houses, stimulated a complete reorganisation of the brewery in Norwich and a modification of the company's activities further afield. At Pockthorpe brewing equipment was renewed in 1846-7, and the letter-book refers to the purchase of vats and pontoons. By February 1847 the company was able to inform Simon Silcock that 'Our brewery department having during the last few months undergone an *entire change* we are quite satisfied that we can offer you now such an article both in XXX and X ale as we are sure will give you satisfaction'.[22] The reorganisation also involved a belated expansion of porter brewing. On taking over responsibility for Bell's public houses, Steward & Patteson wrote to Barclay Perkins, the London brewers, turning down their offer to supply London porter, and two years later, in April 1847, John Preston, the wine and spirit merchant of Cromer, was sent, unsolicited, a sample barrel of the company's porter with the explanation that this was 'in consequence of our having entered very largely into the Porter Trade as *Porter Brewers*'.[23] In Yarmouth, the purchase of Paget's was followed by the appointment of Arthur Steward, Timothy's younger brother, as the company's agent. The brewery site was then sold to the Norfolk Railway Co., which demolished it.[24] Other properties were used to provide a bonded warehouse for the company's wine and spirits trade, and a beer store.[25]

The reorganisation of the brewery and the opening of the railway to London enabled Steward & Patteson to make another assault on the London market. The letter-book indicates that in March 1847 samples of beer were sent via the Norfolk and Eastern Counties railways to Commercial Wharf, Upper Thames Street. Three barrels of XXX and three of X ale were consigned to R. Roberts for 44*s*. [£2.20] and 30*s*. [£1.50] per barrel respectively. This stimulated another inquiry, from John Pickford of Aldersgate Street, who was told on April 20 that the brewery's nett price for XXX ale was 54*s*. [£2.70] a barrel, with the brewery paying the railway or freight charge.[26] Unfortunately, no correspondence survives after this date. However, the partnership deed of 1863 declares that the company established agencies in London, Colchester, Ipswich, and (more surprisingly) Plymouth, in addition to Yarmouth, and it is reasonable to assume that this expansion occurred fairly soon after the brewery reorganisation.[27]

The Brewery Partnership, 1838-63

The brewery partnership of 1838 remained virtually intact for several years. The only change in the 1840's came with the death in May 1841 of William Steward. His 12 per cent share in the partnership passed to his daughter, Anne Palmer Steward, who in 1815 had married Rear-Admiral Sir Eaton Travers of Alverstoke, Hampshire.[28] However, there were more significant changes in the following decade. In July 1852, George Morse, the largest stakeholder, died leaving three-fifths of his share to his eldest son Charles (1820-83). The remainder was held jointly by Charles Morse and Henry Staniforth Patteson (half of this portion having been transferred from George Morse's younger sons).

3. Peter Finch (1840–81) [*John W. Stokes collection*]

In October of the same year Peter Finch also died, marking the end of direct Finch involvement in the brewery. His share was vested in his godson, Peter Finch Steward (1840-81), the second son of Timothy Steward, who took the name 'Peter Finch' as a condition of inheritance. Then, in April 1855, Henry Francis, one of the executors of John Staniforth Patteson's will, died, and control of the estate was confined to the surviving executors, Anne Elizabeth and William Frederick Patteson. Finally, Lucy Steward inherited the share held by Timothy Steward on his death in October 1858. In December 1862 she divided a part of her holding equally among her sons, Donald and Walter, as tenants-in-common.[29] These changes were, on the whole, those of transfer from sleeping partner to sleeping partner. Only Henry Staniforth Patteson, who had joined the brewery in 1832 and obtained a fifth-share in George Morse's estate in 1852, had any practical experience of the business. Lady Travers, J.S. Patteson's executors, and Lucy Steward were principally rentiers. And so too was Charles Morse, who like his father George, took little or no interest in the brewery. After taking his B.A. at Trinity College Cambridge in 1844 he gave up his life to acting, the Alpine Club, and, above all, cricket. Following a successful career with Cambridge he played for Marylebone, *I. Zingari*, for whom he once scored 145 against the Gentlemen of Leicestershire, and the Gentlemen of England. He also represented England in a match against Surrey in June 1849.[30]

By the early 1860's the time was ripe for a new partnership agreement. The contract of 1838 had expired in November 1858 and only three of its eight signatories were still alive. However, a more pressing reason for seeking a new agreement was the need to clarify the financial arrangements concerning the purchase of Paget's property in Yarmouth in 1845. The original aim had been to keep these distinct from the rest of the business. The debt of some £28,000 which had been incurred was to be discharged by means of a sinking fund established with the profits of the Yarmouth Agency. But parts of the fund were later applied to purchase public houses and other buildings in Yarmouth, and on 1 November 1862 a sum of £23,201 19*s*. 3*d*. was still outstanding.[31] A new copartnership agreement was signed on 30 November 1863, operative for twenty-one years from 1 November 1862. It restated the determination of the partners to liquidate the Yarmouth debt out of the agency's profits. The brewery's other monies were not to be used for this purpose. Instead, £10,000 of the company's undivided profits of £11,793 (on 1 November 1862) was transferred to

TABLE 10

Steward Patteson Finch & Co. Partnership, November 1863: Division of £40,000 Capital

Partner	*£100 Shares (no.)*	*%*
Charles Morse	96	24
Executors of J.S. Patteson	60	15
Peter Finch, formerly Steward	50	12.5
Lucy Steward	49	12.25
Lady Travers	48	12
Charles Steward	48	12
Donald and Walter Steward	25	6.25
Henry Staniforth Patteson	24	6
	400	100

Source: Steward & Patteson Partnership Deeds: Indenture, 30 November 1863, BR11/8, N.R.O.

the capital account, making £40,000 in all, and the partners' shares were fixed as shown in Table 10. This arrangement left the widow and three sons of Timothy Steward in control of 31 per cent of the brewery's capital, and with Charles Steward and Lady Travers, the Steward family had a controlling interest of 55 per cent in the new partnership. However, the management of the concern was a matter for Pattesons as well as Stewards. Henry Staniforth Patteson became more closely involved in the brewery, especially after the death of Peter Finch in 1852, and when Timothy Steward died six years later he was left in sole command. By this time the business was too complex to be left to one man, and it was necessary for him to find assistants. Thus, the agreement of 1863, while providing for the appointment of Henry as senior managing partner with a salary of £700 a year, also appointed Donald and Walter Steward as junior managing partners, each with a salary of £400 per annum.[32]

Undoubtedly, the brewery was placed in good hands. Henry Staniforth Patteson had acquired thirty years of practical experience at Pockthorpe after leaving North Walsham Grammar School at the age of sixteen. In 1835-6 he had been trained in malting by Messrs. Taylor & Son of Bishop's Stortford. Furthermore, at the time of the new partnership he had established himself as a prominent member of Norwich's Tory elite. He had already served both as sheriff (in 1858) and mayor (1862), and had been elected a deputy-lieutenant of the county (1859). He was also closely involved in local insurance.

Appointed a trustee of the Norwich Union Fire Society in 1842, he had served as a director since 1848. In addition, he had been appointed to the board of the Norwich & London Accident Insurance Association on its formation in 1856 (he took the chair in 1862) and the General Hailstorm Insurance Society in 1862 (he became chairman in 1882). He went on to act as vice-president of the Norwich Union Fire Society from 1874 to 1877, and as president from 1877 until his death in 1898. He also became a local J.P., director of the Norwich Waterworks Co., and a member of the Great Yarmouth Haven and Pier Commission. Hailed in the press as a 'sincere evangelical', he was an enthusiastic supporter of the Church of England Young Men's Society. Throughout his life his support for the Conservative interest remained strong, and on the death of Col. Charles Bignold in 1895 he became leader of the local party. When he too died, three years later, the *Norfolk Chronicle* declared that 'Conservatism has sustained a severe loss ... His name will ever be held in grateful remembrance by the rank and file of his own party'.[33] In view of Patteson's wider political and business interests, it was natural that he should seek to delegate authority to the junior partners. Here, he was fortunate to find an enthusiastic colleague in Donald Steward. Much of Steward's early life is obscure, and there is no mention of it in his Norwich obituaries. The eldest son of Timothy Steward of Heigham Lodge, the former managing partner of the brewery, he was born in 1829 in Ceylon, according to the *Brewing Trade Review*, and there he spent his early career in coffee-planting. Returning to Norwich, he made much of his opportunities as a junior managing partner. He also settled down. In 1873 he married Mary, the daughter of Alfred Master, a Norwich surgeon. Less committed to politics than Henry Staniforth Patteson, Donald Steward nevertheless served as sheriff of Norwich in 1878, the year of the 'great floods', was chairman of his local parish council (at Catton near Norwich), and was also a director of the Norwich Union Life Society. Described by the *Norwich Mercury* as being of the Liberal persuasion he was the ideal foil for his senior partner. The combination of a Conservative Patteson and a Liberal Steward was effective in maintaining the reputation of a major business in a tightly-knit community such as Norwich. Moreover, Steward possessed other qualities deserving of admiration. He was, according to the *Norfolk Chronicle*, a 'good, all-round sportsman', like many of his brewing colleagues.[34]

Expansion in a Growing Market, 1850-80

In the absence of business records, it is difficult to chart accurately the development of Steward, Patteson, Finch & Co. in the thirty years after 1850, when the demand for beer increased steadily in Britain with the general rise in standards of living. Nor is it possible to establish the details of materials used, types and quantities of beer brewed, markets served, and the equipment introduced as brewing became a more exact science.[35] Occasionally, a glimmer of light appears. In Bayne's history of Norwich published in 1869, for example, it is asserted that Steward & Patteson were producing 100,000 barrels of beer annually, much more than their rivals Bullard, with 60,000, Youngs (40,000), and Morgan (30,000). However, information such as this cannot easily be substantiated, though subsequent data and the company's barley book suggest that a figure of 70,000 barrels would be nearer the mark.[36] The same is true of our fragmentary knowledge of the firm's products. While it is known that the head brewer from 1871 to 1882 was W.A. Provart, the details of his work remain a mystery. The historian's difficulties are exacerbated by the company's decision to spend very little on local advertising. However, an advertisement placed in the *Norfolk Chronicle* of 3 August 1878 offered the public the following range of beers: 'Imperial, XXXX, East India Pale and Light Bitter Ales, and Double Brown Stout'. This indicates that the company was participating in Norwich's growing specialisation in pale ales of the Burton type, which were becoming increasingly popular in late-Victorian Britain. All the company's beer was marketed in barrels. No bottled beer was produced until 1893.[37]

Information on the brewery's labour force is lacking until November 1879. By this time the company was employing about 114 workers at Pockthorpe (with another ten or so taken on at busy periods), and their average weekly earnings amounted to 16*s*. 6*d*. (83p). Brewing had always been a capital-intensive industry when undertaken on any scale, and even at production levels in excess of 100,000 barrels a year a company required only a few operatives at the successive stages. The most numerous at Pockthorpe in 1879 were in the tun-room (26) and stores (13), while nine men were described as 'floats'. But the other specialist duties called for the employment of only a few men, e.g. 'malt grinder' (1), 'boilers' (4), 'worts' (1), 'coolers' (2), 'coppers' (2), 'yeast press' (2), and 'finings' (1). The major problem in terms of industrial relations was thus to secure the loyalty and reliability of small groups of men engaged in a relatively large number of differentiated tasks (there were twenty-eight separate categories in the wage-book in 1879). This necessitated a constant supervision by the managing partners and the head brewer. In return, the company offered relative security of employment - rare in Victorian Britain - and the fruits of a paternalistic tradition which included the payment of pensions to long-serving retired workers and the provision of housing.[38]

There is no doubt at all that market conditions from the mid-1850's were conducive to further growth and profitable trading. G.B. Wilson's estimates of beer consumption in the United Kingdom suggest a rise from 541 million gallons in 1855 to 1,145 gallons at the peak in 1876, an increase in per capita terms from 19.5 to 34.4 gallons, or 76 per cent.[39] While it is not possible to produce a similar estimate for the Steward & Patteson trading area, it seems unlikely that experience there matched the national picture. Agriculture did remain fairly prosperous in the 1850's and 1860's - these were the years of 'High Farming' - and complaints of depression did not appear until the late 1870's. On the other hand, population growth in Norfolk was largely offset by migration, and it is uncertain how much of the general prosperity filtered through to the agricultural labourer.[40] Nevertheless, the excise returns for the Norwich district, although far from reliable, do show an increase in brewers' malt consumption of no less than 186 per cent between 1854-5 and 1875-6, well above the national average. Of course, the disparity may be explained in part by a later (and therefore sharper) decline in home brewing in Norfolk.[41]

TABLE 11

Rateable Value of Leading Norwich Breweries, 1850–80

Brewer	*1850*	*1860*	*1870*	*1880*
Steward, Patteson, Finch	£360	£450	£540	£828
J.B. (& H.) Morgan	£402*	£385*	£373½	£585
Youngs (Youngs, Crawshay & Youngs)	£175½	£189	£211½	£608**
R. Crawshay (C. Crawshay)	£207*	merged with Youngs in 1851		
C. Weston	£90	£190*	bought by Youngs in 1864	
R. Bullard (Bullard & Boyce)	£63	£65	£612	£1067
Arnold (& Wyatt)	—	£78½	£122½	£168

Source: Norwich Poor Rate Books, 1850-80, N.R.O. Rateable values are for brewery site with buildings.
*Includes house.
** R.V. given in error as £108: £608 is probably correct.

How did Steward and Patteson respond to market conditions in the years 1850-80? In Norwich, there was little change in the composition of the industry, as can be seen in Table 11. The only significant events were the amalgamation of Youngs and Crawshay in 1851, the purchase of Weston's brewery by Youngs, Crawshay, & Youngs in 1864 (with its forty public houses it was sold for £15,300), and the expansion of Bullard's premises in Westwick Street in the late 1860's.[42] Unfortunately, rateable values can provide only a rough guide to the comparative position of businesses, and it is difficult if not impossible to estimate the number of public houses supplied by the respective breweries. However, the evidence we have suggests that Steward & Patteson maintained its position in the town, despite the growing challenge of Bullard's. Data on the number of Norwich pubs *owned* by the major breweries, taken from the poor-rate books (which do not provide a complete listing), suggest that Steward and Patteson reduced the number held by about fifty in the thirty-five years to 1880, while the number owned by their competitors, Youngs, Bullard, and Morgan, increased by approximately the same amount (Table 12). Of course, this analysis takes no account of houses held on lease.

TABLE 12

Public House Ownership in Norwich, 1845–80

Owner	*Number of Houses owned*		
	1845	*1860*	*1880*
Steward, Patteson, Finch	183	145	130
Youngs	71	86	100
Crawshay	25	—	—
Weston	32	26	—
Bullard	32	40	81
Morgan	59	53	60

Source: 1845: Table 8, above; 1860 and 1880: Norwich Poor Rate Books, 1860, 1880, N.R.O. I am indebted to Dr P.B. Barnes for this information.

In Yarmouth, Steward and Patteson did not add to the twenty-five public houses acquired with Paget's brewery in 1845. One or two were sold, and one or two were purchased, with the result that the company still owned exactly twenty-five pubs in 1895.[43] Undoubtedly, the main opportunities for further expansion lay outside Norwich and Yarmouth, in the suburbs, large villages, and market towns. For Steward and Patteson, the major developments before 1880 were the purchase in 1866 of twenty public houses previously held on lease from Bell of

Gorleston, the purchase of Bircham's Reepham Brewery with its fifty pubs in 1878, and a steady expansion in the counties of Norfolk and Suffolk, which included the acquisition of about a dozen outlets in King's Lynn and a similar number in Ipswich.[44] These activities certainly stretched the resources of the partners. Public houses were selling for about £500-£600 each in the 1860's and 1870's. The purchase of Bell's properties cost the company £11,875, and the Reepham Brewery and its pubs cost £36,000.[45] Some of the money came from 'ploughed-back' profits, but a considerable amount was found by mortgaging existing properties. The mortgagees were usually friends or relations of the partners, and sometimes the partners acted in an individual capacity. Thus, when the Reepham Brewery was acquired in 1878, Charles Morse, the largest single stakeholder in Steward and Patteson, lent the company £10,000 at 4 per cent on the security of twenty-five of the Reepham pubs. With a complex and constantly changing set of contractual obligations, it is difficult to determine the precise extent of mortgage activity. However, by 1880 at least £23,000 had been raised in this way.[46] It is clear that the brewery was rapidly approaching the limits to further growth caused by dependence for capital upon the resources of the participating families within the private company structure.

4

Steward, Patteson, Finch & Co.: The Last Partnership and the Move to Limited Liability, 1883-95

The Partnership of 1883

The agreement of 1863 was due to expire on 31 October 1883, and on 25 October of that year a new indenture was signed. This recognised several changes of ownership consequent upon inheritance. Whether regular access to the Pockthorpe brewing process enhanced life expectancy is not known, but of the ten signatories of the 1863 agreement, only the managing partners, Henry Staniforth Patteson and Donald Steward, were still alive in 1883. Of the others, Charles Morse had died in March of that year, leaving his share in the brewery to his second son George Henry (1857-1931). The circumstances require comment. Charles had intended to pass on his interest to his first son, Charles II, who had been sent to Pockthorpe after leaving school in the early 1870's. A quite different career had been intended for George Henry. He was sent first to Wellington, then to Cooper's Hill College, the engineering and gunnery college, with the intention of finding him a post in the Public Works Engineering Department in India. Had his elder brother not become seriously ill he would never have involved himself in the brewery. However, in 1878 his father recalled him to Norwich to take Charles's place at Pockthorpe.[1]

It proved to be one of those happy accidents which help to sustain business dynasties. Unlike his dilettante father, George Morse was an ideal recruit to the family business. From the start he took a keen interest in the details of brewing management, and later developed civic and political interests which blossomed into a most distinguished career. Indeed, in many ways, he might have been the son of Henry Staniforth Patteson, for, like him, he not only became successful as a brewing manager but also became an important member of Norwich's Conservative Party. Elected a city councillor in 1887, and an alderman in 1904, he acted as mayor twice, in 1898 and 1922, and led the local party for over a decade. In 1923 he received a knighthood in recognition of his services to Norwich and the Conservative cause. He was also, like Patteson, a director of the Norwich Union. He went on to act as its chairman and president in 1929, but was forced to resign owing to ill-health in the following year.[2] He resembled his father only in his enthusiasm for sport. Unfortunately, a serious eye injury prevented him from hunting and shooting, but he was able to continue with mountaineering, at which he excelled. Having joined the Alpine Club in 1887, he served on its committee from 1892 to 1895, and was elected president in 1926. It was on a climbing holiday that he met his wife, Annie Pasteur (they were married in 1893).[3] But George Morse was not a frivolous man. Austere, even aloof, and abstemious, he pursued his business and political affairs with energy and determination. His entry into the brewery helped to sustain the high quality of management represented by Patteson and Donald Steward, demonstrating once again a great strength in Steward and Patteson - the ability to maintain effective control of the business by drawing upon resources provided by all four of the participating families.

As for the Stewards, Donald was able to increase his stake in the brewery partnership through inheritance. When his brother Walter died in 1869 he took possession of the shares he had held jointly with him, and eight years later he inherited the interest of his mother, Lucy Steward, on her death.[4] His continuing presence as a managing partner ensured that the other changes of ownership involving the Stewards were merely transfers from rentier to rentier. When Charles died in 1870, he was succeeded by his son, the Reverend Charles John Steward of Somerleyton (1839-1909), a graduate of Trinity College, Cambridge.[5] The shares held by Lady Travers, who died in 1864, was transferred to two of her five sons as tenants-in-common: Major-General James Francis Eaton Travers, of Upham in Hampshire, and Captain Francis Steward Travers, of Bwlch in Brecon, formerly of the 60th Rifles.[6] Peter Finch died in November 1881, at the comparatively early age of 41. His widow Eliza retained a life interest in his brewery shares, which were controlled by his executors, Donald Steward, his brother, Charles Fetherstonhaugh, his brother-in-law, and George Lucas, a Great Yarmouth solicitor and family friend. Provision was also made for the subsequent transfer to Finch's children. However, at the time of his death, his second son, Charles Hugh Finch, who was later to become a leading figure in the management of the brewery, was still only a boy. Born at Yately, Hampshire in 1866, he attended Shrewsbury School before joining the firm in 1885.[7]

The Patteson interest remained firmly in the hands of Henry

Staniforth Patteson, who like Donald Steward, had increased his stake in the brewery by means of inheritance. The shares of his father, John Staniforth, which had been controlled by executors for over forty years, finally came into his possession in 1881 after the death of the surviving trustees, his mother Anne Elizabeth (in 1873), and his uncle William Frederick Patteson (in 1881).[8] At the same time, however, Henry passed on a quarter of his holding to his only son, Henry Tyrwhitt Patteson (1851-1915), who was made a junior partner in the firm. Thus, when the new partnership was struck in November 1883 the 400 shares of £350 each were divided into the proportions shown in Table 13. The new agreement, which was to run for a period of nineteen years from 1 November 1883, concerned a capital which had been increased to £140,000, £100,000 larger than in 1863. However, 60 per

TABLE 13

Steward Patteson Finch & Co. Partnership, November 1883: Division of £140,000 Capital

Partner	*£350 Shares (no.)*	*%*
George Henry Morse, The Close, Norwich	96	24
Donald Steward, Catton	74	18.5
Henry Staniforth Patteson, Cringleford	62	15.5
Executors of the late Peter Finch, Hurst Grove, Berks [Donald Steward, Charles Fetherstonhaugh, George Lucas]	50	12.5
Revd Charles J. Steward, Somerleyton	48	12
Maj.-Gen. James F.E. Travers, Upham, Hants. [11/18] and Capt. Francis Steward Travers, Bwlch, Brecon [7/18]	48	12
Henry Tyrwhitt Staniforth Patteson, Cringleford	22	5.5
	400	100

Source: Steward & Patteson Partnership Deeds: Indenture, 25 October 1883, BR11/8, N.R.O.

cent of this considerable increase was explained by the decision of the partners to give up their earlier intention of writing off the capital debt of the Yarmouth Agency. The accumulated profits of this side of the business had been used instead to expand, and future profits were to continue to be 'ploughed back' for the benefit of the whole concern, although the accounts of the two principal branches, Norwich and Yarmouth, were to remain separated. The Yarmouth Agency, which had grown with the acquisition of Bells of Gorleston in 1866, was now represented in the books by a capital of £60,000. The remainder, £80,000, which stood to the account of Norwich, was double the figure fixed in 1863. Most of this increase, however, is explained by the incorporation of the assets of the Reepham Brewery, purchased in 1878 (see Chapter 3).[9]

The holdings of the respective families in this enlarged capital, constrained as they no doubt were by mortgage agreements, remained the same as they had been twenty years earlier. The partnership was effectively a union of three partnerships struck at the time of the major brewing mergers of 1820, 1831 and 1837: Steward, Patteson & Steward, 180 shares (45 per cent); Morse & Patteson, 120 shares (30 per cent); and Finch & Patteson, 100 shares (25 per cent). This gave the Steward/Finch interest 55 per cent, the Morses 24 per cent, and the Pattesons 21 per cent. More important to the effective running of the brewery, of course, was the nature of the active managerial interest. Here, the growing complexity of the business made it necessary to call on the resources of all four families. The partnership deed of 1883 confirmed both Henry Staniforth Patteson and Donald Steward in appointments as senior managing partners, each with a clear annual salary of £700. In addition, two younger partners were appointed as junior managers: Henry Tyrwhitt Staniforth Patteson (salary: £400 a year); and George Henry Morse (salary: £300 a year). The managers were instructed to 'give their constant personal attention to the business', and to that end were granted considerable delegated powers. They were given authority to spend up to £10,000 on any single transaction and up to £5,000 on the purchase of public houses. With the entry of Charles Hugh Finch into the Pockthorpe brewery in 1885 there were no less than five active managers, none of them recruited from outside (see illustration). These men, together with the Yarmouth agent, Thomas Burton Steward (Arthur Steward's son and four times mayor of Yarmouth between 1876 and 1886), and F.E. Doggett, who had succeeded W.A. Provart as head brewer in 1882, filled the key positions.[10] The agreement of 1883 also provided for the admittance of Charles Hugh Finch as a partner when he reached his twenty-fifth birthday. This he did in 1891, and he joined the partnership by acquiring six shares in the business from his late father's executors. There appear to have been no other significant changes before the brewery became a limited liability company in 1895.[11]

The last of the private partnerships undoubtedly gained two able lieutenants in the younger Patteson and Charles H. Finch. Between them they gave the firm a century of service. The precise nature of their duties at Pockthorpe before the incorporation of 1895 has not been

4. Steward, Patteson, Finch & Co. managers, 1888 (standing, left to right: Henry Tyrwhitt Staniforth Patteson; Donald Steward; Charles Hugh Finch; sitting: George Henry Morse; Henry Staniforth Patteson) [*Stokes coll.*]

documented. It is unlikely that they embraced major responsibilities. There were two senior managing partners, and, of the others, George Morse had the longest association with the business. However, H.T.S. Patteson was paid more with his £400 a year, and it is plausible to suggest that he relieved his father, who was sixty-seven years old in 1883, of some of his administrative burdens. Certainly, his involvement in brewery affairs was more unambiguous later on. He became the second chairman of the new company on his father's death in 1898, and served in that capacity until his own death after a heart attack in May 1915. Patteson was, in many ways, a chip off the old block. Outside the brewery he followed his father into local politics and business, successfully maintaining the family place in Norwich's Tory elite. As a member of the Conservative Party he served, like his father before him, as Sheriff of Norwich (in 1901), and also acted as Deputy-Lieutenant and High Sheriff of Norfolk. He also became a director of the Norwich Union Fire Society, the Norwich & London Accident Society, the Norwich Waterworks Co., and Norwich Corn Hall Co., as well as taking an active interest in local charities (including institutions for the blind and mentally-ill). However, his main enthusiasm was for things military. In its obituary the *Norfolk Chronicle* made much of his life-long association with the Volunteer Brigades, first in Berkshire in the 1870's, then with the 4th Volunteers of the Norfolk Regiment, from the mid-1880's. Reaching the rank of Colonel in 1895, he was largely responsible for 'a signalling section at Blofield, the bearer section at Long Stratton, and the very smart cyclist section at Thetford'. Married in 1883 to Annie Chambers (who died in 1904), he left an estate valued at £89,700 net to a surviving son, Robert Wace Patteson (1895-1926), and two daughters, Joan and Ardyn. His eldest son, John Dossie (born in 1889) was killed in France in 1914.[12]

Charles Finch's association with the brewery as apprentice, partner, director, and chairman (1931-45) extended over a period of sixty-seven years. He retired at the end of 1952 and died in March 1954, aged eighty-eight. How much he did before 1895 again is not known. But there is no doubt at all that his influence on subsequent development was considerable. Here he had much to do with the company's pioneering work in pneumatic malting and with the progressive improvement of public houses. Outside Pockthorpe Finch, like his fellow managing partners, became a local political and business figure of some substance. He joined Norwich's City Council in 1905 as a Conservative, retaining his membership until 1932, and was elected Sheriff of the city in 1919, alderman in 1921, and High Sheriff of Norfolk in 1935. He also further strengthened the representation of Steward & Patteson in the Norwich Union Insurance Company, acting as a director of the Life Society, 1920-49 (Vice-President in 1930-41) and the Fire Society, 1925-49 (Vice-Chairman, 1941-8). Finally, like his fellow brewers, he found time for leisure pursuits. Indeed, as a keen all-round sportsman, he must have given a great deal of his time to sporting activities during the period of the last partnership. Not only was he a competent oarsman and footballer - he captained Thorpe F.C. and played at centre-forward for Norfolk v. the Canadian Tourists in 1891 - but he was also an able cricketer, good enough to be given a county trial. Some of his sporting interests were terminated after his marriage in 1900 to Mildred Bertha Long and a subsequent move of house from Sprowston to Costessey House, Costessey. But he still found time for golf, shooting, and steeplechasing, and was accustomed to drive to Ascot Races each year in a carriage complete with postillions. Leaving an estate valued at £112,000 net, he was survived by one of two sons, Peter Charles Finch, of Bracon Ash (1905-79).[13] From the above information it is quite clear that the Pockthorpe brewery was managed by more than mere brewers. Finch, the two Pattesons, Donald Steward, and George Morse were among the most influential political and social figures in the Norwich of their day.

Steward, Patteson, Finch & Co. and the 'brewing revolution' of the 1880's and 1890's

The brewing industry was undoubtedly in a state of flux in the 1880's. Consumption of beer in the United Kingdom, which had been buoyant in the second half of the 1870's (averaging 31.4 million barrels or 33.2 gallons per head), fell by about 8 per cent in the following decade (14 per cent in per capita terms).[14] Pessimism in the trade was also encouraged by the strength of the Temperance Movement, changes in government policy towards the taxation of beer, and the emergence of alternative leisure pursuits for the working classes. The threat of falling demand, further restrictions on licensing, and higher taxation - Gladstone had abolished the malt duty in 1880 but introduced a new beer duty of 6*s.* 3*d.* per thirty-six-gallon barrel of 1057^{0} Specific Gravity [S.G.] - made the general climate a gloomy one.

For Steward, Patteson, Finch & Co., the depressed state of farming in East Anglia was an additional and enduring problem. It heralded a long, painful, period of adjustment in the region which threatened the health of all breweries with a large rural base. Those breweries which had expanded in anticipation of rising demand were left in a critical position in the 1880's. And even those firms whose finances were sound faced several problems. Competition from rival firms in the locality was intensifying, while sales to the more distant urban markets, which the railways had opened up, were hit hard by the success of the Burton brewers, such as Bass and Allsopp. In these conditions it was essential to root out inefficient production methods and improve the quality of the beer. For many provincial brewers this meant a heavy investment in new brewing plant, while further expenditure was required if they were to rise to the technological challenge of producing pale ales, filtered bottled beer, and mineral waters in addition to traditional products. The growing demand for improved standards of comfort in public houses, particularly in the towns, also carried a considerable financial implication. For many smaller breweries the only options were to merge with a neighbour or sell up. Others responded by purchasing public houses in order to protect their market-share. Investment problems were then met by either turning the business into a public joint-stock company, or by acquiring limited liability status and raising capital through the issue of debentures.

The experience of Steward, Patteson, Finch & Co. during its last partnership was typical of many of the larger provincial breweries of the day. Here for the first time in this history there is sufficient documentary evidence to allow some detailed analysis of the firm's problems and response. Many of the ledgers, account books, and statistical tables date from the period 1883-6, a fact which itself suggests that the new partnership began with a determination to improve managerial performance and maintain profitability under more challenging circumstances. The records indicate that the Pockthorpe concern, although absent from Alfred Barnard's brewery survey, *The Noted Breweries of Great Britain*, of 1889-91, was one of the largest provincial breweries. It is true that production at around 80,000 barrels a year (an average of 81,582 barrels over the nine years ending November 1894 [Appendix D, Table 2]) was not particularly large in comparison with the output of urban breweries in the industrial Midlands and North. On the other hand, the number of public houses owned and controlled by Steward Patteson Finch & Co. was very considerable indeed. At the time of a Home Office inquiry in 1892 the firm owned 327 houses in Norwich and the surrounding country districts, plus another 146 through its agencies in Yarmouth, Ipswich and Colchester. This total of 473 owned houses was second only to Greenall Whitley & Co. of Warrington, with 681. In addition, the Norwich company was in the same year leasing another 111 pubs, and serving 103 in the free trade. The company also re-established its interest in the brewing lobby. In December 1883 Donald Steward was elected to the general committee of the Country Brewers' Society, and he helped to form a union of Norfolk Brewers (later the Norfolk Brewers' Association) in the same month, taking the chair at its inaugural meeting.[15]

At a first glance the firm's accounts suggest that the overall profitability of this large 'empire' was fairly sound in the mid-1880's and beyond. Over the decade from 1886 to 1895 beer sales amounted to an average of 75,661 barrels a year, returning an income, before expenses, of nearly £62,000. With the sales of spirits, wines, mineral waters, and malt [the last three items were recorded in *net* terms], total income averaged £70,121 over the same period. After deducting working costs of £48,993 per annum the partners were left with a 'net profit' of £21,128, and from this they took £14,532 a year in dividends, which represented a healthy return of 10.38 per cent on their original capital of £140,000 (see Table 14). However, a more accurate picture of the state of the business is required if we are to understand the factors behind the move to limited liability status in 1895. Here, analysis is hindered by the nature of the accounts. On the revenue side, gross and net items are intermingled, while on the expenditure side, the firm made no attempt to distinguish between items properly chargeable to revenue account, and items properly chargeable to capital. The costs in Table 14, for example, include such elements as 'contingencies', brewery repairs, alterations to public houses, interest on money borrowed, 'depreciation on unsettled purchases', and the wear and tear of horses. Some of the problems may be appreciated if we compare Table 14, the company's own trading or 'profit and loss' account, with Table 15, which represents an attempt to present the available data in a more satisfactory form. In Table 14, 'working costs' exclude two major items: materials, that is, malt, hops, sugar, coal etc.; and beer duty, which was first shown in the accounts for 1895. Thus, the income from beer, while gross of brewery and public house

TABLE 14

Steward, Patteson, Finch & Co. Trading Account, 1886–95

Year ending November	Beer	Spirits	Income [£] Wines (net)	Mineral Waters (net)	Malt (net)	Bottled Beer	Total Income	Working Costs[b]	Net Profit	Partners' Dividends	Retentions
1886	62,146	4,606	207	1,019	1,508	–	69,485	44,523	24,962	15,500	9,462
1887	64,882	4,970	302	1,256	1,548	–	72,959	44,658	28,301	16,000	12,301
1888	63,066	4,944	295	746	1,724	–	70,775	47,404	23,371	15,000	8,371
1889	59,943	4,850	275	1,228	1,352	–	67,649	47,598	20,051	14,000	6,051
1890	59,509	5,285	349	1,113	1,151	–	67,406	51,553[c]	15,853	14,000	1,853
1891	63,081	5,574	252	662	1,091	–	70,661	51,048	19,613	14,000	5,613
1892	61,016	5,504	316	862	1,204	–	68,901	50,366	18,535	14,000	4,535
1893	64,203	5,619	269	1,169	1,171	–	72,431	51,749	20,682	14,000	6,682
1894	58,166	5,701	316	883	1,109	–	66,176	49,162	17,014	13,500	3,514
1895	63,563	5,577	317	1,472	1,325	265	74,762[a]	51,868	22,894	15,317[d]	7,577

Source: Steward & Patteson Account Books, Quarterly Balances, 1886–1908, BR1/104, N.R.O.

[a] 1895 Total Income includes £2,233 from Yarmouth Agency.

[b] This includes interest on money borrowed, pub alterations etc. In 1891–4 includes brewery 'old repair a/c': £1,000; £1,654; £2,293; £1,495.

[c] Includes £3,233 for Depreciation on unsettled purchases.

[d] Company now limited liability: figure in Steward & Patteson Account Books, Expenses and charges on trade, 1884–1957, BR1/107, N.R.O.

TABLE 15

Steward, Patteson, Finch & Co: Estimate of Gross Revenue and Costs, 1886–95 [£]

Year ending November	**Gross Revenue**	Costs: *Malt*	*Hops*	*Other Materials*	*Total Materials*	*Beer Duty*[a]	*Labour*[b]	*Other Costs*	*Total*	**Net Profit**	*Working Ratio*
1886	138,424	33,263	6,625	4,796	44,684	24,255	10,309	34,214	113,056	24,962	82
1887	145,827	34,706	6,495	5,484	46,685	26,183	10,427	34,231	117,526	28,301	81
1888	143,895	34,911	6,610	5,529	47,050	26,070	10,638	36,766	120,524	23,371	84
1889	145,201	35,392	9,559	5,895	50,846	26,706	10,823	36,745	125,150	20,051	86
1890	143,625	35,609	7,863	6,364	49,836	26,383	11,177	40,376	127,772	15,853	89
1891	148,401	34,413	10,062	6,312	50,787	26,953	11,794	39,254	128,788	19,613	87
1892	145,991	35,214	8,934	6,284	50,432	26,658	11,931	38,435	127,456	18,535	87
1893	149,298	33,264	9,983	6,098	49,343	27,522	12,069	39,680	128,616	20,682	86
1894	136,585	31,576	8,663	5,092	45,331	25,078	12,252	36,910	119,571	17,014	88
1895	137,487	27,085	7,023	3,807	37,915	24,810	12,373	39,495	114,593	22,894	83

Source: Miscellaneous accounts, in Steward & Patteson Account Books, BR1/104, 107, 110, and 134, N.R.O.

a Beer duty is first mentioned in the account in 1895, when it amounted to 6*s*. 7*d*. a barrel. The duty for earlier years has been estimated, assuming the following rates per barrel: 6*s*. 3*d*., 1886–8; 6*s*. 5½*d*., 1889–93; 6*s*. 7*d*., 1894. The gross rates of duty were: 6*s*. 3*d*. at 1057° S.G., 1880–9; 6*s*. 3*d*. at 1055° (equivalent to a 2½*d*. increase in duty), 1889–94; 6*s*. 9*d*. at 1055°, 1894–5.

b Labour costs here are salaries shown in the 'trade charges' account in BR1/107 and wages shown in BR1/134.

expenses, is in effect a 'net' item. Assuming that we may obtain an approximate indication of total costs and thus of gross revenue by adding back the data on material costs and beer duty (the latter is estimated for the years before 1895), we may identify some of the pressures acting on the brewery in Table 15.

Here, there are signs that cost pressures may have begun to worry the company before the onset of general inflation from the mid-1890's. Total costs rose by 13 per cent from 1886 to 1891, the relevant factors being a 14 per cent increase in material costs (particularly hops, up by over 50 per cent) and a 14 per cent increase in labour costs. Consequently, the 'working ratio', that is, costs expressed as a percentage of gross revenue, moved up from the low to the high 80's. It is difficult, of course, to analyse the factors responsible for rising costs. However, the explanation for higher labour costs appears to lie in the need to take on additional staff as the brewery's operations became more complex. Comparing the quinquennia 1883/4-1887/8 and 1890/1-1894/5, wages and salaries rose by 16 per cent (salaries: 19 per cent; wages: 14 per cent). Average money earnings at Pockthorpe rose by only 3 per cent, while the average number of workers employed increased by 11.1 per cent, from 133.0 to 147.8.[16]

We should also observe that 'net profits' of £21,000 or so appear more modest when related to the value of the assets employed in the business. Profits amounted to only 6.5 per cent of the value of the total assets shown in the ledgers for 1886-94 (which include liquid assets), and there are grounds for asserting that this is an overestimate of the true return on capital. Much, of course, depends on establishing a correct valuation of the public houses owned by the partners. In the firm's accounts, 'public houses and estates' were valued at only £121,896 on 6 November 1886. Eight years later the figure given was £174,465. However, in the accounts of the new, limited liability company for November 1895, their value was put at £404,275, and net profits for that year, £22,894, or £24,696 before payment of debenture interest, were equivalent to only about 4 per cent of the total issued capital of £580,000.[17] Further evidence that the partners were trading on relatively small margins comes from a detailed analysis of their retail trade. Here, the weakness of a primarily rural business was readily apparent. In the period 1886-8 Steward Patteson Finch & Co. were supplying over 560 public houses directly, and with the agency houses in the Yarmouth, Ipswich, and Colchester areas, the total number of houses supplied was about 710. In addition, the company was sending 8-9,000 barrels a year to the London market, and small amounts to its agencies in Plymouth and Bedfield (Suffolk). For a brewery which was selling only 77,000 barrels or so, this indicates a very low barrelage - the number of barrels sold per public house - scarcely two barrels a week.[18]

In these circumstances of low margins and rising costs, it is not surprising to find that the partners took some action to improve their trading position. First, they sought to reduce their more distant retail trades. Second, they reduced the strength of their beers. Distribution was re-organised on a more rational basis by cutting out some of the agency business. In 1889 London sales fell from 9,000 to 5,000 barrels, and the trade disappeared altogether in 1894. Sales to the Plymouth agency, a long-standing but more modest commitment (sales were running at about 160-70 barrels a year in the late 1880's), ceased in 1891. While it is not clear whether these decisions were forced upon the company by local market factors, further evidence suggests that the moves were probably part of an active policy of rationalisation. Thus, in 1891, the brewery discontinued its supply to twenty-three leased and free trade pubs in Cambridge, and two years later sold its Colchester agency of twenty-eight pubs to Greene King & Sons of Bury St Edmunds.[19] By November 1894, the total number of outlets supplied [including agency houses] had been reduced by about 11 per cent, and the agency trade (as opposed to the 'house trade') had fallen from 40 per cent of total sales in 1886-8 to 28 per cent in 1894-5 (calculated from Tables 16 and 17). At the same time, there were signs of an increasing concentration on the local market, particularly in the city of Norwich. The proportion of total sales going to the city increased from 22 per cent in the two years 1886-7 to 30 per cent in 1894-5 (Table 17). Furthermore, the move to limited liability was accompanied by the purchase of Morse and Wood's Swaffham Brewery and its fifty-one public houses, which strengthened the company's already firm hold on the Norfolk market.

A desire to check the cost of materials may have prompted the company to reduce the strength of its beer. The company's brewing statistics indicate that smaller quantities of malt and hops were being used per gyle towards the end of the partnership. The amount of malt used per barrel fell from 0.488 coombs [four bushels] in 1886-90 to 0.461 in 1891-5 and that of hops from 2.08 lb. per barrel to 1.99. Consequently, the average specific gravity of the beer fell from 1062.77^{0} in 1886 to 1059.44^{0} in 1895, and that of the most popular beer,

TABLE 16

Steward, Patteson, Finch & Co.'s Public Houses, 1886–95 [excluding Agency Houses]

First week of November	NORWICH				COUNTRY				KING'S LYNN		CAMBRIDGE		TOTAL			
	Owned	*Leased*	*free*	**Total**	*Owned*	*Leased*	*Free*	**Total**	*Leased*	*Free*	*Leased*	*Free*	*Owned*	*Leased*	*Free*	**Total**
1886	125	33	12	170	177	62	64	303	26	34	17	9	302	140[a]	119	561[a]
1887	130	28	13	171	184	57	64	305	29	27	17	6	314	133[a]	110	557[a]
1888	131	26	14	171	189	57	64	310	33	25	16	8	320	132	111	563
1889	133	24	13	170	193	61	59	313	30	22	16	8	326	131	102	559
1890	134	21	15	170	195	65	60	320	30	21	16	7	329	132	103	564
1891	131	21	13	165	195	65	56	316	30	24	-	-	326	116	93	535
1892	130	20	13	163	197	63	69	329	28	21	-	-	327	111	103	541
1893	133	18	12	163	198	61	70	329	27	21	-	-	331	106	103	540
1894	134	17	10	161	207	58	67	332	27	18	-	-	341	102	95	538
1895	126	24	10	160	264	63	61	388	24	13	-	-	390	111	84	585

Source: Steward & Patteson Account Books: Quarterly Balances,1886–1908, BR1/104, N.R.O.
[a] Totals include two houses mortgaged.

TABLE 17

Steward, Patteson, Finch & Co. Beer Sales, in barrels, 1886–95

Year ending November	SPF Houses: *Norwich*	SPF Houses: *Country*	Leased Houses: *Norwich*	Leased Houses: *Country*	Free Houses: *Norwich*	Free Houses: *Country*	Total House Trade	Agencies: *Yarmouth*	Agencies: *London*	Agencies: *Essex/ Suffolk*	*Other*[b]	Total Agency Trade	Total
1886	11,989	11,490	3,001	7,095	1,281	8,139	43,063	13,355	8,324	7,411	418	29,508	72,571
1887	13,275	12,880	2,652	6,973	1,350	9,469	46,625	14,481	8,836	7,696	381	31,394	78,019
1888	14,004	11,992	2,521	7,039	1,578	8,988	46,181	14,420	9,007	7,472	377	31,276	77,457
1889	14,866	12,649	2,579	7,883	1,900	9,811	49,736	14,856	5,026	7,678	328	27,889	77,625
1890	15,488	13,621	2,598	7,728	1,561	9,908	50,950	14,498	3,222	7,699	310	25,729	76,679
1891	16,214	14,215	2,407	7,961	2,215	9,625	52,685	14,702	2,318	8,200	247	25,467	78,152
1892	16,212	14,853	2,304	7,067	1,658	9,753	52,198	14,588	2,207	8,235	221	25,251	77,449
1893	17,660	15,445	2,163	7,220	1,908	9,251	53,833	14,801	1,903	8,482	155	25,341	79,174
1894	17,574	15,027	1,937	6,558	1,967	7,766	50,880	14,093	147	4,711[a]	451	19,402	70,282
1895	17,581	15,654	1,851	6,186	1,425	7,026	50,140	13,660	-	4,450	954	19,064	69,204
Average 1886–95	15,486.3	13,782.6	2,381.3	7,171.0	1,684.3	8,973.6	49,630.1	14,345.4	4,099.0	7,203.4	384.2	26,032.1	75,661.2
% Total	20.5	18.5	3.1	9.5	2.2	11.9	65.6	19.0	5.4	9.5	0.5	34.4	100.0

Source: Steward & Patteson Account Books, Quarterly Balances, 1886–1908, BR1/104, N.R.O. Totals are rounded to the nearest barrel. There are numerous pencilled corrections in the accounts, and minor discrepancies are frequent.

[a] Now called 'Ipswich Agency'.

[b] This column includes Plymouth Agency (c.160–70 barrels p.a. until 1891); Bedfield (Suffolk) Agency (c.180–250 barrels p.a.); Private sales (c.40–60 p.a., 419 in 1894–5); Bottled Beer (from 1892–3); and Swaffham Agency (from 1894–5).

XX ale, fell from 1063.0^{0} to 1050.0^{0}.[20] And there was no incentive to maintain high gravities with a taxation system based on a 'standard' barrel of 1057^{0} S.G., 1880-9, and 1055^{0} from 1889.[21] Other signs of anxiety in the period may be found in the partners' decision to reduce dividends in response to falling profits after 1887 (see Table 14, above), and a rise in expenditure on brewery repairs, which amounted to about £12,000 in the period 1891-5. The suggestion that with falling demand and rising costs parts of the business were far from profitable is supported by a reference, in the accounts for the year ending 2 November 1895, to a 'Loss on Ipswich Agency: £379 7*s*.'.[22]

The need to consolidate the business in a period of competitive pressure and uncertainty must have influenced the partners in their decision to change the company's status and raise capital by issuing debentures. Moreover, money was also needed to re-equip the brewery. In the early 1890's it became apparent that as the company diversified its production to keep pace with changing tastes, a great strain was placed on the existing brewing and malting plant, much of it antiquated by this time. In 1887, for example, the company was producing, in addition to small quantities of weak 'X' and table beer, no less than eight different brews: Pale Ale, Light Bitter, 'K', XXXX, XXX, XX, Double Brown Stout, and Porter. In the following year, an experimental 'B' beer was also made, although it was withdrawn two years later, and in 1893 an I.P.A. was introduced, the same year in which bottled beer production was started. The company was also enjoying the benefits of producing its own mineral waters. This branch of the trade, which had been started in 1883, involved a sale of about 140,000 dozen bottles a year, 1886-95, contributing over £1,000 a year net in income, three times that derived from the old-established wine trade.[23] It is true that in spite of this impressive variety, the brewery's mainstay was still the local 'Norwich' beers. XXXX, XXX, and XX ale together accounted for about three-quarters of total production, and the most popular brew was the relatively cheap XX, which made up about 45-50 per cent of the total. In contrast, the newer pale and light bitter ales represented only 5 per cent of total output. And bottled beer production, while expanding rapidly after 1893, was still relatively small. 6,293 dozen bottles were sold in 1894, the first full year (equivalent to 296 standard, 36-gallon, barrels), and 11,341 dozen in 1895 (532 barrels), or under 1 per cent of total output.[24] But however small the new developments were in the early stages, they greatly complicated brewing operations at Pockthorpe, and it was soon accepted

5. The draymen, 1888 [*Stokes coll.*]

6. Four-horse dray, 1888 [*Stokes coll.*]

that investment was essential if the brewery was to maintain its competitive position. C.H. Finch later recalled that when he joined the brewery in 1885 the beer casks were hand-washed. The company also had no less than sixteen floor maltings, most of them small and inefficient.[25] It is almost impossible, of course, to determine exactly how the brewery was organised in this period. A number of photographs were taken in the later nineteenth century, but these usually depict groups of brewery workers, and only one has survived which shows the inside of the brewery (the cask room). All that can be said is that the level of mechanisation appears to have been low, and that local competitors, Bullard's and Morgan's, were reputed to have more modern premises. Finance was certainly required if changes were to be made, and the firm had probably reached the limits of internal funding. The account-books show that the mortgage debt exceeded £60,000 in the late 1880's and early 1890's, and the total amount of indebtedness was about £145,000.[26]

The agreement of May 1895, by which the partners agreed to purchase the Swaffham Brewery of Morse and Woods, together with its fifty-one pubs and two maltings, on 11 October, intensified the pressure for further investment and prompted the decision to change the company's status. Personal and family factors played a major part in the transaction. An interest in the Swaffham Brewery had been held by a branch of the Morse family since 1809, when the brewery was purchased from Page and Lockwood by Thomas Morse of Lound Hall, Suffolk (1744-1844), the elder brother of John Morse (1745-1837), who had established the family's brewing interest in Norwich. Since 1860 the business had been in the hands of Frederick Morse of Lowestoft, Thomas Morse's grandson and youngest son of Thomas Morse junior (born in 1779), and Henry Glasspoole Woods, who were in partnership as brewers and wine and spirits merchants in Swaffham and Lowestoft. The Swaffham enterprise, which had been held in half-shares by the partners, was bought out by Frederick Morse in 1892 for £21,000, the money coming from a 4¼ per cent mortgage provided by Woods. The latter's death in January 1895 prompted Frederick to sell to his cousin's brewery. The surviving legal documentation is not without ambiguity, but it appears that Steward & Patteson put up £21,000 to pay off the Woods mortgage, and at the same time George H. Morse, one of Steward & Patteson's directors, paid Frederick Morse £11,405.[27] Protection of the local Norfolk market was an important consideration in the purchase. And it was made more pertinent by the growing challenge of local rivals, Bullard's and Morgan's. Both had extended their hold on the Norwich tied-house trade, and both had already launched themselves as limited liability companies. In 1890, for example, Steward Patteson Finch & Co. owned 134 pubs in the city, Bullard 94, Youngs 93, and Morgan 71. There was no question of a Pockthorpe monopoly. Indeed, its rivals had strengthened their financial position. In March 1887 Morgan's became a public company with a nominal capital of £185,000. The ordinary shares were retained by the partners, but £75,000 of 6 per cent preference shares were offered to investors. At the time Morgan's owned 106 pubs freehold and held a further eighty-two on lease. In March 1895 Bullard's followed suit, forming itself into a private limited liability company with an issue of £360,000 in 4 per cent debentures to supplement a privately-held ordinary capital of £290,000. The new company controlled a sizeable empire - 441 public houses, 280 of them freehold.[28] The other large Norwich brewery, Youngs, became a limited liability company in 1897. Thus, the move taken by Steward Patteson Finch & Co. in 1895 was not only a response characteristic of the British brewing industry as it reacted to the more difficult conditions of the 1880's and 1890's but also a response to the actions taken by similarly-placed local competitors.

5

Steward & Patteson Limited: Private Limited Liability Company, 1895-1914

The New Company Structure, 1895-1914

On 4 July 1895 the partners converted their business into limited liability form. The brewery valuers, Collins, Tootell & Co. of Queen Adelaide Street, London, valued the company's assets at £450,704. This sum represented the estimated value of 447 freehold public houses, forty-two of the more valuable leaseholds, 286 houses, shops, cottages, and building sites, the brewery premises, and eleven maltings. In addition, 'loose plant', casks, etc. were valued at £16,224, and stock on hand amounted to £33,637. These calculations did not embrace the Swaffham Brewery, which the partners had agreed to purchase on 11 October.[1]

The new company had an initial nominal capital of £300,000, divided equally into ordinary and 5 per cent preference shares. This was held privately, in more or less the same proportions (see Table 18). The Steward/Finch interest now held 54.25 per cent, the Morse family 24 per cent, and the Pattesons 21.75 per cent. The only major change involved a reduction in the stake of Charles J. Steward. 9,000 shares, 3 per cent of the total capital, were taken up by Thomas Burton Steward, the company's Yarmouth agent, and small additions were made to the holdings of Charles Hugh Finch (1.5 per cent) and Henry Staniforth Patteson (0.75 per cent). There were also some adjustments to the Travers family's interest following the death in 1892 of James Eaton Travers.[2] The change of company status did not affect the managerial structure of the brewery, either. The senior partners, Henry Staniforth Patteson and Donald Steward, became, respectively, Chairman and Deputy-Chairman, and the junior managing partners, George Morse, Henry Tyrwhitt Patteson, and Charles Finch, became directors. Together they owned a substantial 67.25 per cent of the capital. The company had obtained powers to issue £320,000 in debenture stock,

TABLE 18

Initial Shareholders in Steward & Patteson Ltd. September 1895

Shareholder	*Shares Held: [£]*			
	Preference	*Ordinary*	**Total**	%
Henry Staniforth Patteson [Chairman]	24,370	24,380	48,750	16.25
Donald Steward [Deputy-Chairman]	27,750	27,750	55,500	18.50
George Henry Morse [Director]	36,000	36,000	72,000	24.00
Henry Tyrwhitt Staniforth Patteson [Director]	8,250	8,250	16,500	5.50
Charles Hugh Finch [Director]	4,500	4,500	9,000	3.00
Executors of the late Peter Finch [D. Steward, C. Fetherstonhaugh, C.F. Lucas]	16,500	16,490	32,990	11.00
Revd Charles John Steward	10,130	10,120	20,250	6.75
Francis Steward Travers	7,000	7,000	14,000	4.67
Executors of James F.E. Travers [Francis S. and Revd Duncan Travers]	7,000	7,000	14,000	4.67
Revd Robert Duncan Travers	4,000	4,000	8,000	2.67
Thomas Burton Steward	4,500	4,500	9,000	3.00
Charles Frank Lucas	—	10	10	—
Total	**£150,000**	**£150,000**	**£300,000**	**100.01**

Source: S. & P. Ltd. Directors Minutes, 24 September 1895, BR1/45, N.R.O. Directors determined at meeting on 4 July 1895, ibid.

and immediately the directors offered £280,000 to the public on the security of their tied-house estate. The issue, which carried an interest rate of 4 per cent, was over-subscribed by more than seven times. Small investors were plentiful, but over half (55 per cent) of the stock was taken up in small amounts of £2,000 and above. While interest was shown by rentiers from a fairly wide area, including London, the prime support was local. Of the larger investments (£2,000 and over), 75 per cent was held by persons living within twenty-five miles of the Pockthorpe brewery. The controlling families together held about 25 per cent of the stock, although the exact position is uncertain due to the existence of numerous trusts and joint-holdings.[3]

The stability of ownership and control was soon disturbed, however. In 1898 the two senior directors died within four months of each other. The loss of Donald Steward in January and Henry Staniforth Patteson in April left only three directors, and the business reins were taken up by Patteson's son, Henry Tyrwhitt, as Chairman, with George Morse acting as his deputy. Although the surviving directors had a considerable experience of brewing by this time, they quickly concluded that fresh managerial blood was required. At an extraordinary general meeting of the company on 23 June 1898 it was agreed that two clerks should be taken on with a view to their subsequent appointment as directors. Once again, members of the participating families were selected. There were no obvious replacements for a Steward and a Patteson. Donald Steward's son, Rupert Donald, was not twenty-five years old in 1898 (he was born in 1880), while Henry Tyrwhitt Patteson's sons, John and Robert, were aged nine and three. So it was Morse and Finch representation that was strengthened (although, as we have seen, the 'Finch' family was of Steward stock). At the same meeting, the names of Arthur Francis Morse, George's younger brother, and Alfred Finch, one of Charles's younger brothers, were put forward. Alfred's nomination was made dependent on his being given the necessary qualification for a directorship by Eliza, the widow of Peter Finch.[4] Both recruits, who were in their late twenties in 1898, proved to be long-standing servants of the brewery. Lt.-Col. Arthur Francis Morse (1871-1959), having been educated at Wellington and Sandhurst, joined the 6th Inniskilling Dragoons. By 1898, however, he was ready, it seems, to abandon a military career. In September he married Annabel Marjorie Haig (1873–1955), the daughter of William Haig of Fife and a niece of Field-Marshall, Later Earl Haig, and the couple moved to Earlham Lodge, near Norwich. Nevertheless, Arthur retained an interest in military matters, for in 1901 he joined the Norfolk Yeomanry. During the First World War he served in Gallipoli, Egypt, Palestine and France, and subsequently was a supporter of the British Legion, acting as president of the Norfolk branch for a number of years. He was also a deputy-lieutenant of the county. Arthur maintained the Morse family's interest in sporting activities. A keen cricketer, he served as president of the county club in 1933. At the brewery, he acquired 400 ordinary shares before his election as a director in 1904, a position he retained for fifty-three years. He served as company chairman from 1945 to 1951.[5]

Alfred Finch (1870-1943) was Peter Finch's fourth son. After an education at Cambridge University he travelled extensively before settling down in Norfolk. His interests were very similar to those of his co-recruit. He was an enthusiastic cricketer, like his brother Charles, and supported the Norfolk County Cricket Club for many years. He also served in the First World War, with the Royal Norfolk Regiment. Having acquired 200 ordinary shares in Steward & Patteson he was appointed assistant secretary in February 1903 - the company secretary was Cubitt L. Page - and became a director two years later, serving in that capacity until his death in 1943. Residing first in Drayton, then in Old Catton, and finally at Berry's Hall, Honingham, he was survived by his wife, Jane.[6] With Arthur Morse and Alfred Finch the reconstituted board of five directors remained unchanged until the death of Henry Tyrwhitt Patteson in May 1915.

The brewing business, 1895-1914

Steward & Patteson's problems did not disappear with its change of status. Indeed, the first twenty years of trading as a limited liability company saw an intensification of elements which had caused concern earlier: stagnant demand for beer, encouraged by the activities of the Temperance Movement, and the development of alternative leisure facilities; a heavy tax burden; and increased competition in the trade, which stimulated brewery sales or mergers and the rationalisation of retail outlets. There were also new factors. Rising prices after 1896 made for a squeeze on working-class living standards, particularly after 1899. Finally, the rise in the price of public houses placed a considerable strain on the financial resources of those breweries which were induced to respond to sluggish demand by increasing their control of the retail trade. The production of beer in the United Kingdom, which had fallen to an annual average of 28.8 million standard barrels in the 1880's, picked up again and by 1898-1900 reached new heights, averaging 36.8 million barrels a year, an improvement of no less than 28 per cent, and 17 per cent higher than in 1875-9. However, although there was no firm trend thereafter, production slipped back to 35.1 million barrels in 1912-14, a fall of about 5 per cent. In per capita terms this deterioration was more pronounced, with a fall of 15 per cent, from 32.0 gallons in 1898-1900 to 27.1 gallons in 1912-14. These fluctuations were set against a background of increased concentration in the industry. The number of common brewers in the United Kingdom fell from 2,649 in 1880 to 1,335 in 1914, and the number of licensed victuallers and beer-retailer brewers fell from 18,574 to 2,357.[7]

At the same time, the licensing environment became much tougher. Justices began to scrutinize applications for the renewal of licences with more care, and moves to refuse such applications on the grounds that the pubs were surplus to requirements were given impetus by the judgements in *Sharpe v. Wakefield* of 1891 and *Boulter v. Kent JJ.* of 1897, where the House of Lords upheld the justices' discretion in the granting of renewals. When the Conservatives introduced their Licensing Act of 1904, they claimed that the measure would accelerate the process of public house closures. In fact, it served to defend the trade against the actions of over-zealous justices. First of all, the Act removed the justices' absolute discretion to grant new licences and refuse renewals, giving ultimate authority to the Quarter Sessions. Second, it established the principle of compensating owners and publicans for the loss of licences, although the money was to come from a levy raised on local licensed premises. Nevertheless, 9,801 on-licences were terminated with compensation awarded in the period 1905-14, and £8,920,000 was paid out in compensation.[8] We can easily exaggerate the effect of the new licensing measures, particularly since many brewers were agreed that there were too many retail outlets. However, the brewers were certainly alarmed by the prospect of much tighter controls. A Liberal Bill of 1908, which had been encouraged by the Temperance lobby, promised to cut the number of on-licences by at least 30,000. There was considerable anxiety before the measure was thrown out in the Lords.[9] The burden of taxation also increased after 1895. In 1900 the beer duty was raised from 6*s*. 9*d*. to 7*s*. 9*d*. [38.75p] a barrel, representing a cost of £38,750 a year to a producer of 100,000 barrels of 1055^0 S.G. Then, in the Finance Act of 1910, the excise liquor licence for brewers was raised to approximately 12*s*. [60p] per fifty barrels, or about £1,200 for a producer of 100,000 barrels. High duties kept brewers' costs high, and encouraged a strategy based on the retention of relatively high retail prices coupled with a close examination of variable costs.[10]

How did Steward & Patteson Limited fare in these years? The company's data suggest that it more than held its own. The production of beer, stimulated by the acquisition of the Swaffham Brewery's fifty-one pubs, increased from 74,818 barrels in the year ending November 1895 to 84,355 barrels in the following year. It then increased steadily, in marked contrast to the national trend. Production reached 100,000 barrels in 1899, 110,000 in 1906, and 115,000 in 1908, with an annual growth rate of 2.3 per cent from 1896 to 1908. Output then fell back to about 111,000 barrels, but there was an increase to nearly 123,000 barrels in the year ending November 1914 (Appendix D, Table 2), putting the company among the leading fifty or so breweries in the country. Beer sales went hand in hand with production. After an initial rise of 10,000 barrels to 78,726 in 1896, sales increased to about 93,000 barrels in 1899, 104,000 in 1903, and 113,000 in 1908. Settling down to a level of about 108,000 barrels from 1909, there was also an upturn in 1914, when sales reached a peak of nearly 119,000 barrels (Appendix D, Table 2).[11] Was this increased business profitable? It has been suggested in the previous chapter that Steward & Patteson's margins had narrowed, and were relatively small in the early 1890's. The firm's trading accounts indicate that there was some improvement after 1895 despite the gloomy national picture (Table 19). Indeed, it is difficult to find many signs of anxiety. Trading income increased by 45 per cent - £91,000 in 1896-8 and £132,000 in 1911-14 - while working costs rose by only 25 per cent, from £52,000 to £65,000. The income from draught beer, still the principal item, increased steadily to 1905-7, although it fell back a little after that. A matter of concern here was the fall in the income per barrel sold, or wholesale price. Averaging 17*s.* 8¾*d.* [88.6p] in 1896-8, it was down to 16*s.* 1½*d.* [80.6p] by 1911-14. Bottled beer income, on the other hand, exhibited steadily improving figures, and the income per dozen bottles sold jumped from 6½*d.* [2.71p] to 1*s.* 1¾*d.* [5.72p]. However, it still accounted for only 3 per cent of total trading income. More important for the overall position was the improvement in profits from the Yarmouth agency, which were under £4,000 in 1896-8 but reached nearly £13,000 in 1911–14 (all figures quoted are annual averages).

The new company must have been delighted to see a doubling of its net profits. Averaging £28,000 a year in 1896-8, they reached £56,000 in 1911-14. The rate of return appears to have been healthy. Net profits, before the payment of debenture interest, increased steadily from 6.7 per cent of total capital (including debentures) in 1896-8 to 11.6 per cent in 1911-14 (Table 20). The ordinary dividend (with bonuses) increased 2½ times, from 6.2 to 15.8 per cent. Was this improved position merely a consequence of increased sales? A more detailed analysis of the company's books suggests that other elements were present. It was observed in Chapter Four that the trading account does not include the cost of materials and the excise duty on beer. These items are included in Table 21, which helps to provide further insights into the brewery's business strategy. With inflation amounting to just over 30 per cent in the period 1896 to 1914 (the Board of Trade's wholesale price index shows a rise of 32 per cent), cost control was

TABLE 19

Steward & Patteson Ltd. Trading Account, 1896-1914 (annual averages) [£]

Year ending November	*Beer*	*Spirits*	*Wines*	**Income** *Mineral Waters*	*Malt*	*Bottled Beer*	*Yarmouth Agency*	**Total Income**	*Working Costs*	*Debenture Interest*[b]	**Net Profit**	*Distributed Profits*
1896–8	72,549	6,650	398	1,555	1,645	565	3,868	91,001	52,028	10,827	28,146	16,500
1899–1901	80,120	7,864	463	1,813	1,799	795	4,913	103,700	57,686	10,714	35,300	17,674
1902–4	85,806	8,191	417	1,542	2,596	1,316	7,722	113,162	61,296	10,598	41,268	20,597
1905–7	92,149	8,360	323	1,684	2,655	1,544	9,714	124,615	62,418	10,640	51,677[c]	24,125
1908–10	91,576	7,254	474	1,302	1,397	2,321	10,570	128,204	62,509	10,593	55,101	31,594
1911–14	90,041	6,379	544	1,781	1,677	4,025	12,764	132,063	64,978	10,541	56,544	30,684[a]

Income per unit (p) [Annual averages]

	Beer per barrel	*Spirits per gallon*	*Wines per doz bottles*	*Mineral Waters per doz bottles*	*Bottled beer per doz bottles*
1896–8	88.6	26.5	36.5	1.15	2.71
1899–1901	83.4	25.8	31.2	1.18	3.18
1902–4	84.1	25.4	29.9	1.08	4.12
1905–7	86.8	25.7	23.3	1.13	4.17
1908–10	83.1	25.5	34.7	0.98	5.03
1911–14	80.6	25.6	37.3	1.12	5.72

Source: Steward & Patteson Account Books: Quarterly Balances, 1886–1908, BR1/104, and 1909–38, BR1/101, N.R.O.

[a] Includes bonuses.
[b] Included in working cost totals.
[c] As reported in accounts. A discrepancy of £360 for 1905 (£120 p.a., 1905–7) is indicated.

TABLE 20

Steward & Patteson's Rate of Return on Total Capital, and Ordinary Share Dividends, 1896–1914 (three-year averages)

Year ending November	*Rate of Return on Total Capital (%)*	*Ordinary Share Dividend (%)*
1896–8	6.7	6.2
1899–1901	7.9	7.0
1902–4	8.9	9.0
1905–7	10.7	11.3
1908–10	10.8	16.3*
1911–14	11.6	15.8*

Source: Taken from Appendix D, Table 3.

* Includes bonuses.

clearly vital. Beer duty and labour costs increased by 43 and 37 per cent respectively over the period 1896-8 to 1911-14, matching the increase of 41 per cent in gross revenue. However, material costs were more successfully contained. The cost of malt, by far the most important raw material, increased by only 21 per cent, that of hops by only 29 per cent. Although other materials (coal, sugar, and isinglass) exhibited a sharper rise, overall material costs did not exceed the inflation rate. Here, there was both a substitution of materials and a reduction in the quantities used in brewing. The trend towards a lower malting and hopping rate, evident in the early 1890's, was continued. The amount of malt used fell by 19 per cent, from 0.461 coombs per barrel in 1896-8 to 0.374 coombs in 1911-14. The hopping rate was cut by 37 per cent. While 2.106 lb. per barrel were used in 1896-8, the amount had fallen to 1.33 lb. by 1911-14. On the other hand, 46 per cent more sugar was introduced: 7.73 lb. per barrel in 1896-8, and 11.27 lb. in 1911-14. This tendency to substitute sugar for malt might have been more marked but for the rise in their relative prices. Malt cost 33*s*. 6*d*. a quarter or 16*s*. 9*d*. [84p] a coomb in 1896-8, and 19*s*. 1¼*d*. a coomb [95½p] in 1911-14, an increase of 14 per cent, while sugar, only 11*s*. 4¾*d*. [57p] a cwt. in 1896-8, cost 14*s*. 5¾*d*. [72p] in 1911-14, or 26 per cent more. The differential in favour of sugar thus narrowed appreciably. The overall effect of the brewery's response was to reduce the strength of the beer sold. The specific gravity fell from 1059.9^{0} to 1057.5^{0} in the period examined.[12] At first sight, Steward & Patteson appear to have been less successful in restraining labour costs. However, the increase in the wage-bill was largely due to the fact that about 25 per cent more men

TABLE 21

Steward & Patteson Ltd: Estimate of Gross Revenue and Costs, 1896–1914 (annual averages) [£]

Year ending November	**Gross Revenue**	*Malt*	*Hops*	*Other Materials*	**Costs** *Total Materials*	*Beer Duty*	*Labour*[a]	*Other Costs*[b]	*Total*	**Net Profit**	*Working Ratio* [%]
1896–8	166,876	33,955	7,277	5,301	46,533	29,342	13,149	49,706	138,730	28,146	83
1899–1901	195,003	38,065	10,245	7,487	55,797	35,506	14,101	54,299	159,703	35,300	82
1902–4	209,778	38,972	10,148	8,318	57,439	39,177	15,017	56,877	168,510	41,268	80
1905–7	220,483	36,449	9,410	9,574	55,433	40,435	17,172	55,765	168,806	51,677	77
1908–10	226,848	39,390	6,939	10,575	56,904	41,740	17,599	55,504	171,747	55,101	76
1911–14	235,444	40,991	9,390	10,947	61,328	42,053	18,068	57,451	178,900	56,544	76
Percentage change: 1896/8–1911/14	+41%	+21%	+29%	+107%	+32%	+43%	+37%	+16%	+29%	+101%	-8%

Source: Steward & Patteson Ltd. Account Books: Quarterly Balances, 1886–1908, BR1/104, 1909–38, BR1/101; and BR1/107 and BR1/134, N.R.O.

[a] Salaries (excluding directors' fees, and pensions) from BR1/107; Wages for 1895/6 to 1897/8 from BR1/134; for 1904/5 to 1913/14 from BR1/107; for 1898/9–1903/4 from BR1/134 x 1.2 to produce comparability with the later series in BR1/107, which was produced on a new basis from 1904/5.

[b] Includes debenture interest of c.£10,500 p.a.

were taken on as production was stepped up. The employer's response to the problems of inflation was far from generous. The Pockthorpe Wage-book indicates that average money wages increased by only 5 per cent from 1896-8 to 1911-14 - from 89.6p to 94.2p - well below the 30 per cent increase in wholesale prices, and the 17 per cent rise in Bowley's cost-of-living index, over the same period. In this way, the company was able to contain the wage-cost per barrel brewed, which rose only slightly, from 8.5p to 8.6p. Thus, by keeping a tight rein on labour and material costs, the brewery was able to reduce the 'working ratio' (costs expressed as a percentage of revenue) from 83 in 1896-8 to 76 in 1911-14.[13]

Under these conditions, the incentive to rationalise the company's retail trade was much reduced. As we have seen, significant moves had been made in this direction before 1895. The public house statistics in Table 22 reveal that only minor adjustments were made in the period to 1914. Unfortunately, the complete picture is obscured somewhat by a change in the method of recording the data. From 1897 the information shown in the accounts included the agency houses of Yarmouth and Ipswich, previously omitted, but merged the Norwich City and 'Country' returns, took the King's Lynn *owned* pubs and all the Swaffham houses out of the 'Country' category and excluded all reference to the free houses supplied (there had been eighty-four of these in 1895). Nevertheless, the data given in Table 22 shows that by 1914 the total number of pubs supplied (excluding the free trade) had

TABLE 22

Steward & Patteson Ltd.'s Public Houses, 1897–1914
[Including Yarmouth/Ipswich Agencies, excluding Free Houses]

First week of November	*Norwich/ Country*	*Swaffham*	*King's Lynn*	*Yarmouth*	*Ipswich*	*Total*	*Of which: Owned*	*Leased*
1897	409	47	58	95	47	656	528	128
1899	407	48	54	95	45	649	538	111
1902	413	50	52	95	43	653	549	104
1905	405	48	51	92	41	637	552	85
1908	402	43	45	94	36	620	543	77
1911	393	43	42	92	33	603	535	68
1914	403*	40	42	94	32	611	548	63

Source: Steward & Patteson Account Books, BR1/104, 101, N.R.O.

* Includes Eye brewery houses, later distinguished as a separate agency.

fallen by only 7 per cent, from 656 to 611. The reduction is accounted for by a substantial fall in the number of houses leased, from 128 to 63, while the number of freehold houses increased slightly, from 528 to 548.

Of course, the global statistics hide the fact that the company was continuously engaged in buying and selling properties. In 1897 the Weybourne brewery was bought for £17,000, and in 1914 the company purchased the Eye brewery in Suffolk, with twenty pubs, from Adnams of Southwold. The price paid was £16,000.[14] In addition, ten of the fifty-one Swaffham Brewery pubs had been sold by 1914, five of them before the operation of the Licensing Act of 1904, whose compensation provisions encouraged the termination of licences. The closure of pubs certainly accelerated after 1905. In Norwich twenty pubs were 'closed by compensation' in the years to 1914, and in all sixty-two Steward & Patteson licences were lost. The brewery collected £23,000 in compensation, and sold off the properties for £15,500, more than covering its contributions under the Act. Whether the brewery was actively involved in the decisions to refuse licences is hard to determine, but the effect of such transactions was undoubtedly to improve the average barrelage (number of barrels sold per annum). Most of the Norwich pubs closed were selling under one hundred barrels, and the average barrelage in the city increased from 193 in 1903-4 to 249 in 1913-14. There were modest increases in the other sales areas, too.[15]

The data on beer sales (Table 23) reveal that no dramatic changes occurred in the nineteen years after limited liability. The House or Home Trade (which included the Swaffham and King's Lynn areas) made up about 71 per cent of the business, and the agency trade 27 per cent, and the annual deviations from this average for 1896-1914 were comparatively slight. However, there was a hint at least of further moves towards a concentration of sales in the more profitable areas of Norfolk and district. The Yarmouth agency flourished in the period, increasing its share of the total business from 19 per cent in 1886-95 to nearly 22 per cent in 1896-1914. The other agencies, on the other hand, were financially disappointing. The Ipswich agency, for instance, made losses of about £5,400 or £450 per annum in the period 1896-1907, and separate accounts for the Swaffham and King's Lynn areas (whose sales were incorporated in the House Trade) showed losses of a similar magnitude.[16] Two growth sectors can be identified, although they remained insignificant in relation to the total volume of beer sold.

7. The 'Free Trade Tavern', Norwich, c.1900 [*Colman & Rye Library, Norwich*]

TABLE 23

Steward & Patteson Ltd. Beer Sales, in barrels, 1896–1914 (annual averages)

Year ending November	House or Home Trade	*Yarmouth*	Agencies *Ipswich*	*Bedfield*	Total Agency Trade	*Bottled Beer*	Total
1896–8	60,446	14,902	4,900	110	19,912	957	81,315
1899–01	70,009	18,699	5,210	75	13,984	1,091	95,086
1902–4	72,638	22,242	4,802	67	27,129	1,464	101,233
1905–7	75,776	23,897	4,610	84	28,591	1,692	106,061
1908–10	78,467	24,252	5,315	94	29,661	2,127	110,256
1911–14	76,449	25,983	6,088	14 [55 in 1911 only]	32,085	3,152	111,686
Average 1895–14	72,516	21,890	5,206	71	27,167	1,655	101,505
% Total	71.4	21.6	5.1	0.1	26.8	1.6	100.0

Source: Steward & Patteson Account Books, Quarterly Balances, BR1/104 and BR1/101, N.R.O.
Note: Columns may not add across due to rounding. Swaffham was included in the Home Trade from 1895–6.

Bottled beer sales increased from 957 barrels in 1896-8 to 3,152 in 1911-14, but they were still under 3 per cent of the total. The increased demand for beer in bottled form also stimulated purchases of beer brewed by other companies. Beer 'bought in' in this way, which had averaged only 146 barrels a year in 1898-1900, jumped to over 400 barrels from 1901 as the company began to distribute the products of Bass and Guinness. But even the 492 'foreign' barrels sold each year in 1911-14 represented under half a per cent of the total beer sold.[17]

The history of Steward & Patteson Limited in the years 1895-1914 is thus one of a company enjoying a profitable existence in spite of the problems facing many brewers elsewhere and the general climate of anxiety in the trade. To a large extent this happy position was due to the company's regional dominance, based on a large tied-house business which had been built up and rationalised before the great scramble for pubs began. It enabled it to respond to change without experiencing sudden crises. The company certainly made progress in the years to 1914, but it remained a mixture of the advanced and the antiquated, of the progressive and the conservative. This can be observed in a number of different aspects of the business, in retailing, in the production process, and in labour relations.

Turning first to the public houses, the more detailed information on Steward & Patteson's twentieth-century operations indicates that while there was a conscious move towards the concentration of sales in outlets of higher consumption, the company retained a large number of low-profit pubs in its empire. In Norwich, its biggest single market, Steward & Patteson responded quite well to the new market conditions. We have already mentioned the disposal of twenty pubs with low annual sales. This was accompanied by the opening of new, large houses in areas of high population density. In October 1895, for example, the company opened the 'Branford Stores', in the north of the city, and in the first year it sold 335 barrels of draught beer. Trade grew steadily, and in 1913-14 sales totalled 719 barrels and 737 dozen bottles of beer. The average barrelage for 1895-1914 was 437. There were similar returns at the 'Marlborough Stores' in Pockthorpe, opened in 1892, where sales rose from 336 barrels in 1893-4 to 701 barrels in 1913-14 (plus 878 dozen bottles), averaging 597 barrels in the period 1895-1914. A high volume of sales was also characteristic of the 'Cricketer's Arms' in Lakenham, the 'Red Lion' in St Paul, and the 'Denmark Arms' in Heigham.[18] On the other hand, it is clear that Steward & Patteson persisted with public houses where the consumption was meagre. In 1895-6, for example, the brewery supplied only twenty-two barrels to the 'Prince Regent' in Union Place, and only twenty-six to the 'Bull' in St Clement.[19] The situation was similar in the county. While there were very successful houses, such as the 'King's Head' at Hoveton, the 'Robin Hood' at Sheringham and the 'Black Horse' at Leiston, with annual sales of 400-500 barrels, 1902-14, there were also several marginal outlets, such as the 'Queen Adelaide' at Wells-next-the-Sea (thirty-seven barrels per annum), the 'Woolpack' at Yaxham (fifty-one barrels), and the 'Dove' at Poringland (fifty-seven barrels), which were presumably retained for social reasons. [At the time of writing the 'Dove' is still open.] The impression that the company was not responding aggressively to the problem of low barrelages in the rural areas is also reinforced by the data for Swaffham and King's Lynn. Here the average barrelage per house in 1902-14 was only seventy-five and ninety-two respectively.[20]

The brewery's response to technological change was surprisingly firm for a provincial business. While certain features of the brewing process remained much as they had been fifty years earlier, there were significant changes also. Strengthened by its limited liability status, the company introduced much needed improvements at the turn of the century: a new cask-washing and cooperage department (circa 1898), with five 16-cask machines; and a new fermenting room (circa 1900). However, the most spectacular development, which attracted the attention of the trade journals, was the pneumatic maltings, installed in 1907-8. The process of pneumatic malting, in which hot moist air was passed over the barley, had been popular in Germany and the United States for some time, but only a handful of British brewers had adopted it. Steward & Patteson's investment in the Gallard-Henning drum malting, which amounted to at least £20,000, was a considerable one. The plant, with its twenty-one malting drums, eight pneumatic steeping tanks, and four kilns, was designed by the brewery's architect, Walter Trollope, and installed by R.J. Hanbury, the British distributors of the Gallard-Henning system. The machinery was supplied by the prominent East Anglian engineering firm, Robert Boby, of Bury St Edmunds, and the contractors were J.S. Smith of Norwich. The installation was described in the *Brewing Trade Review* in August 1908 as 'the largest ... of its kind in the United Kingdom'.[21]

The company's approach to labour relations remained, as before, a mixture of an old-fashioned stress upon discipline and a strong belief in the value of benevolent paternalism. Brewing had a long tradition

8 and 9. The pneumatic maltings, 1908: i] The steeping cisterns; ii] The malting drums [*Brewing Trade Review,* 1 August 1908/*Brewers' Society*]

of relatively stable employment prospects, and this was taken to justify low wages for many grades of work. Wage rates were not noticeably volatile. Thus, during the inflationary period, 1896-1914, as we have seen, a 5 per cent increase in average money wages at Pockthorpe left the workers considerably worse off in real terms. On the other hand, the company was developing a 'welfare' policy, with an emphasis on the provision of housing and retirement pensions. In the period 1895-1914, pensions were awarded to forty-eight workers, a third of whom had served the brewery for forty years and more.[22] Nevertheless, the company often displayed a rather relaxed attitude to discipline and to punishment for brewery misdemeanours. The survival of the Yarmouth Agency's 'Offences Book' for 1901-16 gives a good indication of the way in which the brewery treated its workforce (see the extracts at the end of the chapter). Control was vital where drink and money were handled in large quantities, but while the Yarmouth Agent, Richard Grand (who had succeeded Thomas Burton Steward in 1898), and the foreman, Mr King, emphasised that offences would lead to instant dismissal, they were in practice more generous. Problems connected with excessive drinking were at the root of many incidents, as the following entry indicates:

'1900 Aug.21. Bullock (Drayman) came home very drunk. In charge of Horse & Cart. Fell down in a heap in Harness-House and went to sleep. Whines [Storekeeper] thrashed him with a Whip-Stalk but unable to rouse him.

22. R.G. severely cautioned him. Told him next occasion this thing happened he would be discharged.'[23]

Intemperance was also a problem among the supervisory staff. Both Whines, the Storekeeper, and Hurrell, the Bottling Stores Foreman, gave particular cause for concern at the turn of the century, and, as the extracts in the appendix show, both received lenient treatment until matters got out of hand. The Offences Book also records other examples of the company's attitude to the personal problems of the staff. A warning to a vanman in 1906 about an allegation that he was using the stables at night for 'immoral purposes', the treatment of a careless drayman who drove his horse into the river, a distressing case of attempted suicide, and a junior clerk's fraud - all in 1907 - suggest a mixture of uncompromising severity and enlightened leniency. Steward & Patteson's reaction to fraud seems to have been much tougher when it was committed by the wages staff. Thus, while F.H. Wade, a junior clerk, and A.E. Penney, the third clerk, were given every chance to redeem themselves, Sidney Alexander, a vanman, was 'summarily discharged' after discrepancies in the invoices had been discovered. The treatment of Penney was particularly sympathetic. Both Grand, the Yarmouth agent, and the interested directors, showed themselves anxious to do all they could to encourage him to pull himself round. This was an indulgence which was rarely extended to the wages staff where the risk of drinking was great, the rules had to be obeyed, and recruits were not difficult to find (see appendix).

Whatever the Offences Book reveals about the treatment of brewery staff at Yarmouth, it indicates that the directors and their senior staff remained in close contact with the business as the trade expanded. This can also be seen in the directors' management of their public house empire. Notes drawn up by Charles Hugh Finch in connection with the Yarmouth Agency pubs and properties for 1896-8 reveal the close personal attention to the retailing of beer, wines and spirits that is essential to success in the trade. Finch supervised the outlets, whether tied or free, monitored expenditure on improvements, sales, and the prices charged to tenants (which varied with the status of the house), and was also involved in property transactions. An extract from his 'notes' (others are given at the end of the chapter) will serve to convey the attention to detail characteristic of Steward & Patteson's management:

'**Queen's Hotel, Weston** July 3rd, 1896

	barrels sold	*waste returned*	
1891–2	31½	6	
1892–3	29	4	
1893–4	31½	4	= 13½%
1894–5	36½	3½	
1895–July 96	12	1½	
	140½	19	

Trade: 1892 $\frac{97*}{122}$ 1893 $\frac{89}{148}$ 1894 $\frac{102}{124}$

1895 $\frac{100}{154}$ = P.A. 15 XXX 69 DBS 16

Prices 32/- XXX 50/- DBS and XXXX

Trade: 1893 $\frac{107½}{55}$ 1894 $\frac{100¾}{69}$ 1895 $\frac{91¼}{61½}$

This does not include pieces of DBS returned. Our draymen report that the waste pipe runs only into our cask. Settled to do nothing for a bit and try with bitter ale again as soon as we find a definite improvement in it.
Queen's Hotel sold to Nightingale Jan 1897.'[24]

This and the other transactions described by Finch were vital to the successful management of a large and dispersed business empire. The minutes show that between July 1895 and July 1914 the company bought ninety-seven public houses, leased twenty-five, and disposed of twenty-one properties. The purchases ranged from the 'Lion' at Martlesham, which was bought for £3,325 in 1896 to a beerhouse at Lessingham, acquired for £250 in 1910, and the average price paid was £1,226. Over the same period, Steward & Patteson spent a total of £106,800 on trade alterations, most of which went on improvement to pubs.[25] The personal involvement of the directors and a firm grasp of business details helped to make a success of this large regional brewery, at a time when several large breweries were facing difficulties, particularly in London and Burton-on-Trent, where the cost of amalgamations, and the purchase of public houses at inflated prices took their toll.[26]

Appendix

A. Extracts from the Yarmouth Punishment Book, 1901-16

1. Excessive drinking

'1900 Aug.21. Bullock (drayman) came home very drunk. In charge of Horse & Cart. Fell down in a heap in Harness-House and went to sleep. Whines [*Storekeeper*] thrashed him with a Whip-Stalk but unable to rouse him.

22. R.G. [Richard Grand, Yarmouth Agent, 1898-1935] severely cautioned him. Told him next occasion this thing happened he would be discharged.'

'1900 Dec.4. Darn (Drayman) and Duffield (Groom) had a fight in Stores Yard 6p.m. R.G. fined them 1/- to be paid into Hospital Box and told them if such a thing occurred again on the Premises, instant dismissal would follow.'

'1901 Feb.1. Powley (Drayman) whilst taking 2 gals. Gin to Carrier in afternoon broke the Bottle and lost all the contents. As he was the worse for drink on his return to Stores Whines ordered him home.

R.G. left this case for Mr C.H.F. [*Charles Hugh Finch, Director, 1895-1952*] to deal with. Mr C.H.F. instructed R.G. to see Powley and tell him he would be fined 10/- to be paid by him at the rate of 1/- per Week for the loss incurred.'

'1901 July 20. Henn 'Lord Nelson' Gorleston met R.G. in the morning outside Stores and complained that when he came to see Whines this morning relative to non-arrival of Beer ordered last evening by Savory (A.W. Vanman) Whines swore at him. Whines walked up as Henn was making his complaint and swore at him again and made as if to strike him. Subsequently R.G. summoned Whines before him and told him very seriously such an exhibition must never be seen again at Stores.'

'1903. Oct.17. Hurrell. Bottling Stores about 3pm applied to Eastoe [*C.R. Eastoe, Brewery Clerk. Joined Yarmouth staff June 1895 (Wages: 25/- a week, 30/- by July 1898)*] for leave to be absent for a short time to attend a Forester's Meeting. As R.G. was expected back from Norwich 3.30 p.m. Eastoe told Hurrell to await his return (R.G. ard. 3.35). Hurrell appears thereupon to have taken himself off and up to 6.30 p.m. had not returned although a tradesman (Geo. Read Painter Gorleston) who had attended the same meeting and who stated he had stayed until its conclusion called to see R.G. at 5 p.m.'

'1904. Feb.8. 4.30. Upon R.G.'s return from Oulton Rail Journey to-day, he found Whines had been drinking and upon R.G. enquiring if Beer Stock - as taken on Saturday night - was found to be correct Whines said it was a lot out...

R.G. when at work in his room about 7p.m. heard Whines - now evidently drunk in room adjoining - shouting to his Wife at the top of his voice.

The following were some of the expressions made use of:

"To Hell with Steward & Patteson, Blast Steward & Patteson. I won't have it put upon me. I always was an honest man and I intend to die one - for all the lot of bloody monkeys in the Office. A lot of scum. Who are they? Bloody rotters. I'll do for the buggars some day. I'll push four of them in the bleeding river and then I'll show Steward & Patteson. I am a Man -I am not a bloody jumped up fool.

What are Steward & Patteson to me. Blast them. I'll damned well chuck the buggars up. There's only you and my dog I care for in the whole bloody world. I've got a bit and shan't go to the bloody Workhouse".'

'1905. Mar.31. Grey Horse 'SILVER' when being driven by drayman Carter this morning went down on Southtown Bridge and took hair off 'near' knee (as large as a crown piece). Whines did not report this but R.G. saw it for himself about 5pm. R.G. told Whines that he (Whines) knew it was his duty to report the matter and cautioned him not to keep things back in future. (There has been too much of this of late - notably 2 gals. S.W. lost last quarter and not reported until R.G. found it out when taking stock 4th Feb. - It is becoming difficult at times to know who is at the head of Yarmouth Agency R.G. or Whines.'

'1906. Sept 3. On R.G.'s return 5.15pm from Oulton Road Journey he found Hurrell (Bottling Stores) slightly the worse for drink. Upon R.G. again going in Bottling Stores (5.45pm) he found Hurrell leaning upon his desk and in the act of drinking more Beer. R.G. cautioned him.'

'December 7th 1907. 11.30. Upon R.G. going into Bottling Stores he found Foreman Hurrell in the act of drinking a glass of Beer.

2 PM. Hurrell came into Counting-Room for orders in a 'fuddled' state (R.G. present).

5.30PM. As Hurrell's 'Weekly Statement' was not to hand R.G. sent for it. Message was returned that 'Stock' was not correct but that 'Statement' would be sent in within half-an-hour.

7.10PM. As 'Statement' not to hand and Clerks having all gone home R.G. went for it. Found Bottling Stores locked. After repeated knocking Hurrell (still in the same fuddled condition) opened the door. Upon R.G. requesting 'Statement' Hurrell said as he could not get it right, he was leaving it until Monday and going home. R.G. thereupon challenged Hurrell with being the worse for drink. Hurrell appeared to think this a joke and declared he had not had a drink all day. R.G. asked Hurrell why it was necessary to lie about it and reminded him that he (R.G.) saw him drinking a glass of Beer in the morning. R.G. assured Hurrell that about the only chance he had of keeping his present situation was for him to become a teetotaller. Hurrell replied 'very well: I will turn teetotaller from now'.'

'1908. Nov.7 7.40PM. Quarter Day. Hurrell's Bottled Beer Stock Sheet for Quarter not being to hand R.G. Inquired of Wade (Bottled Beer Clerk) about it. Wade reported he could make nothing out of Hurrell as he appeared dazed and unfit for work. R.G. found Hurrell incapable of counting up Stock or getting out figures and R.G. was of opinion that he had been drinking. Hurrell denied this and said he was unwell. R.G.

ordered him home and to come again next morning (Sunday) at 9 a.m. to go through Stock with Wade afterwards to 'stand off' until Wednesday when the matter should be brought before Mr C.H. Finch.'

'Nov.9. Hurrell called at Office and saw R.G. and produced Medical Certificate from Doctor T.P. Devlin ... Influenced by [this] ... R.G. re-instated Hurrell ... fining him 2/6 and cautioning him that this was his last chance.'

'1909. Mar.9. 5.15 P.M. Upon R.G.'s return to Office found Hurrell 'fuddled' - although not actually drunk -'

'1909. Sept.15. R.G. reported to Mr C.H. Finch that for Week ending 11th inst. he had ordered in writing 16 bbls L.B. and 19 bbls D.B.S. to be bottled. At end of Week he found that but 16 bbls L.B. and only 13 bbls Stout had been bottled and the shortage in bottling had not been reported to R.G. by Hurrell as it should have been. Also that Hurrell's habits were not always temperate especially when R.G. was away from Office - and R.G. had on different occasions cautioned him about this.'

'Mr C.H. Finch summoned Hurrell before him and told Hurrell he must thoroughly understand that on the next occasion R.G.'s orders were not carried out or he were found under the influence of drink, he would be discharged. He (Mr Finch) was emphatic on the point.'

'1909. Oct.15. 5PM (Friday). R.G. on going into Bottling Stores found Hurrell seated upon a Stool in front of his Desk apparently dosing. He had before him a Weekly Statement Sheet on which were some figures in pencil. R.G. inquired if he had no work to do. Hurrell replied he was making a start on his Weekly Statement. R.G. pointed out that this was a matter of impossibility as, it being but Friday, Hurrell could not possibly know what either his Sales or his Stock would be at the end of the Week.'

'1909. Oct.19. R.G. found Hurrell very 'hasy'. R.G. told him that he had had more to drink than was good for him. Hurrell replied (*not* rudely) that perhaps R.G. could not tell the difference between too much drink and 'brain fag'.'

'Oct.22. R.G. pd. Hurrell his Wages and gave him a weeks notice.'

'Oct.25. Hurrell strange in his manner, occasionally crying. 4.45 Fell down in Stores in a fit. Dr Shaw summoned to attend to him. Hurrell sent home on S & P's Cart. During the night (12.5 am) R.G. sent for to Hurrell's house to soothe him as he was out of his head. R.G. went and found him suffering from 'delirium tremens'.'

'Oct.29. Hurrell left S & P's service.'

2. **Personal problems**

'1906. Decr. 1. A.W. Foreman King reported that it is rumoured Vanman Loades has been seen taking women into A.W. Stables of a night time for immoral purposes, but King could find no absolute proof of this. R.G. saw Loades (with King). Loades denies the allegations. R.G. told him as there was no necessity for him to go to the Stables at night - nor, in fact, down 'Cellar House' Loke at all - if R.G. heard of his being seen down there again, in the absence of a satisfactory explanation he would be discharged.'

'1907. Jan.12. Town Drayman Carter (doing duty for Country Drayman - Moore - who is sick) at 9.20am took Bay Horse 'SHERIFF' from loose-box in A.W. yard to bring round into Beer Stores Yard. Instead of taking it round by roadway past Cellar House - as was his duty - he brought it over Quay next River with the result that by some means 'SHERIFF' tumbled into River. Two Men put off in a Boat from opposite side of Harbour and succeeded in keeping up Horse's head and in guiding him thro' the Bridge to 'slip-way' below Bessey & Palmer's yard. 'SHERIFF' was then taken to Shipley's given a drink & brought home. The two Men referred to came to Office and asked for 10/- each remuneration - which R.G. ordered should be paid them. R.G. fined Carter 10/- to be paid by weekly instalments of 2/6d each - and sharply reprimanded him.'

'1907. Aug.21. R.G. laid Drayman Page's case before Mr C.H. Finch. Taking into consideration the previous warnings Page had received and particularly on July 5th 1905 and the grave danger of allowing a man - known to be addicted to drink - to be in charge of horses Mr Finch decided there was no other course open but to discharge Page for misconduct. Mr Finch came to this conclusion very reluctantly as Page had put in close upon 30 years service. Had there been any other position open in the Agency not connected with horses to which Page could have been transferred, he should have been so transferred but there was no such position open. Mr Finch directed that there should be handed to Page as a gratuity on account of long service and to give him time in which to obtain other employment:-£1 on Aug 24th £1 on Aug 31st £1 on Sept 7th £1 on Sept 14th.'

'1907. June 28. **Report by C.R. Eastoe on J. Cross's act of self-wounding**

On Friday June 28th on returning to the Office from dinner about 1.58pm I found Cross with a towel in his hand. The towel was covered with blood and Cross was endeavouring to stop the bleeding from a wound in his neck. He had an open pocket-knife in his hand. I asked him what was the matter. He replied 'I have cut my throat'. I asked him why he had done so and he answered 'I do not know'. I immediately called for Store-Keeper Whines to take charge of the Office, there being no one else available. I then sent for a Cab and took Cross to Dr Shaw who put two stitches in the wound which was about one and half inches long and about 1/8 inch deep. ...

July 3. At Mr Finch's request Dr Shaw called at the Yarmouth Office to day re above ... Dr Shaw said he was of opinion that the act was one of sudden impulse - occasioned by recent family trouble and bereavement - ... The Doctor added that it was a very half-hearted attempt and that a fortnight's holiday should be sufficient to set him up again.

July 4. R.G. went to Brewery to see Mr G.H. Morse [*George Henry Morse, Director, 1895-1931*] and Mr C.H. Finch re above. They decided, Cross (who had been suspended by R.G. since 28th ult) should be re-instated on the following conditions:

That he leaves Yarmouth for a holiday not later than 8th inst. and remains away until 20th inst.

That he thoroughly understands a second similar occurence - however slight - will bring immediate dismissal.

That he abstains from drinking Spirits during office hours.

That he conforms to certain new regulations concerning his work.'

3. **Fraud**

'1907. Aug.29. Eastoe reported to R.G. that he had discovered falsifications in the a/cs of Management Houses as under:

[*amounted to £9 10s.*]

Seeing that the handwriting of alterations resembled that of Junior Clerk (F.H. Wade) Eastoe challenged him with the falsifications. Wade admitted his guilt stating that he had had great trouble & temptation owing to trouble of a private nature which he would not divulge. R.G. telephoned to Brewery to Mr G.H.M. [*George Henry Morse, Director, 1895-1931*] (Mr C.H.F. being away) for instructions in the matter.

... 1907. Aug.30. Mr A Finch [*Alfred Finch, Director, 1905-43*] investigated the matter against Wade. He had Wade before him R.G. also being present. Wade again admitted the frauds and upon being pressed for the cause stated that it was owing to a girl blackmailing him with whom he had had connection the former part of 1905 ...'

'Aug.31. Mr A. Finch telephoned R.G. that Directors considered the offence so great that they could not possibly overlook it, therefore Wade must be told to leave their service tonight. R.G. discharged Wade and relieved his keys but R.G. wrote Directors that September being a busy month and some of the Clerks having arranged their holidays for that month (August being 'barred' to them) if Wade left at once September business would occasion much anxiety and asking that Wade might be permitted to stay the month.'

'Sept.2. Mr A. Finch telephoned R.G. at 'Wherry' Oulton that for R.G.'s convenience Wade might stay on for a month ...'

[*Wade does not appear to have been discharged at this time. See entry for 7 Nov. 1908.*]

'1911. Sept 25. A.W. Foreman King reported that he had discovered discrepancies between carbon-copies of Invoices and Invoices themselves in Sidney Alexander's (2nd A.W. Vanman) Book and produced 4 Invoices with their Carbon Copies in verification. R.G. summoned Alexander before him (King being present) and he admitted the falsifications and fraud urging in excuse that his pay 14/- per week was insufficient (Alexander is 19 years of age). R.G. summarily discharged him.'

'1911. Jan.21. Penney today asked R.G.'s permission to borrow £8 on his salary. Seeing that Penney's salary is but £4.3.4 per month and that on 9th Novr 1910 R.G. granted Penney permission to borrow £4- which sum is repayable 4th prox. R.G. closely questioned Penney as to why this money was needed. Penney stated that he had lately been buying a lot of clothes and was being pressed for payment. From Penny's personal appearance R.G. disbelieved this story ... It then occurred to R.G. that Penney had not yet paid in the Rents of two Cottages in Tyrolean Square Cobholm which he collects and these should have been paid in a fortnight ago and it then further occurred to R.G. That Penney was late in paying in these Rents last quarter and also that they were not paid in until Penney had borrowed the £4 previously referred to. R.G. accordingly asked Penney where were the Rents now due ... [Penney] admitted he had used the money for his own purposes and appeared to think by so doing he had committed no fault. R.G. thereupon questioned Eastoe and Eastoe gave it as his opinion that Penney was in an unfortunate position at home. His mother was an epileptic and his Father away at sea on a Light Ship for weeks at a stretch leaving insufficient means behind him and that Penney in consequence kept making up deficiencies besides his 10/- standing contribution. Eastoe further stated he believed Penney to be free from vice. R.G. severely censured Penney and pointed out that his action was clearly deliberate dishonesty to his employers and should he misconduct himself in any similar manner in future R.G. must bring the matter to Mr Finch's notice and there would be no hesitation about it. R.G. agreed that £8 should be advanced and in repayment £1 pr month should be deducted from Penney's salary ...'

'1912. Aug.19. Upon R.G. inquiring of third clerk (Penney) this morning as to Rents of Cobholm Cottages ... and requesting production of the money Penney admitted that he had been using it for his own purposes, stating in extenuation that the whole of the quarter's collection would be forthcoming on quarter-day. R.G. assured Penney that the matter of taking his employer's money was an extremely serious one ...'

'Aug 20. R.G. upon thinking over foregoing incident insisted upon Penney laying all the facts before his Father and that his Father should call and see R.G. on the matter. 7.15p.m. Penney Senr called at R.G.'s House and expressed surprise and sorrow at his Son's conduct. He asserted that he believed his Son to be free from any particular vice but he had of late got too fond of company and billiard-playing ... Upon the understanding that Penney Senr would warn his Son very seriously that this must be his last chance R.G. consented not to report ...'

'Aug.21. R.G. assured Penney that this would be his last chance and obtained from him a promise that he would abstain from billiard-playing on licensed premises for 12 mos. After Sept.29th Penney no longer to collect Rents of Cobholm Cottages'.

'1913. Feb. 19. Eastoe having reported to R.G. that Burnham 'Ferry Boat' Southtown was pressing 3rd Clerk - A.E. Penney - for repayment of £5 - money lent - R.G. demanded from Penney a full list of his debts which - not without difficulty owing to Penney's untruthfulness in the matter - R.G. eventually received purporting to be a full, true and complete a/c:-

Burnham 'Ferry Boat'	£5 Borrowed
Canham 'Lichfield Arms'	2 Do
Drummee 'Mitre'	1 Do
Jackson & Lunn (Tailors)	3 Clothes
Martins "	2-3s Do

Bearing in mind his record and as Penney collects money on Lowestoft Journey, R.G. laid the matter before Mr C.H. Finch to-day, who, after severely reprimanding Penney, instructed R.G. to advance £14:10 on Penney's I.O.U. and with the money R.G. was to pay the debts. Penney to repay the amount by monthly instalments of £2.'

B. Extracts from C.H. Finch's Notes on Public Houses, 1896-8

'Waggon and Horses June 1896

Leasehold of charity trustees 1875 for 21 years expires March 1896 @ £25 Rental. Tenant pays £26 10. Have spent £35 a year for last 20 years and allow £5 a year on licence of £25.

Trade:	1892	$\frac{97^*}{122}$	1893	$\frac{89}{148}$	1894	$\frac{102}{124}$

			PA	XXX	DBS
1895	$\frac{100}{154}$	=	15	69	16

Prices 32/- XXX 50/- DBS and XXXX

Present tenant went in March 1896 horse dealer and if we hire would like to stay on. Hill [*Frank Hill, brewery clerk*] says could always reckon house to do over $\frac{80}{100}$. Hill says nothing now standing in books for repairs and dilapidations. House would probably cost £15 per year repairs in future. Rent at auction not likely to be under £60 a year. Received letters July 1896 saying dilapidations £43 which we must pay at end of lease. Auction is held on Aug 10th 96 at 6 for 7 pm at Star Hotel by Aldred.

Hill came to Nch 8th Aug 1896 and settled to bid up to £75 p.a. 10.8.96: Hired this house by auction £71, 14 years from Sept 29th 1896. De Caux bid for us run up by Lemmon for Syndicate (Fitt & Co [*Geo. Fitt & Co., Norwich, auctioneers and valuers*]).'

* top figure gives annual sales of beer in barrels; the bottom figure probably refers to sales of wines and spirits in gallons.

'Queens Hotel, Weston July 3rd, 1896

	barrels sold	waste returned	
1891-2	31½	6	
1892-3	29	4	
1893-4	31½	4	= 13½%
1894-5	36½	3½	
1895-July 96	12	1½	
	140½	19	

This does not include pieces of DBS returned. Our draymen report that the waste pipe runs only into our cask. Settled to do nothing for a bit and try with bitter ale again as soon as we find a definite improvement in it.

Queens Hotel sold to Nightingale Jan 1897.'

'Barge, Unicorn, Two Necked Swan July 13th, 1896

Mr. S.J. Ramsey, 47, Wellesley Road, Gt Yarmouth, wanted to buy a house in Yarmouth for his brother. He suggested Barge or Unicorn. D.S. [*Donald Steward, Deputy-Chairman, 1895-8*] asked £2,000 for Barge, £1,000 for Unicorn.

Barge: As regards this house Hill says it has been at low ebb for some years owing to excess in competition and heavy working expenses but now have put a young man in who has the place Rent Free, licence free and No. 1 prices (32/- XXX, 50 DBS) and so he will probably do $\frac{100}{120}$ this year and has promised next year to pay £20 off the £25 licence. Settled to keep this house.

Unicorn: Hill to offer Mr Ramsey this house and report how he gets on.

T.A. Hewson, 11 Lancaster Road, Gt Yarmouth wrote 25.6.96 offering £450 for the Unicorn as it stands with Fixtures, but refused offer £750. He also offers £900 for Two Necked Swan, also promises us a fair turn in DBS and beer if we sell either house.

Two Necked Swan:

Trade: 1893 $\frac{107\frac{1}{2}}{55}$ 1894 $\frac{100\frac{3}{4}}{69}$ 1895 $\frac{91\frac{1}{4}}{61\frac{1}{2}}$

Both prices refused by us. Hewson wrote TBS [*Thomas Burton Steward, Yarmouth Agent to 1898*] again 5.8.96 re. buying Unicorn, and D.S. said he would not refuse £750. T.B.S. asked him £900 11.8.96 - he refused.
Two Necked Swan was sold to Joseph Steele 26.3.97 for £2,500, Steele afterwards in September 1897 sold the house to Whitbread & Co for £4,000.'

'Live and Let Live, Burgh St Margaret

plus 13 acres and beerhouse. 8 miles from Yarmouth
Annual hire from exors of late Mrs Hunt.
Rent paid by S & P £72.10 Rent paid by tenant £40
Prices 30/- XXX, 50/- DBS and XXXX
Repairs av £15
Trade: 1893 138, 1894 134, 1895 125
July 96. Hill says this house will probably be sold before long and helps to cover our Kings Arms, Burgh St Margaret.

March 26th, 97: Mr Lee Hunt [*milliner and fancy draper, Yarmouth*] came to office and we (DS and self) arranged for 10 years lease from March 97 @ £72. 10 per ann - we do repairs - and also spend about £50 on house at once.
Bought this house £2,000, - annuity of £20 on a lady 86 years old, Aug 6 1897, with 14 acres land worth from £60 to £70 per acre.'

'White Lion, Gorlestone Aug 4th, 1896

Hill says this house will have to be rebuilt in a couple of years, it is tumbling down and in a very bad state. This is the best public house or hotel site in Gorlestone and Mr Spelman [*of H.W. and C. Spelman, auctioneers, valuers, &c., Norwich and Yarmouth*] told me he reckons the site and house without a licence worth £1000. It is now doing $\frac{150}{238}$ and Hill says if rebuilt would do $\frac{250}{400}$.

Hill came to Norwich 8.8.96 and we settled to rebuild this house early in 98. Hill said a good house should be built from £1,600-£1,700. Rooms wanted - ground floor - 2 bars and smoking room in front, club room, sitting room, kitchens, etc., Upstairs 8 BRs and 2 sitting rooms.

15.7.97. Plans passed and contracts must not exceed (D.S.) £2,100 (not including architect's fee).'

BUILDING PLOTS

'Danby Estate
If this land is to be built upon before Dec 31st 1899 we are to have the first option of a site for a public house @ £1 a foot footage for 72 feet @ depth to be 100 feet.'

'Land at Carlton
Went with T.B.S. Sept 7 1896 and attended sale of sites. We bought Public House Plot no 196 for £14 per ann @ 20 yrs' purchase.'

6

War and Inter-War Years: Steward & Patteson, 1914-36

The First World War and its Aftermath

The Great War intensified the national trend towards a lower level of beer consumption. Not only did taxation increase - the beer duty was raised from *7s. 9d.* to *23s.* in 1914 and reached *100s.* by 1920 - but there were restrictions on raw material supplies, output, and gravity, and shorter licensing hours. Consequently, beer production declined in terms of both quantity and quality. U.K. production, in standard barrels, which had amounted to 35.1 million barrels in 1912-14, fell by 38 per cent to 21.8 million in 1915-19. At Pockthorpe, Steward & Patteson's war-time brewing followed suit, although there were some quite sharp fluctuations from year to year. Production, which had reached nearly 123,000 barrels in the year ending November 1914, slumped to only 67,000 barrels in the corresponding period in 1918, a decline of some 45 per cent. Sales also matched this fall (See Appendix D, Table 2). The short-lived post-war boom was reflected in the company's revival, and over 100,000 barrels were brewed in each of the three years to November 1921. However, any hopes of a return to 'normal' pre-war conditions were quickly dashed with the sharp contraction in activity in 1921-2. Thereafter, production and sales stabilised at about 84,000 barrels a year, 25 per cent down on the pre-war level.[1]

For Steward & Patteson, the War was not quite the disruptive force it proved to be for the larger brewers in the industrial heartlands of Britain. One of East Anglia's principal industries, agriculture, benefited from Government support and import-controls, and its prosperity helped to maintain consumer spending in rural areas. Nevertheless, the company's main problems, of supply, production limits, and marketing restrictions, were common to all in the brewing industry, and Steward & Patteson reacted to these in much the same way as others. The rising price, and restricted supply of barley, sugar, and hops, particularly after 1916, was followed by a considerable reduction in the strength of the beer produced. In the United Kingdom the average specific gravity fell from 1053.20° in 1909-10 to 1030.55° in 1918-19 (Year ending 31 March). At Pockthorpe, the average S.G. fell from 1057.5° in 1911-14 to 1033.06° in 1917-18. The use of malt, hops, and sugar was reduced as prices soared, and high prices in the early 1920's prevented a return to pre-war production methods (Table 24). Consequently, with average raw material prices in 1920-2 greatly in excess of those in 1911-14 - up by 159 per cent for malt, 267 per cent for sugar, and 173 per cent for hops - consumption per barrel fell by 24-30 per cent for these items (derived from Table 24). At the same time, the average S.G. of the beer brewed, at 1040°, although an improvement on the low point of 1917-18, remained about a third lower than that of pre-war, and indeed was slightly down on the national average (1042.61°, for example in 1920-1).[2] In the more depressed demand conditions of the 1920's, which accompanied the slump in world trade and the contraction of Britain's staple industries, there was little incentive for brewers to restore pre-war production standards. In fact, there was a positive financial incentive to brew weaker beer. From April 1923 the beer duty of 100*s*. a *standard* barrel was subject to a rebate of 20*s*. per *bulk* (i.e. selling) barrel. The weaker the beer, the more bulk barrels

TABLE 24

Pockthorpe Brewery: Average Gravity, Raw Material Consumpton and Prices, 1911-36

Year ending November	*Average Specific Gravity*	*Raw Material Consumption (per barrel)*			*Raw Material Prices (or costs)*		
		Malt (coombs)	*Sugar (lb.)*	*Hops (lb.)*	*Malt (coomb)*	*Sugar (cwt.)*	*Hops (cwt.)*
					s.	*s.*	*s.*
1911–14	1057.50°	0.374	11.27	1.33	19/1¼*d.*	14/5¾*d.*	136/10*d.*
1915	1055.28°	0.375	10.07	1.24	19/8*d.*	16/8*d.*	112/0*d.*
1916	1050.00°	0.346	9.12	1.17	26/10¾*d.*	27/2*d.*	102/8*d.*
1917	1043.61°	0.308	6.83	1.12	34/0½*d.*	35/10*d.*	130/8*d.*
1918	1033.06°	0.244	4.53	0.94	39/3*d.*	60/9*d.*	149/4*d.*
1919	1034.44°	0.230	7.13	0.95	42/4½*d.*	64/0*d.*	175/0*d.*
1920	1039.17°	0.258	8.21	1.00	55/2*d.*	66/9*d.*	336/0*d.*
1921	1040.28°	0.259	8.46	1.06	54/0*d.*	52/4*d.*	392/0*d.*
1922	1041.39°	0.263	8.94	1.16	39/4*d.*	40/5*d.*	392/0*d.*
1923–9	1040.71°	0.262	8.49	1.23	34/2*d.*	33/6½*d.*	253/7*d.*
1930–6	1038.72°	0.243	8.68	1.29	31/6¾*d.*	25/10*d.*	191/5½*d.*

Source: Steward & Patteson Account Books, BR1/101, 110, N.R.O.
Note: Malt prices are unit costs of malt produced by the company.

could be produced against the taxable standard. Given the demand and fiscal circumstances, it is no surprise to find that although malt and sugar costs/prices fell by 31 and 37 per cent respectively between 1920-2 and 1923-9, consumption settled down at a level close to that of 1920-2. There was an important exception. The hopping rate was restored. The average consumption of hops in the period 1923-9 was 1.23 lb. per barrel, only 7.5 per cent down on the figure for 1911-14. Steward & Patteson may have been content to produce a weaker beer, the average of 1040.71° for 1923-9 being lower than that of many of today's premium bitters. But the company was clearly anxious to restore the beer's characteristic hoppy flavour.[3]

How was the brewery's profitability affected by the more volatile price and supply conditions of the First World War and its aftermath, and by depressed demand? Net profits, after payment of debenture interest, which had averaged £56,500 a year in 1911-14, held up in money terms until the early 1920's. The results for 1921-3 were then particularly disappointing - £38,000 a year, compared with £68,500 in 1919-20. Recovery in the rest of the decade saw net profits reach £64,000 a year in 1927-9 (Table 25). The reality of the position was masked by inflation, however. As Table 25 shows, in constant values

TABLE 25

Steward & Patteson Profits (annual averages), 1911–36

Year ending November	*Net profits (after deducting debenture interest) current values* £	*Net profits in constant 1911–14 values* £	*Rate of Return (before debenture interest)* %	*Ordinary Share Dividend†* %
1911–14	56,544	56,544	11.6	15.8*
1915–18	59,561	36,898	11.8	14.0*
1919–20	68,448	29,636	8.7	5.5
1921–3	38,252	19,745	5.3	5.5
1924–6	61,980	35,632	8.0	5.8
1927–9	64,378	38,983	8.3	7.0
1930–2	76,288	51,131	9.9	7.0
1933–6	92,228	64,995	11.8	10.6*

Source: Taken from Appendix D, Tables 3 and 4. Constant values of net profits derived from index of retail prices in C.H. Feinstein, *National Income, Expenditure and Output of the United Kingdom, 1855–1965* (Cambridge, 1972), T140.

* Includes bonuses.
† Dividends were paid gross to 1925, then free of tax (the company paying the tax).

the brewery's net profits never approached pre-war levels. The 1921-3 results were barely a third of those for 1911-14, and after the recovery of the mid-late 1920's, profits (in 1927-9) were still only two-thirds as high as they had been before the war. Nevertheless, the rate of return appears to have been reasonably high, the period 1921-3 excepted, stabilising at about 8 per cent on an expanded capital. In 1919 the company had increased its ordinary share capital from £150,000 to £450,000 when it capitalised its reserve fund. Two bonus shares of £10 nominal value were distributed for each share held. This step, which was taken to provide a better indication of the brewery's capital value and to 'make for increased stability',[4] naturally reduced the size of the ordinary dividend per share. But even on an ordinary capital which had increased three-fold Steward & Patteson were able to pay 5.5 per cent free of income tax, 1919-23, rising to 7.0 per cent, 1927-9, and still transfer sizeable sums to reserve accounts.[5] Trading conditions may have been more difficult after the war, but they were not able to disturb the solid foundations of a business which had been conservatively and successfully managed in pre-war years.

Further indications of the brewery's position in the 1920's emerge from a more detailed analysis of the trading account, and from a reworking of the profit and loss account, as was done in Chapter Five. The trading account, summarised in Table 26, reveals that the only significant change for the company was the marked increase in income from bottled beer sales, which rose from £4,000 a year in 1911-14 to nearly £38,000 a year in 1927-9 (in current prices). This reflected a national switch in consumers' tastes from draught to bottled beer, however, and in the case of Steward & Patteson the combined income from draught and bottled beer in 1927-9 was in real terms no higher than that of 1911-14 (Table 26). With income from the Yarmouth agency a third lower than in 1911-14 in constant values, the brewery's income showed no improvement on the years before the First World War. Unfortunately, on the other side of the account, working costs increased faster than the inflation rate, and in constant values were 35 per cent higher in 1911-14. All this is evidence of squeezed trading margins in the more difficult conditions of the 1920's.

Where did the problem lie? It was certainly not a question of falling unit income. The revenue from both draught and bottled beer was maintained both in current and constant prices. Draught beer, which had earned 80.6p a barrel in 1911-14, produced £1.421 a barrel in 1927-9, or 86.0p in 1911-14 values. Bottled beer had earned 5.72p a dozen

TABLE 26

Steward & Patteson Ltd. Trading Account, 1911–29 (annual averages) [£]

Year ending November	Income					Working Costs		
	Draught Beer	*Bottled Beer*	*Yarmouth Agency*	*Total*[a]	*Debenture Interest*	*Total*	*Net Profits*	*Distributed Profits*[b]
1911–14	90,041	4,025	12,764	132,063	10,541	64,778	56,544	31,125
1915–18	103,025	5,727	13,526	146,559	8,794	86,998	59,561	28,500
1919–20	140,201	4,635	24,798	202,033	7,840	133,585	68,448	32,250
1921–3	128,600	11,668	11,131	179,735	8,190	141,483	38,252	32,250
1924–6	128,706	21,921	12,882	195,474	8,828	133,495	61,980	33,750
1927–9	117,968	37,618	14,256	208,901	8,960	144,523	64,378	39,000
1927–9 in constant 1911–14 values	71,433	22,779	8,632	126,496	5,426	87,513	38,983	23,616

Source: Steward & Patteson Ltd. Account Books, BR1/73, BR1/101, N.R.O.

[a] Includes Spirits, Wines, Mineral Waters, Malt (all under £8,000 p.a.)

[b] With bonuses. Note that the tax position was as follows: preference shares – tax deducted by company; ordinary shares – tax paid by company (distributions are *free* of tax), from 1926. Prior to 1926 ordinary dividends were paid gross of tax, leaving the shareholder to deal with inland revenue.

TABLE 27

Steward & Patteson Ltd: Estimate of Gross Revenue and Costs, 1911–29 (annual averages) [£]

Year ending November	**Gross Revenue**	Costs								**Net Profit**	*Working Ratio [%]*
		Malt	*Sugar*	*Hops*	*Total Materials*	*Beer Duty*	*Labour*[a]	*Other Costs*[b]	*Total*		
1911–14	235,444	40,991	8,372	9,390	61,328	42,053	18,612	56,097	178,900	56,544	76
1915–18	288,517	39,560	8,968	5,253	56,616	85,342	22,132	64,866	228,956	59,561	79
1919–20	569,121	66,922	24,874	12,660	109,412	257,676	39,247	94,338	500,673	68,448	88
1921–3	546,312	50,073	15,533	17,248	87,488	279,089	45,227	96,256	508,060	38,252	93
1924–6	466,924	38,176	11,308	11,926	65,770	205,679	41,368	92,127	404,944	61,980	87
1927–9	472,240	37,241	9,323	10,042	60,900	202,439	44,014	100,509	407,862	64,378	86
1927–9 in 1911–14 values	285,957	22,551	5,645	6,081	36,877	122,583	26,652	60,861	246,974	38,983	
As % of 1911–14	121	55	67	65	60	291	143				

Source: Steward & Patteson Ltd. Account Books, BR1/101, BR1/107, N.R.O.

[a] Salaries (including directors' fees and remuneration), wages, and pensions. Figure for 1911–14 differs from that shown in Table 21, above.

[b] Figure for 1911–14 affected by revised calculation of labour costs.

in 1911-14; in 1927-9 the figure was 11.5p, 6.96p in 1911-14 values.[6] Changes in real costs were responsible for reduced margins, as can be seen in Table 27, which provides estimates of 'gross revenue' and 'total costs', repeating the procedure carried out in Chapter Five. The marked rise in the cost of raw materials, and, above all, the considerable increase in beer duty, particularly evident to 1923, had the effect of increasing the 'working ratio' (costs expressed as a percentage of gross revenue) from 76 in 1911-14 to 93 in 1921-3. The improved conditions of the mid-late 1920's produced a recovery to 86, but this represented lower margins than those experienced by the brewery before the war. The company was able to reduce its bill for raw materials, such that in real terms its expenditure in 1927-9 was about 40 per cent lower than in 1911-14. But labour costs, including pensions, where expenditure rose steadily after 1925, increased by 43 per cent in real terms, and beer duty was almost three times higher in 1927-9 than in 1911-14 (£122,583, compared with £42,053, in 1911-14 values, Table 27).

The impact of the new, post-war conditions on Steward & Patteson's retail trade also needs to be examined. The War had brought with it a determined government assault on drunkenness. Brewers' pessimism was further increased by the threat of nationalisation, which gathered pace after the creation of the Central Control Board in 1915 and its acquisition, a year later, of the breweries and pubs in the Carlisle and Gretna area. The rationalisation of the trade which followed in Carlisle sent a chill down brewers' spines.[7] In the event, nationalisation did not come, but the demand for beer, which had been hit by supply restrictions in wartime, failed to recover. In peacetime, there was the competition of the club trade and the growing popularity of other pursuits, including sports, the cinema, and radio. The retention of high beer duties kept the price of beer up. In terms of standard barrels, production fell from 21.8 million in 1915-19 to only 19.6 million in 1927-9 (though in fact, 25.0 million bulk barrels [of any gravity] were actually produced).[8] In the country at large, brewers responded by rationalising and improving their licensed properties in an attempt to maintain profits. Licences in areas of over supply were surrendered in return for new licences in suburban areas; new public houses run by salaried managers were opened by some of the larger breweries to provide food as well as drink. All this was encouraged by the government, supported by the recommendations of, first, the Southborough Committee on the Disinterested Management of

Public Houses of 1927, and second, the Report of the Royal Commission on Licensing (England and Wales) of 1932.[9]

For Steward & Patteson, with its large number of small rural pubs, war-time restrictions put pressure on supplies and must have exposed many marginal houses. The scope for improvement outside the larger towns of Norwich, King's Lynn, Yarmouth and Ipswich was limited by small barrelages. Nevertheless, the same conditions affected the free trade, the public house estates of Steward & Patteson's major rivals, such as Bullard, Morgan, and Youngs Crawshay, and the remaining publican-brewers. The indications are that S. & P. maintained its regional dominance by means of a conservative policy of consolidation. The brewery's estate changed very little in size over the period 1914-18. As Table 28 indicates, the total number of tied houses fell slightly, from 611 in 1914 to 596 in 1928. Of course, the global figures hide the numerous transactions carried out in the property market. The most important were in 1917, when the company's Mildenhall pubs were exchanged for Greene King's Fakenham pubs (formerly those of Charlton's brewery), and in 1922, when Charles Pearse's Crown Brewery of East Dereham was purchased for £26,500. This was largely responsible for the net gain of nineteen public houses in that year. Judging by the data for subsequent years, the acquisition was followed by the weeding out of the Crown Brewery's least desirable properties, and the brewery itself appears to have been disposed of in 1925.[10] The minute books refer to several purchases of individual houses, which were balanced by an equal number of sales. Many redundant pubs were sold off for compensation under the Act of 1904. To the fifty-four sold in this way up to 1914 were added another forty-seven to 1929.[11] Sales usually realised small sums, exclusive of compensation, rarely over two or three hundred pounds. Purchases, on the other hand, cost much more. The largest in the 1920's occurred in 1927, when the 'Crown and Anchor', Great Yarmouth and the 'King's Arms', North Walsham were bought for £6,250 and £7,000 respectively.[12] Steward & Patteson continued a policy of gradual change, of selling off the worst properties and buying better ones. And another pre-war trend to be continued in the 1920's was the reduction in the number of pubs leased, which fell from sixty-three in 1914 to only thirty-one in 1928 (Table 28).

In August 1929 Steward & Patteson bought the brewery and properties of W. & T. Bagge of King's Lynn. This was without doubt the most substantial transaction since the War. Bagge's was a medium-

TABLE 28

Steward & Patteson's Public Houses, 1914–36

Date: November	*Norwich City*	*Norwich County*	*Swaffham*	*King's Lynn*	*Eye*	*Yarmouth*	*Ipswich*	*Total*	*Of which: Owned*	*Of which: Leased*
1914	403* (City and County)		40	42	–**	94	32	611	548	63
1918	129	255	40	36	20	96	32	608	561	47
1921	128	253	39	36	18	98	29	601	567	34
1922	126	264	41	41	20	99	29	620	583	37
1928	120	288*** (County and Swaffham)		41	23	95	29	596	565	31
1929	119	287	Bagge's 75	42	23	94	29	669	638	31
1936	112	275	111 (Bagge's and King's Lynn)		22	91	32	643	618	25

Source: Steward & Patteson Account Books, BR1/101, N.R.O.

* City and County first separated in account in 1918, total 384.
** Eye area first separated in account in 1918 (previously, pubs in Norwich County).
*** Swaffham area merged with Norwich County in 1926 (last separate entry, for 1925, lists 40 pubs).

sized concern with seventy-five tied houses, run by one of Norfolk's oldest merchant families, who had been leading members of Lynn's elite for three centuries.[13] Why the brewery was sold to Steward & Patteson and how much they paid for it remain something of a mystery. Since 1908 Bagge's had been managed by Robert Ludwig Bagge of Gaywood Hall (1872-1933), following the death of his grandfather, Robert, in 1891, and uncle, Thomas Edward, in 1908. Robert Ludwig, who was knighted in 1927 for his services to the Conservative party, had joined the brewery straight from his public school, Charterhouse, in 1890. A combination of factors - bereavement, ill-health, and the lack of a male heir - probably induced him to sell. He had five daughters but no son, and his wife Anna had died in February 1929, six months before the sale. Robert himself died within four years.[14] His brewery had been running at a modest level in the 1920's, with annual sales of some 7-9,000 barrels, an income from beer of £50-60,000 a year, and an annual wage and salary bill of about £5,000.[15] For Steward & Patteson the purchase gave it a stronger position in the town of King's Lynn, with twenty-two additional pubs, plus fifty-three new outlets in west Norfolk and the border with Lincolnshire and Cambridgeshire, including three houses in Wisbech.[16] These acquisitions took the total number of S. & P. tied houses to 669, a record figure and one which maintained the company's position as one of the largest provincial owners of licensed property.[17] The price paid for Bagge's was not referred to in the company's minute book, but the valuation of property and fixed plant shown in the balance sheets for November 1928 and 1929 shows an increase of nearly £144,000. One thing is quite clear. In order to finance the purchase, the company increased its borrowing powers, then in October 1929 secured a loan of £100,000 from the Norwich Union Life Insurance Society. There were close links between the two concerns. The two leading directors of the brewery, Sir George H. Morse, the Chairman, and Charles H. Finch, were also directors of the Norwich Union. The loan was secured by a mortgage on £210,000 of the company's debenture stock, and a redemption policy was taken out to redeem the loan in twelve years with interest at 6.675 per cent.[18]

By acquiring breweries and public houses as they came onto the market, Steward & Patteson were merely following the policy of gradual consolidation adopted by other breweries in the 1920's. Bullard's, one of Steward & Patteson's major competitors in Norwich, followed exactly the same course.[19] In the (still) gentlemanly world of

10. Horses at the loading platform, 1928 [*Stokes coll.*]

11. The lorry fleet outside the pneumatic maltings, in the 1920's [*Stokes coll.*]

brewing, there appears to have been no attempt by the larger breweries to try to swallow up rivals of comparable size, and follow this with an aggressive policy of rationalisation. Other national trends in the 1920's included investment in bottling facilities, motorised beer delivery, improved public houses, and a shift to managed houses. How far did S. & P. move in these directions? The evidence suggests that the company exhibited a mixture of above average enterprise and provincial caution. The swift rise in popularity of bottled beer forced all breweries to respond by improving their plant, although for most companies this meant rather piecemeal additions. But at Pockthorpe Steward & Patteson built a new bottled beer store in 1926, with the building contract fixed at £21,413.[20] A refrigeration plant was also installed, and two years later, a completely new office building was erected. The company also followed national trends by making greater use of motor lorries for longer distance deliveries.[21]

There was more caution with public house management. Here, the impetus came chiefly from the very large breweries in urban areas. Hawkins records that Mitchells and Butlers, the Birmingham brewers, had put salaried managers into nearly 800 of their 1,300 pubs and off-licences by the early 1920's.[22] Outside the big cities the incentive to do the same was more limited. Greene King, the Bury St Edmunds brewers, increased the number of managed houses from about six in 1924 to over a hundred (over 20 per cent) twelve years later, the change coming in the larger towns and in coastal resorts where consumption was highest. This occurred in a provincial concern where the demand per house was low, on average barely three barrels a week.[23] Steward & Patteson was producing about the same amount of beer - 80,000 barrels - as Greene King, but had nearly 200 more tied houses, suggesting an average demand of barely two barrels a week. Although the number of its managed houses is not recorded, this must have been small in the 1920's. The change in the control of pubs from tenancy to management usually followed a considerable investment in improving existing houses or in building new ones. Greene King apparently spent £12-13,000 a year on its pubs in the early 1920's. This brewery also built new houses to a high standard, encouraged by Basil Oliver, the head brewer's brother, who was the author of the standard work on public house improvement, *The Renaissance of the English Public House*.[24] For Steward & Patteson, information is once again rather elusive. However, the account books provide evidence of increased spending. The entries showing trade alterations to public houses

TABLE 29

Beer Sales and Agency Income, 1914–36 (annual averages)

Period	Beer Sales (Barrels)				Agency Income				
	Total	*Home* %	*Agencies* %	*Bottled* %	*Yarmouth*	*Ipswich*	*Swaffham*	*King's Lynn*	*Eye*
1911–14	111,686	68	29	3	£12,764	£370	-£296	£52	£107*
1921–3	88,073	67	28	5	£11,131	-£389	-£1,306	-£34	-£484
1924–6	85,043	63	27	10	£12,882	-£1,173	-£347	-£143	-£86
1927–9	83,006	56	26	18	£14,256	-£1,031	—	£2,035	-£13
1930–6	85,111	41	27	32	£14,273	£60	—	£6,345	£358

Source: Steward & Patteson Account Books, BR1/101, N.R.O. Woodbridge sales and income omitted, 1932–3.

* Figure for 1914.

12. 'George', brewery percheron, c.1935 [*Stokes coll.*]

reveal an annual expenditure of £5,340 in the period 1895-1914 and £1,840 in 1915-19. Thereafter, expenditure jumped to £4,860 per annum in 1920-4 and £9,880 per annum in 1925-9.[25] This does suggest that the company appreciated the value of refurbishing pubs, though no doubt many of the smaller rural outlets escaped attention.

In relation to marketing and sales the company again exhibits both conservatism and dynamism. The beer sales data show a continuation of poor results in the brewery's peripheral distribution area, but there was little or no attempt to alter radically the market area. The 'agencies' of Yarmouth, Ipswich, Swaffham, King's Lynn and Eye together accounted for 37 per cent of the tied estate in 1922 and took about 28 per cent of the beer sold. But the income generated was very small, as it had been in the past, and all but Yarmouth made losses in the 1920s (Table 29). At the same time, it is clear that the company had some success in the marketing field with its 'Buy British' slogan. Under Charles Finch's direction, the brewery decided to produce beer made from English barley only, despite the fact that most brewers considered foreign barley, and especially the long thin kernelled variety, to be necessary for good drainage in the mash tun. After experimental brews had proved successful, S. & P. launched a new

Norfolk Brown Ale (Gravity: 1037.5^{0}) in the summer of 1928, and reported that demand greatly exceeded expectations. The purchase of foreign barleys was then phased out and from 1931 the company was able to boast that its beers were brewed entirely from English barley, English hops, and British Empire sugar (see illustrations). The success of the advertising campaign which accompanied the change in brewing practice was demonstrated by country-wide orders for S. & P. beer. The company even supplied the House of Commons, where the 'Buy British' slogan no doubt appealed to Conservative protectionists.[26] With this exception, there was a fair amount of stability in the product range after the post-1914 reduction in gravities. Porter was dropped after May 1918, and the XXX draught beer was another war-time casualty. The brewery's extremely strong 'Double Brown Stout' became a more modest 'Stout' in 1920. Two strong bottled beers were added in the 1920's: 'BK', a Stingo, and 'Nips', a barley wine, introduced in 1922 and 1929 respectively. But the mainstay of the brewery's sales - Pale Ale, Light Bitter, XXXX, XX and Stout - scarcely changed at all in the period 1920-36, as Table 30 demonstrates.

TABLE 30

Steward & Patteson Beer Range, 1914–36

	Specific Gravity in November			
Beer	*1914*	*1920*	*1929*	*1936*
Pale Ale	1055°	1047°	1047°	1046°
Light Bitter	1047°	1029°	1029°	1030°
K	1082°	1070°	1053°	1053°
XXXX	1065°	1047°	1047°	1045°
XXX	1053°	—	—	—
XX	1047°	1029°	1031°	1030°
Double Brown Stout	1073°	—	—	—
Porter	1054°	—	—	—
Stout	—	1047°	1039°	1040°
BK (Stingo)	—	—	1070°	1067°
Nips	—	—	1083°	1083°
Norfolk Brown Ale	—	—	1038°	1038°

Source: Steward & Patteson Quarterly Cost Account Book, 1908–51, BR1/117, N.R.O.

13. Steward & Patteson advertising: the 'Buy British' campaign, early 1930's

Figure 1

Correspondence between B.G.C. Wetherall, Head Brewer, Steward & Patteson, and supplying firms, November 1931, re guarantees that raw materials would be British or Empire Made

November 9th 1931

Dear Sirs,

Buy British Goods

This movement is one which has our entire support, and as we are anxious to produce Beers which will enable our Customers to conform with this National Appeal, we should like to have your assurance, in writing, which some other firms from whom we purchase Brewing materials have given to us, that the............ which you are supplying to us is wholly the product of British Empire grown material.

Hoping we may have your favourable reply in the near future.

Yours faithfully

per pro. B.G.C. Wetherall

Manbré & Garton, Limited
Winslow Road
Hammersmith
London W.6.

4th November 1931

Messrs. Steward & Patteson Ltd.,
Pockthorpe Brewery
Norwich

Dear Sirs,

Mr Wetherall was speaking to us yesterday with regard to the origin of the Raw Sugars that we use in our Refinery, and we hereby have pleasure in giving you our assurance that the Brewing Sugars with which we supply you will be manufactured from Raw Sugars imported from the British Empire. We trust this assurance will give you every satisfaction.

As you are probably aware, we have our own Estates and Sugar Refinery in Kenya Colony, and for many years have done all we can to further Empire produce.

Yours faithfully

A.R. Higgins
MANBRÉ & GARTON LIMITED

Edward Fison Limited
Manufacturers of Malt
Extract Etc.
Ipswich

B.G.C. Wetherall Esq.,
Messrs Steward & Patteson Ltd.,
Pockthorpe Brewery,
Norwich.
Friday Nov. 27th 1931
Dear Sir,

Replying to your enquiry of the 26th inst. we are prepared to guarantee that any delivery of Diastasic Malt Extract we make to you will be solely manufactured from Empire barley, and this guarantee will hold good with all deliveries. We shall much appreciate an order from you.

We hope you are finding business fairly well maintained, in spite of the fact the reports we have hardly confirm this position.

Yours faithfully
p.p. Edward Fison Ltd

The Depression of the 1930's

For most breweries, the 'Great Depression' of 1929-33 merely exacerbated problems already established in the 1920's. Annual beer production in the United Kingdom fell by 17 per cent, from 25.0 million bulk barrels in 1927-9 to 20.7 million in 1930-3, and by 20 per cent in relation to barrels of standard gravity. Profits fell by similar margins.[27] At the same time, the burdensome tax on beer was raised to new heights in the 'crisis' budgets of April 1930 and September 1931: from £5 per standard barrel (less £1 rebate) to £5.15 and £6.70 respectively. For a company brewing beer at an original gravity of 1037⁰ this represented a rise in tax from £4 per barrel to £5.70, an increase of 42.5 per cent. The changes added *2d.* a pint to the price of beer at a time when prices were in general falling.[28] There was some improvement for the trade after the budget of April 1933, which introduced a new method of taxing beer. A duty of £1.20 per bulk barrel was imposed for beer with a gravity of 1027⁰ or less, with an additional duty of 10p for each degree above 1027. For brewers of 1037⁰ beer, this involved a tax of £2.20 a barrel, much lower than in the crisis years, and about half of the tax paid in the period 1920-30.

Nevertheless, the trend to weaker beer continued. The average gravity fell from 1043° to 1041° by the late 1930's. This said, the combination of lower taxation and an upswing in industrial recovery made the years 1934-9 relatively prosperous ones for the brewing trade. There was a modest recovery in consumption. Production rose to 21.9 million bulk barrels a year in 1934-6 and 24.7 million in 1937-9.[29] But behind the fluctuation in fortunes caused by the Depression and the subsequent recovery there lurked the factors which continued to cause anxiety. First, the club trade continued to grow. In the period 1930-8 3,000 more clubs were established, at a time when the number of on-licences fell by more than 4,000.[30] Changing consumer tastes and a rapid increase in suburban house-building again made it imperative for brewers to improve and re-locate their public houses. Finally, the climate of opinion reflected by government remained critical of private enterprise, and continued to examine the worth of the 'Carlisle scheme'. All this made for relatively unsettled conditions, and the trend towards concentration in the industry was maintained.[31]

The experience of Steward & Patteson in Norwich matched that of the country as a whole. A rural base in East Anglia may have been a little more secure than that in an industrial area where depression struck hardest, but only a little. The agricultural sector was far from buoyant, given import penetration stimulated by a sharp fall in world food prices after 1929. Indeed, beer production at Pockthorpe fell quite as much as the national average in the depth of the depression: from 90,300 barrels to 69,300, 1930-2, a fall of 24 per cent, identical to the reduction nationally. And beer sales fell by 22 per cent in the same period (See Appendix D, Table 2). The company then shared fully in the revival of the later 1930's. In the years to November 1935 and 1936 95,000 barrels were produced and sold, a figure which was higher than at any time since the early 1920's (ibid.). What distinguished Steward & Patteson from many other breweries was the fact that the profits of this still private limited company remained good. There was no 'crisis' reduction after 1929. The amount available for distribution increased steadily from 1926 to 1931, and although net profits, after deducting debenture interest, fell by 25 per cent, 1931-2 - from £82,500 to £62,100 - they rose by no less than 38 per cent, from £68,600 to £94,900, in 1933-4 (Appendix D, Table 4). The strength of the company's position may also be judged from the data in Table 25, above. Net profits jumped from £64,000 per annum in 1927-9 to £76,000 in 1930-2 and £92,000 in 1933-6. In constant 1911-14 values, the increase was from £39,000 to £51,000 and £65,000 - the profits in 1933-6 being 15 per cent higher than the previous peak of profitability in 1911-14. The rate of return fell from 10.7 per cent in 1931 to 8.3 per cent in the following year, but then rose steadily to a peak of 13.2 per cent in 1935 (Appendix D, Tables 3 and 4). As Table 25 shows, the average return in 1930-2 was in fact higher than in 1927-9, and in 1933-6 it matched pre-war rates. Ordinary dividends, paid free of income tax, were maintained at an annual rate of 7 per cent, 1927-32, and with bonuses averaged 10.6 per cent over the period 1933-6. At the beginning of 1936, the company could boast of a financially strong position. Free reserves amounted to £400,000, and in addition there were benefits deriving from the policy of buying in the debenture stock, which had been followed consistently over a number of years. In the period 1905-22 £177,500 had been bought up by the directors, and £224,000 was transferred to Steward & Patteson Ltd. in 1923. At the beginning of November 1935 the company held £238,720, or 85 per cent of the debenture stock, having acquired it at an average discount of 22 per cent (£78/£100).[32] Thus, at Pockthorpe the drop in sales and net profits was a cyclical setback but one which was not reflected in a fall in returns to shareholders or a reduction in financial security. Holders of ordinary shares fared much better in the 1930's than they had done in the 1920's.

Much of the company's trading experience in the 1920's also applied to the period to 1936, when the decision was taken to convert the brewery into a public limited liability company. Table 24 shows that in the 1930's some response was made to falling input prices, by increasing the amount of sugar and hops used in the brewing process. However, the amount of malt used was reduced, and the average gravity of the beers produced in 1930-6 was fully two degrees lower than it had been in 1923-9 (Table 24). Like other breweries, Steward & Patteson benefited from the reduction in excise duties after 1933. The cost per barrel fell from £3.29 in 1932 to £2.12 in 1935 and 1936, a reduction of 36 per cent,[33] but this did not lead either to an increase in the strength of the beer produced or to a significant reduction in its retail price. In Norwich, as indeed in other parts of the country, beer prices were largely determined by an informal cartel, in this case the Norfolk and Suffolk Brewers Association. Wage rates were handled in the same way. Thus, when the beer duty was raised in September 1931, the Association agreed to increase retail prices by 1*d*. a pint, and when the duty was reduced in April 1933 the Association responded by cutting the price by 1*d*. There was little or no scope for Steward &

Patteson to take unilateral action, nor is there any evidence that such a course was ever contemplated.[34] In fact, the company's unit income from sales fell a little during the 1930's. The income per barrel fell from £1.42p in 1927-9 to £1.32p in 1933-6, and the income from bottled beer fell from 11.5p a dozen in 1927-9 to 8.8p in 1933-6. The reduction was matched by the general deflationary conditions which obtained after 1929. Thus, in constant 1911-14 values, the income from draught beer actually rose, from 86.0p to 93.1p, while that from bottled beer fell slightly, from 6.96p to 6.20p.[35]

The trading position in 1930-6 is summarised in Table 31, in both current and constant values. In current values the company experienced a stablisation of income from beer, both draught and bottled, and an estimated gross revenue of about £485,000, a little higher than in the late 1920's. Costs, on the other hand, were successfully reduced, by no less than 21 per cent (comparing 1933-6 with 1927-9). As already observed, economies were evident in the use of malt, and the reduction in beer duty from 1933 had predictable effects on overall costs. Labour costs, on the other hand, remained high. While wage costs were held down - they fell from £28,900 per annum in 1927-9 to £23,950 (17 per cent), helped by a cut in the wage rate of 1*s*. a week in May 1932 - pension costs rose sharply. The annual cost of pension provisions increased from £420 in 1921-4 to £2,275 in 1928-9. A new pension and life assurance scheme, arranged with the Legal & General Assurance Company, took effect on 30 June 1934. By 1935-6, pensions were costing Steward & Patteson £8,780 a year.[36] Nevertheless, there was an improvement in margins, with the 'working ratio' (costs expressed as a percentage of gross revenue) falling from 86 in 1927-9 to 81 in 1933-6 (Table 31). A rather different picture emerges if the same data are expressed in constant values. Here, the emphasis falls on an improvement in real revenue, with real costs actually rising at a time of deflation. The brewery's costs in 1933-6 were some 12 per cent higher than in 1927-9 in constant 1911-14 values, and labour costs were 22 per cent higher. The excise duty paid also remained greater in real terms than in 1927-9, and raw material costs increased in the late 1930's, due mainly to a rise in hop prices, which, always volatile, jumped from £5.39 a cwt. in 1931 to £13.48 in 1934. The improvement in margins is best interpreted as coming from the ability to keep real income high. The income from bottled beer in 1933-6 was 58 per cent higher than in 1927-9, and gross revenue was 19 per cent up. In a period of falling prices, the company strengthened its position by maintaining revenue.

TABLE 31

Steward & Patteson Ltd. Trading Position, 1930–6, with comparisons for 1911–14 and 1927–9 [£]

Period	Income		Gross Revenue	Costs				Net Profit	Working Ratio
	Draught Beer	Bottled Beer		Raw Materials	Beer Duty	Labour	Total		[%]
[1: in current values]									
1911–14	90,041	4,025	235,444	61,328	42,053	18,612	178,900	56,544	76
1927–9	117,968	37,618	472,240	60,900	202,439	44,014	407,862	64,378	86
1930–2	110,359	51,396	486,473	49,384	221,351	45,290	410,185	76,288	84
1933–6	116,664	51,066	484,524	58,600	196,647	46,062	392,296	92,228	81
[2: in constant 1911–14 values]									
1911–14	90,041	4,025	235,444	61,328	42,053	18,612	178,900	56,544	
1927–9	71,433	22,779	285,957	36,877	122,583	26,652	246,974	38,983	
1930–2	73,967	34,447	326,054	33,099	148,359	30,355	274,923	51,131	
1933–6	82,215	35,987	341,455	41,297	138,581	32,461	276,459	64,995	

Source: Steward & Patteson Ltd. Account Books, BR1/101, 107, N.R.O. Constant values derived from Feinstein's retail price index: Feinstein, *National Income, Expenditure and Output of the United Kingdom, 1855–1965* (Cambridge, 1972), T140. Format as for Tables 26 and 27, above.

In the retail trade, the policies of the 1920's were extended into the 1930's. The number of tied houses fell from 669 in 1929, after the acquisition of Bagge's, to 643 in 1936 (Table 28, above), repeating the pattern evident in 1922-8. The only market to see a small expansion was the Ipswich agency, where three pubs in the Woodbridge area were added with the purchase of Messrs Lockwoods for £6,000 in July 1932. In Norwich, the brewery's biggest market, Steward & Patteson continued its policy of exchanging the licences of small inner-city pubs for licences for new houses to serve the expanding suburbs and council estates. Often action was forced upon the company by the slum clearance and road-widening activities of the local authority. For example, in January 1935 the 'Woodcock' in Woodcock Road was opened in place of the 'King's Head' in St James, where the property was required for a road improvement scheme, and in the following October the 'Morrison Lodge', Harvey Lane, replaced the 'Dun Cow'. Pockthorpe, which had been affected by slum clearance.[37] New pubs were also opened to serve the Larkman and Mile Cross estates: the 'Larkman', Dereham Road (capital cost: £3,400, 1932); the 'Park House', Catton Grove Road (£4,700, 1933); the 'Bull Road Inn', Reepham Road (£3,750, 1935); and the 'Health House', Gertrude Road (£4,400, 1936).[38] The company also bought the 'York Hotel' in Norwich from the Licensed Victuallers' Association for £4,500, in 1932, and the 'Wellington' in Cromer for £5,900 in 1935, and spent sizeable sums on rebuilding works, including £3,795 for the 'Dunstable Arms' in Sheringham (1931-2) and £5,410 for the 'King's Arms', Caister (1935-6).[39] Finally, there is evidence that the brewery began to operate some managed, as opposed to tenanted, houses after 1928.[40] All in all, the scale of improvement of the tied estate in 1930-6 was greater than it had been in the 1920's. Reserve funds in excess of £90,000 were established for property and property improvement. The trade alterations account reveals an annual expenditure of £8,530 in 1930-6, compared with £7,370 in 1920-9, and this presumably excludes the sums used to acquire pubs and to build new ones.[41]

The new public houses of the 1930's were in the main successful, attracting above average sales. In Norwich, for example, the average sale of draught beer amounted to 145 barrels a year per house in 1935 and 1936. The newly-built 'Park House' sold an average of 260 barrels in the same years, and the 'Woodcock' sold 323 in 1936. The 1930's also saw an improvement in the profitability of the brewery's agency trade, with higher returns from Yarmouth, King's Lynn, and Eye, leaving only Ipswich as a continuing disappointment (see Table 29).[42] But notwithstanding the move to higher-volume outlets and the numerous sales of small properties - a further nineteen pubs were sold off for compensation in 1930-6 - the tied estate continued to include numerous pubs of marginal worth in both village and town. These were in every way social rather than profit centres. In the Norfolk area, annual sales of draught beer over the period 1920-6 averaged only sixty-four barrels per pub, barely one and a quarter barrels a week each, and some houses experienced very low demand levels. The 'Black Lion' in Reepham, for example, sold only 23.3 barrels a year, 1930-6, under half a barrel a week. Norwich too had its small pubs with sluggish demand, pubs like the 'Black Horse', St Gregory, where in the three years 1934-6 sales amounted to only seventy-eight barrels of draught and 1,194 dozen bottled beers a year - equivalent in total to a weekly consumption of two and a half barrels.[43] Clearly, the extent to which the company pursued a more vigorous retailing policy should not be exaggerated.

The 1930's, like the 1920's, witnessed a mixture of cautious development and conservative brewing practices. On the development side, S. & P. decided to bottle its own cider instead of buying it in, and in August 1931 agreed to purchase machinery for the purpose, at an estimated cost of £600. A modest business began in 1932, yielding about £900 a year.[44] The company also continued to pursue a modest marketing policy. The 'Buy British' campaign was maintained, and the firm supported the Brewers' Society's national advertising, which included the slogan 'Beer is Best' from December 1933. A marketing advantage was also gained from the grant of a Royal Warrant appointing Steward & Patteson brewers to H.M. King George V in 1934. The warrant had been obtained by the company's agent at King's Lynn, A.E. Massingham, following the supply of beer to the Royal Household at Sandringham.[45] In addition, modest prizes were won for bottled stout and light ale, at the Brewers' Exhibition of 1931 and at the Brewing Trade Review Exhibition of 1933.[46] The company also successfully tendered for the supply of beers at the ground of Norwich City Football Club, and began trading in the 1935-6 Season.[47] Brewing equipment was also renewed, though there were no dramatic technological changes. The company replaced its steam engines with electric power, lined its fermenting vessels with copper - thirteen were modified in 1933-4 at a cost of £1,800 - scrapped its old wooden malt vats in favour of steel bins, and in 1935 purchased a malt conveyor to take malt to the grinding machine.[48]

It is not certain how far these changes placed Steward & Patteson ahead of its rivals in East Anglia - Bullard, Morgans, and Youngs Crawshay & Youngs in Norwich, Lacons in Yarmouth, and other regional companies such as Greene King in Bury and Adnams of Southwold. The impression is that Steward & Patteson were neither the most dynamic nor the most profitable of these enterprises, although this is not to say that they lagged behind very far in an industry where comfort was preferred to radical change. Comparisons of balance sheets and ordinary dividends are difficult, if not dangerous, to make, but they suggest that S. & P. may have been the largest company, but was not the most prosperous, as Table 32 indicates.

TABLE 32

East Anglian Brewers to 1936

Brewery	*Paid-up Nominal Capital (incl. debentures)* £	*Tied Houses (no.)*	*Average Annual Ordinary Dividend (incl. bonuses)* %	*Period Covered*
Steward & Patteson	888,000	643 (1936)	7.85	1924–36
Bullard	644,000	c.530 (1937)	19.23	1924–36
Lacon	644,673	—	10.83	1931–6
Greene King	790,000	509 (1936)	16.31	1924–36
Adnams	121,500	—	15.96	1924–35

Source: The Stock Exchange Official Yearbook, 1938, and R.G. Wilson, op. cit. pp.270, 275.

Ownership and Management, 1914-36

The founding families of Steward, Patteson, Finch and Morse continued to hold all the shares in Steward & Patteson Limited until the firm was converted into a public limited liability company in March 1936. As time went on, the clear division of interest between the four groups, evident in the first listing of shareholders of September 1895 and shown in Chapter Five, was blurred a little by a more complex pattern of ownership, with shares transferred to children, relatives, and spouses, and to numerous executors and trustees. Shares were also exchanged by members of the participating families, often at generous prices. In 1895 the ordinary and preference shares were divided into only twelve parts; by 1936, the ordinary shares were

TABLE 33

Steward & Patteson Ltd. Ordinary Shareholders, 1895–1936

Family	Nominal Value of Holding [£]				Percentage Held [%]			
	Feb. 1895	*Feb. 1914*	*Feb. 1920*	*Feb. 1936*	*1895*	*1914*	*1920*	*1936*
Morse	36,000	55,260	177,000	180,600	24.0	36.8	39.3	40.1
Patteson	32,630	27,000	55,980	57,590	21.8	18.0	12.4	12.8
Steward/ Finch	81,370	67,740	217,020	211,810	54.2	45.2	48.2	47.1
Total	150,000	150,000	450,000	450,000	100.0	100.0	100.0	100.0

Largest Shareholders with Percentage Held [%]

Feb 1895		*Feb. 1914*		*Feb. 1920*		*Feb. 1936*	
George H. Morse	24.0		33.2		30.1	Executors of late G.H. Morse	14.1
						George Geoffrey Morse	9.7
						Francis John Morse	7.1
Donald Steward	18.5	Executors of late Donald Steward	18.5		18.5	Eirene Steward and Donald Charles Steward	9.4
Henry S. Patteson	16.3	H.T.S. Patteson	18.0	Robert Wace Patteson	9.8	A. Finch/G. Wyllys (solicitor)	8.1
Executors of late Peter Finch	11.0		12.1	Charles Hugh Finch	7.1		5.8
				Alfred Finch	7.0		6.9

Source: Steward & Patteson Share Ledger, 1895–1920, BR1/71, and Annual Summary of Share Capital and Lists of Directors and Shareholders, 1908–36, BR1/74–7, N.R.O.

divided into thirty-six holdings, the preference shares into thirty-three, and there were forty-five separate individuals and groups named in the register. Clearly, with a limit of fifty shareholders for private company status, the time was ripe for conversion to the public form.[49] Nevertheless, it is still possible to isolate the main divisions of interest, in spite of the growing complexities of ownership. In 1895, the Steward/Finch family had held 54.3 per cent of the ordinary and preference capital, the Morse family 24 per cent, and the Pattesons 21.7 per cent. The balance then shifted in favour of the Morses as George Henry Morse acquired shares, and the trend intensified after the death of Henry T.S. Patteson in May 1915 and the capitalisation of reserves in October 1919. By February 1920 the Morses owned 37 per cent of the capital, while the Pattesons' share had dwindled to 14 per cent. There was little change in the distribution over the next sixteen years.[50] A similar pattern may be observed when the controlling ordinary capital is analysed (see Table 33). The Morse family increased its share from 24 per cent in 1895 to 40.1 per cent in 1936, while the Patteson holding fell from 21.8 to 12.8 per cent. The Steward/Finch family retained much the largest share, and for most of the period enjoyed a controlling interest above 50 per cent. However, we should distinguish between theoretical and effective control. The Steward and Finch holdings were too dispersed to constitute a managerial dominance. The real power lay with those who held large stakes and were also directors, and, above all, with the directors who were interested enough in the brewery to play an active part in its management. In 1914, for example, four men either owned or controlled no less than 86 per cent of the ordinary capital - George Morse, Henry T.S. Patteson, and the 'active' executors of the estates of Donald Steward and Peter Finch, namely the Finch brothers, Charles and Alfred. Time and the expansion of the capital account eroded this dominance. But as late as 1936, the two Finches and the two Morses on the Board, George's brother, Arthur Francis, and his eldest son, George Geoffrey, controlled at least 60 per cent of the equity capital.[51] For much of the twentieth century, then, the firm of Steward & Patteson was to all intents and purposes the firm of Morse & Finch.

The brewery's board of directors was a stable and enduring body throughout the forty-one year life of the private limited company. Continuity was the keynote. The first five chairmen had all been founder-directors in 1895: Henry Staniforth Patteson, Donald Steward, H.T.S. Patteson, George Morse, and Charles Finch. In the period 1914-

36 only death or ill-health produced changes. Thus, on the death of H.T.S. Patteson in May 1915 George Morse became chairman. His failing health resulted in the appointment of his son Geoffrey, in February 1927, and his death in April 1931 was followed by the appointment of Charles Finch as chairman, a post he held until 1945 (Table 34). The only other appointment was that of Peter C. Finch, the son of Charles Finch, who was brought onto the Board in February 1933 to assist his father, who by this time was sixty-six years old. After H.T.S. Patteson's death in 1915 the brewery was dominated by George Morse. Not only was he Chairman and an active manager, but he was also the major individual shareholder. In the period 1911-21 he held over 30 per cent of the equity and retained at least a quarter until the late 1920's. His full life as a local councillor in Norwich - Lord Mayor for the second time in 1922-3, the year of his knighthood - certainly did not preclude an active business contribution, which embraced the Norwich Union Insurance Company as well as Steward & Patteson. He was a rather severe, naturally shy man, who was 'very sparing of words'. But all who knew him recognised his devotion to management and his great capacity for hard work. As one of his obituarists put it, 'he had a great gift for seeing to the core of things; never fussing about irrelevant trifles; keeping his mind on main issues'.[52] Of the other directors, A.F. Morse and A. Finch contributed comparatively little, but Charles Hugh Finch proved to be an able lieutenant to George Morse and for much of the period 1915-31 the indications are of a business competently run. However, signs of strain became evident with Morse's declining health in the late 1920's and in particular after an operation in 1929, and his death in April 1931 left something of a vacuum which no-one quite managed to fill.

It was at this stage that signs of a recruitment problem for this family business began to emerge. After the War, two new recruits were brought into Pockthorpe at a junior level in the hope that, like George Morse and Charles Finch before them, they would blossom into active directors and possibly future chairmen. Unfortunately, neither did so. In May 1919 Geoffrey Morse, George's eldest son, joined the brewery's office as a clerk with an annual salary of £100 a year, and in the following November Robert Wace Patteson, the surviving son of H.T.S. Patteson, was appointed to a similar position (also with a salary of £100 a year). Both men were in their early twenties and both had had distinguished war careers which made it difficult for them to adjust to the more mundane concerns of a provincial brewery in

TABLE 34

Steward & Patteson Board of Directors, 1914–36

Director	*Born*	*Appointed*	*Chairman*	*Left*	*Ordinary Shares Held in Own Name*		*Salary in*	
					Feb 1920	*Feb 1936*	*1931*	*1936*
H.T.S. Patteson	1851	1895	1898–1915	May 1915 [died]	—	—	—	—
G.H. (Sir George) Morse	1857	1895	1915–31	April 1931 [died]	30.1%	—	£1,200	—
C.H. Finch	1866	1895	1931–45	Dec. 1952 [retired]	7.1%	5.8%	£1,200	£1,200
A.F. Morse	1872	1904	1945–51	Feb. 1957 [retired]	3.9%	3.8%	£1,100	£1,200
A. Finch	1870	1905	—	May 1943 [died]	7.0%	6.9%		
G.G. Morse	1896	1927	—	Aug. 1936 [resigned]	—	9.7%	—	£1,000
P.C. Finch	1905	1933	—	June 1947 [resigned]	—	1.8%	—	£642

peacetime. Captain, later Lieutenant-Colonel Patteson was a particular disappointment. Educated at Wellington and Sandhurst he had joined the Norfolk Regiment and won the Military Cross during the War. However, he showed little appetite for the brewing business, and did very little to earn his salary (£350 per annum in 1925-6). On his sudden death after a minor throat operation in 1926, at the early age of 31, much of his considerable shareholding passed to his sisters, Ardyn Barton and Joan Perowne, and their families.[53] Geoffrey Morse made a more substantial impact. He was earning £450 a year when he was brought onto the Board in February 1927. But he too found that the War had left a mark on him. A Captain in the East Surrey Regiment, he too had been awarded the Military Cross (in 1917), but unlike Patteson had been torpedoed and wounded. An unhappy personal life contributed to his decision to leave the brewery and the Board. After a spell on leave in April 1936 he resigned with effect from 1 August 1936, only a few months after the brewery had been converted into a public company.[54]

Two further recruits from the participating families also failed to inject vigour into the enterprise. On Patteson's death, Peter Charles Finch, Charles's son, joined the brewery office, at the age of twenty-one. He subsequently joined the Board in February 1933, and served until his resignation in June 1947. However, he failed to share his father's interest in the day-to-day administration of the company. On the Steward side, there had been no-one to replace Donald Steward, who had died in 1898. His son, Captain Rupert Donald, of Spexhall, near Halesworth in Suffolk, showed more interest in farming after attaining his majority, and it was left to his son, Donald Charles (1907-81), to make a contribution at Pockthorpe. He joined the office in 1928 at the age of twenty, after an education at Radley and Cambridge, with an initial salary of £50 a year. After his father's death in 1933, he and his mother Eirene held the largest single portion of his grandfather's stake in the brewery (see Table 33, above). His salary advanced to £450 a year by 1935-6, and in November 1936 he too joined the Board. He had some positive qualities and fostered good relations with public house tenants, but after the war his influence on the company was more often eccentric than dynamic.[55] Further evidence of the continuing search for able managers from within the families is provided by the appearance of Sydney Arthur Morse, the son of A.F. Morse, in the salary book. Born in 1902, he had been educated at Charterhouse and Trinity College Cambridge, but did not join the brewery immediately. In June 1935, shortly before his thirty-third birthday, he was appointed at a starting salary of £450 a year, and within eighteen months was on the Board.[56]

There are no letter books, and the company's minute books provide only a bare outline of the business. However, there are some indications that all was not well at Pockthorpe in the years immediately after George Morse's death. Supervision seems to have declined when Charles Finch was allowed special leave of absence to go to South Africa to represent the Norwich Union Life Office.[57] On his return he found the brewery in a poor state of cleanliness, and there had been numerous complaints from customers about the condition of the beer produced. A letter to the brewing department from the directors of 7 October 1932, following a two-day inspection, expressed dissatisfaction with the state of the yeast and fermenting rooms. 'The Yeast Room is particularly dirty, with mould on the walls and ceiling and slime on the floor, which must be detrimental to the yeast ... In the Fermenting rooms many of the outsides of the squares are mouldy and dirty, the copper and brass cocks and fittings are covered with verdigris, and the walls of the long room have patches of blue mould on them'.[58] Ten days later, Finch noted that 'for some 6 or 8 weeks past we had had serious complaints of our beer, especially P.A. [Pale Ale]; this was mainly due to shortages of beer stock - several P.A. gyles being sent out the day they were racked - This was thoroughly gone into by the Directors and in their opinion the cause was mainly owing to friction between Mr Wetherall [the Head Brewer] and Mr Hunter [an assistant brewer] and their not getting on together ... Wetherall had certainly shown signs of weakness in management'.[59]

B.G.C. Wetherall had joined the brewery in 1923 at the age of fifty, replacing W.B. Paterson as Head Brewer at a salary of £1,200 a year. For a time things appear to have gone well, and as late as July 1932 Wetherall was nominated as company representative on the research scheme of the Institute of Brewing.[60] However, production problems continued to concern the directors, and after more difficulties with the Pale Ale Wetherall was challenged by Finch, in January 1933, about his having concealed complaints about a consignment. On 6 March Finch saw Wetherall again and told him that 'the directors were very concerned that he had not reported it and told him that if he did not report in future we should make change of Brewer'.[61] A month later, matters came to a head. Wetherall had been absent from the brewery with 'fluid on the knee'. From his home he made allegations about the quality of the malt supplied to the brewing room. Charles Finch noted, on 11 April, that the directors were 'practically of an opinion that a change of management is necessary - as we feel we cannot carry on our business any longer where the Head Brewer is and has been so out of touch with heads of other departments'. In May Wetherall was replaced as Head Brewer by F.C. Hipwell.[62] The episode is difficult to interpret conclusively. It might be evidence of a swift and strong management response to production problems and the crucial (for a brewery) matters of cleanliness and quality. We can find occasional references to similar action, as in 1925 when A.J. Bland [sic], tenant of the 'Recruiting Sergeant' at Great Yarmouth, was given notice after being accused of diluting the Strong Ale with Mild.[63] But the overriding impression is that in 1932-3 brewery supervision had gone slack in the wake of George Morse's death, and that a firmer response was forced upon the surviving directors by external pressures.

Taking a more general look at the brewery's organisation, the salaried staff remained a compact team. In 1919 there were thirty staff at Pockthorpe in the various departments, and a handful of employees at the company's outposts in Yarmouth, King's Lynn, Ipswich, Swaffham, and Eye (Table 35). By 1936 numbers had increased to forty

TABLE 35

Steward & Patteson Salaried Staff, 1919, 1936

Total employed	*1919*	*1936*
Pockthorpe	30	40
Agencies	12	17
Departmental heads		
Secretary	S.S. Base (£400)	W.J. Culley (£600)
Cashier	G. Lugden (£400)	R.S. Mills (£390)
Head Brewer	W.B. Paterson (£1,200)	F.C. Hipwell (£1,200)
Malting Manager	R.E. Chichester (£1,000)	R.E. Chichester (£1,100)
Architect [Surveyor]	W.A. Trollope (£370)	W.H.H. Middleton (£550)
Head Traveller	G. Holmes (£460)	F.H. Hill (£530)
Mineral Water Manager	J.H. Gunnell (£270)	S.F. Baker (£260)
Transport Manager	———	J.J. Chapman (£350)
Agency Managers		
Yarmouth	R. Grand (£480)	R. Grand (£540)
Ipswich	J.A.W. Josselyn (£460)	C. Spinks (£310)
King's Lynn	A.E. Massingham (£280)	A.E. Massingham (£480)
Swaffham	G.A. Walker (£390)	———
Eye	W. Hunt (£270)	C. Hunt (£380)

Source: Steward & Patteson Salaries Account Book, BR1/141, N.R.O.

in Norwich and seventeen in the agencies. The brewery's 'architect', W.A. Trollope, died in 1933 and was replaced by a 'surveyor', W.H.H. Middleton. A Transport Manager, J.J. Chapman, was appointed in 1925. Otherwise, long and uninterrupted service was the norm in all departments. S.S. Base, the Company Secretary, joined Steward & Patterson in 1881 at the age of twenty and served as Secretary from 1919 to 1929. His successor, W.J. Culley, was taken on at the age of seventeen in 1893 and acted as Secretary until 1946. Between them, they put in 101 years' service. Francis Hipwell, Wetherall's successor as Head Brewer, was a company employee from 1910 to 1950, and Trollope served from 1892 to 1933. Chichester, the maltster, Lugden, the cashier, and the agents Grand, Josselyn and Massingham, were all long-serving managers.[64]

Less is known about the wages staff, for no wage books appear to have survived for the period after 1916. It may be suggested, however, that departmental changes in the inter-war years were limited except in distribution, where motor lorries replaced horses except over short distances, and S.S. Annie, the wherry used for Norwich-Yarmouth traffic, was sold in 1937.[65] There are also indications that the old paternalism which had characterised labour relations in the brewery

14. S.S. Annie, prior to sale in 1937 [*Stokes coll.*]

was beginning to break up in the 1920's and 1930's. We can see this in the General Strike of May 1926. Contrary to the expectations of Sir George Morse Steward & Patteson workers came out on strike in support of the miners, along with other brewery workers in Norwich. The strike, together with the punitive terms exacted from strikers prior to reinstatement, was a severe blow to the deference and loyalty of the past.[66] Thereafter, the board minutes refer to wage rate adjustments in which negotiations with a 'Men's Committee' are recorded, for example in July 1927 and April 1928.[67] Coopers' wages were fixed in accordance with the deliberations of a National Joint Industrial Council.[68]

Of course, to a certain extent the old ways continued - the works outings, the long service awards, support for the territorial army - and the company's outings, concern for the individual, and progress with sick pay and pensions provision is remembered affectionately by brewery pensioners.[69] But in a world of fluctuating economic activity - of inflation and deflation, wage increases and wage cuts - it became more difficult to sustain the concept of the large, independent, gentleman brewer. The more hard-headed world of management accountants, graduate trainees, and brewing room scientists, lay in the future. Steward & Patteson at least had the right company form - the public company - and the right size to facilitate a transition from the old to the new. But in the 1930's its management appears to have been more old-fashioned and nostalgic than anything else.

Figure 2

Draft letter of reinstatement for brewery workers after the General Strike, 1926

TO:- Messrs. Steward & Patteson, Ltd.,

I, the under-signed, hereby request you to allow me to re-enter your employment as and I hereby express my sincere regret that I broke my previous contract of employment with you by leaving your service without giving you the legal notice to which you were entitled, and that if you are prepared to permit me to re-enter your employment, I undertake to carry out my duties in a proper and satisfactory manner, and I fully realise that if you do so re-employ me, that the re-employment may be of a temporary nature only, and is strictly subject to one week's notice on either side.

DATED this day of 1926.

I have read the above and fully understand the same

Steward & Patteson Breweries and Agencies

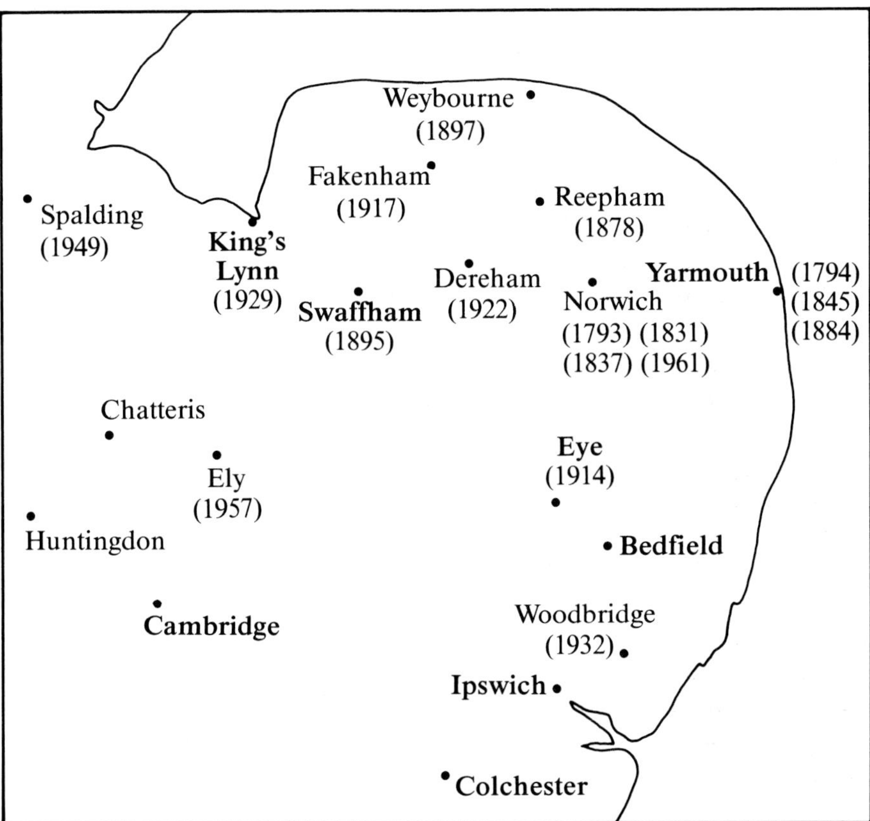

Note: Dates = dates of acquisition by Steward & Patteson.
Agencies are in bold type

15. Steward & Patteson Ltd. Board of directors, 1937 (standing, left to right: Sydney Morse; Francis John Morse; Peter Finch; Donald Steward; sitting, left to right: Arthur Francis Morse; Charles Hugh Finch (Chairman); Alfred Finch) [*Stokes coll.*]

7

Steward & Patteson and the Modern Brewing Industry, 1936-63

Public Company Status and the Second World War

The timing of Steward & Patteson's decision to go public in March 1936 owed a great deal to rather negative factors, and in particular the financial burden of death duties payable on the estate of Sir George Morse (who died in 1931), which was rendered more difficult to bear by the limitations imposed by private company status. But positive elements were also present. One of these was the restored reputation of Steward & Patteson's beer after its brewing difficulties in the early 1930's (see above, pp.127–8). Consistency of production under Frank Hipwell, Head Brewer from 1933, and the granting of a Royal Warrant in 1934 undoubtedly gave the directors confidence. The improvement in the general conditions in the trade had the same effect. In January 1936 Charles Finch sought the advice of the company's auditors, Collins, Tootell & Co., about a conversion scheme. This was to involve a reduction in the denomination of the share capital from £10 to £1, and the capitalisation of undivided profits held in reserve. An issue of £150,000 ordinary shares was to be made, allotted to existing shareholders on the basis of one share for every three shares held, and the new shares were then to be offered to the public.[1] The auditors concurred with the plan, and in March, the shares were placed with Rowe, Swan & Co., a firm of stockbrokers, which had agreed to underwrite the issue at a net purchase price of 53*s*. [£2.65] a share (55*s*. less expenses). The new shares were described by the *Investors' Chronicle* as 'a very sound brewery investment'. Dealings opened at prices ranging from 55*s*. to 60*s*. [£2.75 - 3.00].[2] Company conversion enabled the ordinary shareholders to benefit from what was, in effect, a tax-free distribution of accumulated profits. The company took its place among the country's quoted breweries at a time of upswing in the economy, and for a time conditions continued to improve. U.K. beer production, which had amounted to 21.9 million bulk barrels per annum in 1934-6, increased to 24.7 million in 1937-9. Steward & Patteson's own production had been 95,000 barrels in 1935 and 1936,

16. The 'Royal Oak', Oak St., Norwich, August 1938 [*G.A.F. Plunkett/Colman & Rye Lib.*]

higher than at any time since the early 1920's. Output then increased to about 100,000 barrels in 1937 and 106,000 in the following year (See Appendix D, Table 5). At this point the Second World War intervened to transform the market environment.

The conflict of 1939-45 produced many of the same conditions as that of 1914-18: raw material shortages, higher prices, government controls, and raised levels of taxation. But the general climate was very different from that experienced by brewing during the First World War. Churchill's government did not repeat Lloyd George's efforts to limit beer consumption, nor was there much incentive to do so, since both the average strength of British beer and the incidence of drunkenness had greatly diminished over the first forty years of the twentieth century. On the contrary, beer production actually increased during the Second World War. In spite of a fall in the alcoholic content of the beer brewed - the average specific gravity was cut from 1040.9⁰ in 1937-9 to 1034.7⁰ in 1945 - U.K. production, in *standard* barrels of 1055⁰, increased by 12 per cent, from 18.4 million per annum in 1937-9 to 20.6 million in 1945. In terms of *bulk* barrels (of any gravity), output increased by a third, from 24.7 million per annum in 1937-9 to 32.7 million in the last year of the war. Far from being seen as a threat to munitions production beer drinking was commonly regarded as a necessary accompaniment of social intercourse, an important factor in the maintenance of civilian morale and industrial productivity.[3] Lack of alternative leisure activities also helped to maintain demand in the public house, in spite of higher prices and the brewers' difficulties in maintaining the quality of the beer.[4]

This is not to say that the war years provided an easy time for the trade. In the first place, the burden of taxation became very heavy indeed. As Table 36 shows, the duty charged on a barrel of 1027⁰ gravity, £1.20 before the outbreak of war, had been increased to £7.03 by April 1944, a rise of 486 per cent; for beer of 1037⁰ gravity, the duty was raised from £2.20 to £9.63 a barrel, an increase of 338 per cent. The shift to higher thresholds was particularly marked in the period September 1939-April 1942, but there was no respite in the latter stages of the war. Indeed, no move was made to reduce the beer duty until April 1949.[5] Raw material shortages were another pressing problem. On the outbreak of war, the government imposed a 'barley levy', collected at the rate of 9*d.* a standard barrel,[6] heralding a range of allocative and import controls which provided many a headache in the brewing room. All the major inputs were affected: sugar rationing

TABLE 36

War-time Beer Duties

Date		Duty on *Barrel 1027°* *(i)*	*Barrel 1037°* *(ii)*	*Standard barrel 1055°* *(iii)*	*Index (1933–9 = 100)* *(i)*	*(ii)*	*(iii)*
April Sept.	1933– 1939	£1.20	£2.20	£4.00	100	100	100
Sept.	1939	£2.40	£3.40	£5.20	200	155	130
July	1940	£4.05	£5.55	£8.25	338	252	206
April	1942	£5.91	£8.09	£12.03	493	368	301
April	1943	£6.92	£9.47	£14.08	577	430	352
April Nov.	1944– 1947	£7.03	£9.63	£14.39	586	438	360

Source: Brewers' Society, *U.K. Statistical Handbook* (1980), p.54.

began in April 1940; malt supplies were hit by import controls and a poor barley crop in 1941; the Ministry of Food regulated purchasing and encouraged the use of inferior substitutes for malt, first flaked malt and maize, and then, in 1943, the use of flaked oats and potatoes.[7] Brewers could of course compensate in part for higher costs and scarce raw materials by shifting to lower gravity beers as far as the baseline gravity of 1027°, but the evidence suggests that they were rather reluctant to do so. It was the government who insisted that the 1940 output (in standard barrels) be pegged at 1939 levels. This was followed by instructions that average gravity be cut by 10 per cent from February 1941, a figure subsequently raised to 15 per cent, with effect from 1 January 1942.[8] Shortages of labour and petrol also served to hamper production and distribution in wartime. Irish workers were drafted into the maltings, and an increasing number of women was employed throughout the brewery, but the trade reported severe shortages of labour, particularly in the ancillary departments such as bottling. Transport arrangements were hit by petrol shortages, necessitating inter-brewery pooling arrangements. Finally, bombing destroyed or badly damaged a great many public houses: 3,000 were reported to be out of use by 1944.[9]

Steward & Patteson certainly shared the common experience of the nation's breweries during the Second World War. In some ways, however, the company fared better than most. Like the other major producers in East Anglia, the Pockthorpe brewery benefitted from the extra demand for beer generated by full employment in agriculture and an influx of troops which intensified in the latter stages of the war. Consequently, brewery production, which had faltered in 1940 and 1941 - 108,000 and 110,000 barrels compared with 112,000 barrels in 1939 - climbed to new heights, reaching 130,600 in 1942, 134,700 in 1943, and 148,400 in 1944, when sales topped the 150,000-barrel mark for the first time (Appendix D, Table 5). Profits also remained healthy as the annual reports and accounts make clear. Despite complaints about the burden of taxation - the annual beer duty paid increased from £235,000 in 1939 to £1.1 million in 1944 - the company was able to declare a comfortable and stable dividend of 12½ per cent [less tax] on its expanded ordinary share capital from 1937 to 1945.[10] Other local breweries did equally well, with average ordinary dividends in 1939-45 amounting to 16.8 per cent for Bullard's, 14.1 per cent for Morgans, and 12.6 per cent for Youngs Crawshay & Youngs.[11] On the debit side, Steward & Patteson's public houses suffered from the damage inflicted by air raids, particularly in 1942. A summary of the position in August 1943 revealed that fourteen pubs had been destroyed, twenty-one had been seriously damaged, and 139 had been slightly damaged. Rebuilding and repair costs were estimated to total about £100,000. A more detailed account of April 1945 listed 215 pubs damaged by enemy action over the period 1940-5. The government provided some relief with its war damage legislation, but there is no doubt that the company's retailing was disrupted in Norwich, where most of the serious bombing had occurred. The company also lost its Woolhall Maltings, and experienced some damage at the brewery itself. However, it escaped the fate of Morgans, whose brewery was so badly hit in June 1942 that it was forced to ask Steward & Patteson to brew for its houses in 1942-3.[12] There were other problems too. Steward & Patteson, in common with other brewers, lost labour - 168 employees joined the armed forces. And transport difficulties led to a recommendation from the Ministry of Transport that a temporary exchange of public houses with Lacons of Yarmouth be arranged. This rationalisation agreement began in June 1943.[13] The company also was forced to cut its production of mineral waters by about 45 per cent in 1943.[14]

Production costs naturally escalated. The company's beer duty payments more than doubled, from £219,900 per annum in 1937-9 to £551,100 per annum in 1940-2, and then doubled again to £1,043,800 in 1943-5.[15] Raw material costs also rose sharply, although the company was able to cushion itself against the worst effects of the malt shortage by continuing to supply most of its own needs. But the price of sugar increased by about 140 per cent in the period 1939-43, that of hops by 60 per cent (90 per cent, 1939-44), while the cost of the malt made by Steward & Patteson was 150 per cent higher in 1943 than it had been in 1939.[16] Inevitably, given the high levels of demand for beer, the brewery was forced to offer a weaker, lower quality product. As in the First World War, raw material inputs per barrel fell sharply, but this time new lows were reached. Mash tun ingredients in 1943-5, at 0.209 coombs of malt per barrel, 5.72 lb. of sugar, and 0.71 lb. of hops, were respectively 11, 29 and 43 per cent lower than in 1937-9 (see Table 37). Flaked barley was introduced early in 1942 and its use continued after the war. Flaked oats and flaked malt were added in 1943 and 1944. In 1937-9 the company had brewed beer with an average gravity of 1037.2°. In 1941-2 some of the stronger ales were abandoned, and the strength of the premium beers such as Pale Ale and XXXX was cut from 1046° to 1038°; at the same time, the gravity of the weak beers such as Light Bitter and XX fell from 1030° to 1026°. Average gravity fell to 1031.1° in 1942, and to 1030.8° in 1943 and 1944.[17]

TABLE 37

Pockthorpe Brewery: Gravity, Raw Material Consumption and Prices, 1930–55

Year ending November	*Average Gravity*	**Raw Material Consumption (per barrel)**			**Raw Material Prices (or costs)**		
		*Malt** *(coombs)*	*Sugar* *(lb.)*	*Hops* *(lb.)*	*Malt** *(coomb)*	*Sugar* *(cwt)*	*Hops* *(cwt)*
1930–6	1038.7°	0.243	8.68	1.29	£1.58	£1.29	£9.57
1937–9	1037.2°	0.234	8.06	1.25	£1.64	£1.54	£10.29
1940–2	1033.6°	0.218	5.75	0.90	£2.45	£2.68	£11.87
1943–5	1031.1°	0.209	5.72	0.71	£3.44	£3.20	£18.44
1946–9	1031.2°	0.206	5.96	0.77	£3.25	£3.28	£24.17
1950–2	1033.4°	0.219	6.61	0.85	£4.36	£3.76	£26.95
1953–5	1034.4°	0.221	6.99	0.98	£5.00	£3.68	£29.94

Source: Steward & Patteson Account Books, BR1/101, 102, 111, N.R.O.

* 'Malt' includes other materials – malted and flaked oats, and flaked barley. Flaked barley represented c.15–25 per cent of malted materials in 1945–55, but was cheaper than the company's malt only in 1945–8.

Rising raw material prices and higher tax meant that from 1937-9 to 1943-5 Steward & Patteson's brewing costs increased by over 300 per cent, but this produced conditions which were by no means catastrophic. Trading income rose by 32 per cent over the same period, and most of the increase in beer duty (equivalent to about 5*d.* a pint retail) was passed on to the consumer. Net profits did fall - by 26 per cent, but the company was able to maintain its ordinary dividend and set aside reasonable sums for contingencies. Between 1938 and 1945, £50,000 was transferred to general reserve, £87,000 to a contingency fund (including war damage contributions), £36,000 was provided for property improvement, and £97,000 for future tax purposes - making £270,000 in all.[18]

The Brewing Business, 1937-55

In many ways, of course, the war did not end in 1945. Austerity conditions persisted for almost a decade of peacetime, and brewers continued to experience high levels of taxation and shortages of raw materials. In 1946 food shortages restricted the supply of grain for brewing purposes. In May the government limited brewers to 85 per cent of their monthly output (standard barrels) in the year ending September 1945, and in August introduced a 10 per cent cut in average gravities. After lobbying by the trade the cut in gravity was withdrawn in May 1947 and the period for determining output was changed to the year to March 1946. But the economic crisis of 1947 led to the government's insistence, in January 1948, on a further reduction in output - to 82 per cent of the 1945-6 level - and there were two more tax hikes, in November 1947 and April 1948, amounting to an increase of 2*d.* a pint in retail prices. For 1037^{0} gravity beer, the new duty of £12.26 a barrel was now five and a half times higher than it had been in 1939 (cf. Table 36). Sugar supplies were also affected by restrictions on dollar spending. The overall result was a dearer, lower quality beer, which did nothing to stimulate demand. At the same time, public house conditions remained poor, since building licensing in the post-war period prevented brewers, like others, who had postponed essential repairs and renewals in wartime, from making the necessary investment. By the time they were free to do so, and the government had relaxed its grip on the industry - the Finance Act of 1950 allowed beer to be brewed at 3^{0} higher for the same duty, for example - the climate facing brewers was gloomier.[19] United Kingdom output, 32.7 million barrels in 1945, fell by 10 per cent or 3.4 million barrels in the following year, and by a further 11 per cent (3.5 million barrels) in 1948. By 1953-5 annual production was averaging 24.4 million, about the same as in the late 1930's. However, because the strength of the beer

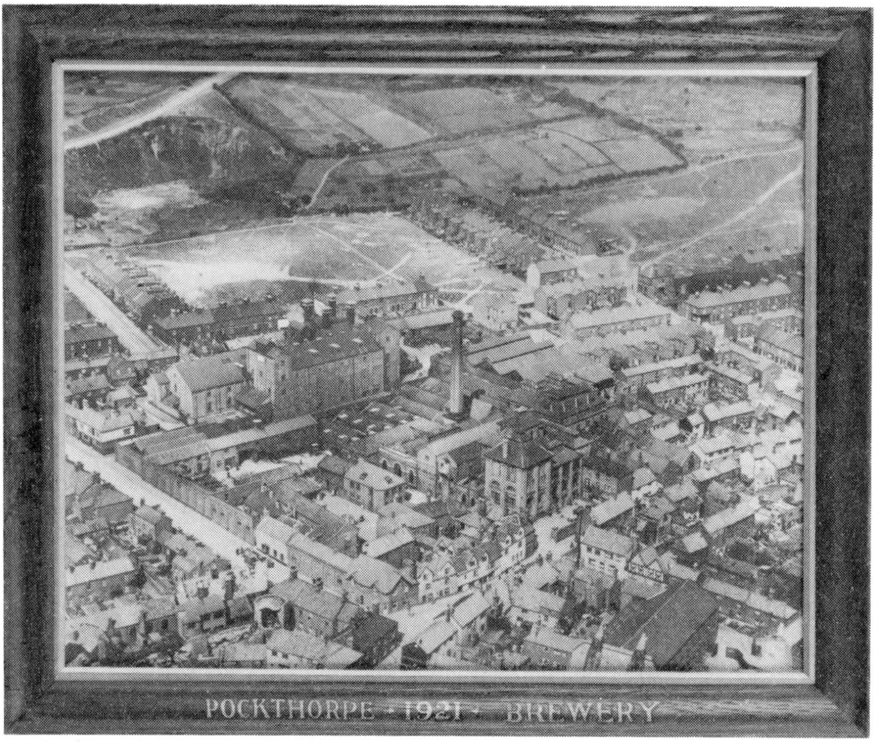

POCKTHORPE · 1921 · BREWERY

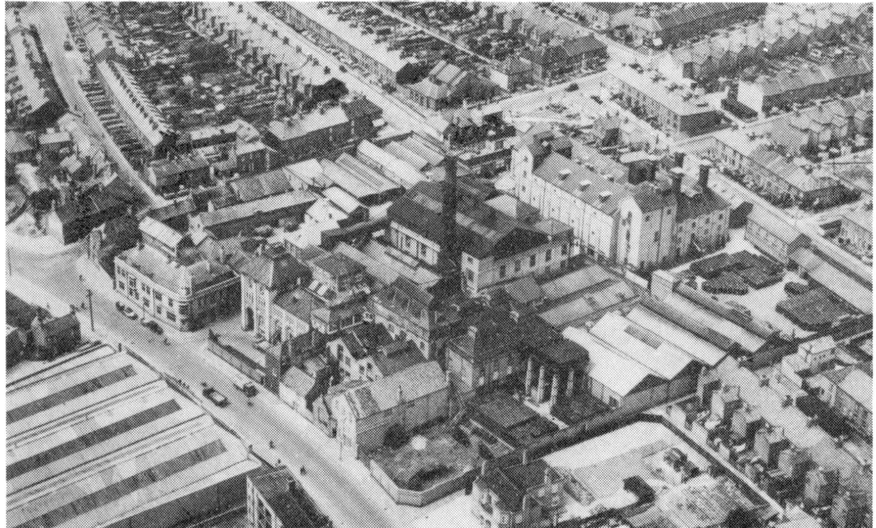

17 and 18. Aerial views of the brewery:
i] 1921 [*Bridewell Museum, Norwich*]
ii] 1946 [*Stokes coll.*]

had been reduced, annual output in standard terms fell from 18.4 million barrels in 1937-9 to only 16.4 million in 1953-5.[20]

Given these conditions, it is important to assess the experience of Steward & Patteson over a longer time-span, from the late 1930's to the mid 1950's. Here, it is clear that high raw material prices and lower input levels persisted after 1945, as Table 37 indicates. The Pockthorpe brewery's average gravity increased by about three degrees after 1949, but this improvement still left the company's beer significantly weaker than it had been before the war. The price of brewing materials continued to increase steadily, causing many a complaint at the annual general meetings. Thus, while average United Kingdom prices rose by about 35 per cent from 1937-9 to 1953-5, the cost of sugar increased by 140 per cent, hops by 190 per cent, and malted materials by 205 per cent. It is scarcely surprising to find that the brewery maintained a policy of economy. While brewing inputs climbed out of their end-war trough, they were still down on the pre-war position - by 6 per cent for malt, 13 per cent for sugar, and 22 per cent for hops (calculated from Table 37).

How far did Steward & Patteson's financial fortunes reflect the rise and subsequent decline in demand for beer, and the steady rise in costs? The position is complicated by the company's takeover of Soames & Co., the Spalding brewers, in 1949, and by a number of smaller acquisitions in the 1950's. The published accounts were altered radically in 1950, and no detailed accounts are available for the period after 1955. Nevertheless, it is possible to give a broad indication of the company's profitability. Table 38 summarises the results for the two decades from 1937 to 1956, the year before the brewery's results were once again affected by merger, this time with East Anglian Breweries of Ely and Huntingdon. Net profits, which had sagged during the war, picked up in the late 1940's and increased to a fairly comfortable level in the mid-1950's, boosted of course by the acquisition of Soames & Co. of Spalding. But since inflation was a persistent feature of the period, the real value of the company's profits dropped sharply. Of course, with no sign of current cost accounting methods in business balance sheets, the picture looked comforting. And the rate of return after tax, measured on the historic value of the company's paid-up capital, was sufficient for the directors to distribute a healthy 12½ per cent dividend, 1937-45, 12½ per cent plus a 2½ per cent bonus, 1946-53 (income tax deducted by the company), and a special 3 per cent bonus to celebrate the firm's 160th anniversary in

TABLE 38

Steward & Patteson Profits (annual averages), 1937–56

Year ending November	*Net Profits (after paying debenture interest) current values*	*Net Profits in constant 1937–9 values*	*Rate of Return (before deducting debenture interest)*	*Ordinary Share Dividend (percentages are gross: tax deducted by co.)*
	£	£	%	%
1937–9	99,562	99,562	13.3	12.5
1940–2	71,515	56,504	9.5	12.5
1943–5	75,189	52,350	10.0	12.5
1946–8	99,405	61,122	13.3	15.0*
1949–53	107,173	53,151	9.5	15.6*
1954–6	113,084	46,958	8.0	13.0*

Source: Taken from Appendix D, Table 6. Constant values from Feinstein, op. cit. T140, as in Table 25 above.

* Includes bonuses.

1953. Returns naturally fell when the company increased its capital by £217,660 (£147,360 in ordinary shares) to finance its merger with Soames in 1949. But the company had not been milked hard for profit. Thus, in 1954 the directors were confident enough to capitalise part of the capital reserve in order to provide dividends equivalent to the regular 2½ per cent bonuses to ordinary shareholders. Two £1 6 per cent cumulative preference shares were distributed for every five £1 ordinary shares held, adding £298,944 to paid-up capital.

A lack of data on a comprehensive and consistent basis for the company's trading as a whole makes it difficult to interpret the changing experience of Steward & Patteson with accuracy. However, some elements may be isolated with confidence. Beer sales held up fairly well after the war. Although the number of barrels sold fell from the war-time peak of 146,000 per annum in 1943-5 to only 103,000 in 1953-5, this level of sales was much higher than in the 1930's (see Table 39). Unfortunately, some disturbing trends lay behind the average. The mainstay of the company's business had always been the 'Home Trade' - sales in Norwich and Norfolk. Here, as Table 39 shows, sales fell by 56 per cent from 1943-5 to 1953-5, double the decline for the brewery as a whole. It is clear that sales of draught beer were inflated artificially by the shortage of glass for bottled beer during the war and austerity periods. In consequence, bottled beer sales fell to about 20 per cent of the barrelage. When they recovered in the early 1950's the decline in draught beer sales was exposed. Sales through the agencies also deteriorated. Two were actually closed after 1939 - Eye, which was merged with the Ipswich agency in May 1940, and then Ipswich itself, where from November 1947 deliveries were made direct from Norwich.[21] This meant that the decline in distribution to the 'Home Trade' by the early 1950's was worse than the figures suggest, since the Ipswich business, 8,200 barrels in 1947, was now incorporated in the 'home' statistics. In fact, the maintenance of reasonable levels of production and sales was due principally to the company's takeover of Soames & Co. of Spalding in August 1949.

TABLE 39

Steward & Patteson Beer Sales, 1930–55 (annual averages)

Period	**Beer Sales (barrels)**								
	Total	*Home Trade*	*%*	*Agencies***	*%*	*Bottled Beer*	*%*	*Soames*	*%*
1930–6	85,111	34,896	41	22,980	27	27,235	32	–	–
1937–9	106,139*	42,082	40	32,990	31	31,087	29	–	–
1943–5	146,169	71,289	49	49,120	34	25,760	18	–	–
1946–8	124,005	57,913	47	41,194	33	24,898	20	–	–
1950–2	116,850	40,269	34	22,414	19	40,252†	34	13,915	12
1953–5	102,660	31,511	31	18,930	18	39,223	38	12,996	13

Source: Steward & Patteson Account Books, BR1/102, N.R.O. Excluded: beer purchased: c.2,700b. 1937–9, 5,000b. 1949 and 1950.

* Discrepancy of 60 barrels in total for 1939.
** Includes sales to Morgans and Lacons.
† Includes 'bottled beer bought' (1950) – 1,684 b. p.a.

Soames & Co., an expanded family brewery, had grown by amalgamation in Lincolnshire from the late nineteenth century, and had been operated as a private limited company since 1909. The paid-up capital of £101,000 was held by only eighteen shareholders, who were, for the most part, members of the Soames, Peacock, and Harvey families. The brewery operated in territory adjacent to that of Steward & Patteson: from its Spalding headquarters it distributed beer to branches in Sleaford, Boston, Peterborough and Bourne. Twice before 1949 it had been approached by Steward & Patteson about a merger, only for the suggestion to be rejected. However, the time now appeared ripe. In common with many British brewers, the Soames directors were gloomy about the prospects for the industry given the government's existing hostility to it, which culminated in the Licensing Act of 1949. They were also depressed by their recent poor results and pointed out that 'it will be almost essential if the Balance Sheet is reconstructed that a Valuation of the Company's Assets would be made with its attendant heavy cost and delay'. Finally there was the matter of 'the advancing years of two of the Directors and the retirement contemplated by Mr MacLeod' [Charles C. Macleod, the Managing Director].[22] The Board therefore resolved to dispose of the business, giving Steward & Patteson first refusal. In May an offer was agreed, confirmed in August, by which Steward & Patteson acquired the whole of Soames's issued capital: an allotment of £217,660 in Steward & Patteson shares was made to Soames shareholders.* The business was then run as a subsidiary company, with separate accounts, until 1957. However, this was certainly not a merger of equals. For Steward & Patteson, the principal motive for the merger was to extend its trading area at a time of falling demand. Brewing ceased at Spalding in November 1949, and the 240 Soames pubs were then supplied from Pockthorpe, making up 12 per cent of total sales in the period 1950-5 (see Table 39). The Lincolnshire business contributed about 20 per cent of the expanded company's net profits after tax.[23]

Was the strategy a sensible one? The directors clearly thought so, and successive annual reports referred to the benefits obtained from the acquisition. Press comment was also favourable. The *Lynn News and Advertiser* pointed out that the merger with Soames gave Steward & Patteson an enhanced position as the largest brewery in East Anglia. It also enabled S. & P. to maintain higher sales than its major Norwich rival, Bullard.[24] On the other hand, it may be argued that all the company did was to add to its already large number of marginal, low barrelage, public houses. An additional capitalisation of £217,660 may not have been very much to pay for a brewery with 240 pubs, but many of these were located in remote areas of the Fens. Steward & Patteson supplied under 13,000 barrels of draught beer a year to Soames in the mid-1950's (Table 39, above). Assuming that no brewing at all was carried out by Soames after November 1949, this indicates an average consumption per pub of only one barrel a week.[25] In the increasingly competitive world of brewing after the war, a more appropriate policy was either to secure profitable urban outlets by merger, or to ward off the penetration of national brands such as Guinness, Bass and

*The offer was ten £1 Steward & Patteson 5 per cent cum. pref. shares for each £10 Soames 5 per cent cum. pref. share, and five £1 Steward & Patteson 5½ per cent cum. pref. and twenty-four £1 Ord. shares for each £10 Soames Ord. share. Thus, the Soames share capital of £39,600 pref. and £61,400 ord. was exchanged for £70,300 pref. and £147,360 ord. in S. & P.

Worthington by improved marketing of superior, locally-brewed products. Steward & Patteson did neither. It did rationalise its agency distribution and reduced its existing tied estate by about 7 per cent, from 642 houses in 1937 to 595 in 1955. But the merger with Soames increased the company's total to about 870 pubs, and by 1955 it was producing 102,000 barrels for 842 pubs (Table 40), equivalent to only two and a third barrels each per week, and lower than in the 1930's.[26]

TABLE 40

Steward & Patteson's Public Houses, 1937–55

Date:	Norwich		*Ipswich*	*Eye*	*King's*	*Yarmouth*	*Soames*	*Total**
November	*City*	*County*			*Lynn*			
1937	111	275	32	22	111	91	–	642 (25)
1943	106	277	50		109	90	–	632 (22)
1949	103	276	49**		107	90	[247] †	[872] (35)
1955	99	244	63**		100	89	247	842 (30)

Source: Steward & Patteson Account Book, BR1/102, N.R.O.; 'Steward & Patteson Ltd. Norwich. Licensed Houses – 6th November, 1955' [showing book values], J.W. Stokes collection.

* Figures in brackets give no. of leaseholds, included in the total.
** Ipswich data shown separately, but houses supplied direct from Norwich from November 1947. 20 houses were transferred from 'County' to 'Ipswich' in 1951.
† Soames data available for November 1955 only: 1949 figure may be a little higher.

Note: data include off-licences, but exclude Smith & Carman (1).

Other aspects of the company's trading after 1936 reveal a similar picture of steady progress but with no radical changes of policy. The wines and spirits business improved, with income rising from £9,375 a year in 1937-9 to £26,417 a year in 1953-5. This may be explained in part by the popularity of spirits during the war, when the quality and strength of beer declined, but demand also grew from the late 1940's. Steward & Patteson consolidated this side of the business by acquiring a controlling interest in Green & Wright Limited, a Norwich firm of grocers and wine and spirits merchants, in October 1955. The ill-health and subsequent death of Herbert Wade, managing director of the firm for many years, was a factor in the move, but poor results also contributed to the takeover. Green & Wright's accounts reveal net losses of £2,951 for April-November 1955, and £1,742 in 1956.[27] The controlling interest was gained to use the company's trading name in off-licences. The grocery business was soon closed down, and the opportunity taken to centralise wine and spirit operations. Even so, the financial results were satisfactory. Steward & Patteson paid £63,743 for most of the company's paid-up capital of £22,500 (nominal value). Net profits averaged £7,172 per annum in the period 1957-62, representing a return of 11.25 per cent.[28] Steward & Patteson's soft drinks and mineral water business also exhibited growth. Income rose impressively during the war, from a modest £7,035 per annum in 1937-9 to £24,482 per annum in 1941-5, but much of this was due to the government's rationalisation of production and pooling arrangements. Over 70 per cent of income in 1944-5 was for the Soft Drinks Industry and was therefore passed to firms which had been required to shut down. However, there was a strong post-war demand for non-alcoholic drinks, and income rose to £25,500 per annum in the early 1950's.[29] Once again, the brewery's position was strengthened by company acquisition. Dawson's Mineral Water Company Limited of Norwich was another ailing local firm ripe for takeover. Financial irregularities had surfaced in 1949, and the company had been forced into receivership by May 1950. Steward & Patteson then stepped in and in December bought the share capital of £2,400 in ordinary shares plus the goodwill for £15,300.[30] Operated as a subsidiary, Dawson's accounts revealed small but adequate net profits of £1,744 in 1952, £4,144 in 1955, and £2,224 in 1956.[31]

As already stated, it would be rather dangerous if not futile to attempt the construction of trading and profit and loss summaries to match those produced for earlier chapters. However, some indication of turnover and margins can be assembled, and it is important to gain information here, since the strong suggestion emerging from the rise in costs with the war and the merger with Soames is that margins may well have been cut. The data presented in Table 41 are necessarily speculative, but for the first time it is possible to utilise new accounts, presented in a special typed statement and inserted into the company's profit and loss ledger, which give the agencies' gross revenue and net profits, and not merely the net profits, as hitherto, for 1939-49. The results confirm our a priori expectations. The 'new basis' data indicate narrowing margins during the war, and there appears to have been no significant improvement in the early post-war years. The 'old basis' results are more difficult to interpret, since they exclude the full accounts of the Soames subsidiary and the established agencies, but these too suggest that reduced margins were experienced after 1939. They also indicate that there was little change into the mid-1950's. Of course, both sets of data are affected by transfers from reserves for repairs and maintenance deferred during the war, and the 'old basis'

TABLE 41

Estimates of Steward & Patteson's Trading Position, 1937–55 (annual averages)

Period	'Trading'		'Profit & Loss'		*NET*	*MARGINS*	
	Gross Revenue	*Costs*	*'Gross Revenue'*[1]	*'Costs'*[1]	*PROFIT*	*(ii)/(i)*	*(iv)/(iii)*
	(i)	*(ii)*	*(iii)*	*(iv)*	*(v)*	%	%
	£	£	£	£	£		
	1. Norwich brewery and agencies – new basis						
1939	324,111	223,356	627,914	527,159	100,755	69	84
1940–2	374,881	303,366	1,022,274	950,759	71,515	81	93
1943–5	465,794	390,605	1,658,619	1,583,430	75,189	84	95
1946–9	510,768[2]	413,258	1,618,683	1,521,173	97,510	81	94
	2. Norwich brewery plus agencies' net revenue only – old basis						
1937–9	271,430	171,867	559,272	459,709	99,562	63	82
1943–5	434,665	359,476	1,627,490	1,552,301	75,189	83	95
1949–52	476,156[3]	388,447	1,632,431	1,544,722	87,708[3]	82	95
1953–5	596,014[4]	472,177	1,684,671	1,560,834	123,838[4]	79	93

Source: Steward & Patteson Ltd. Account Books, BR1/101, 102, N.R.O.

Notes

1 'Profit & Loss' figures are trading results plus raw material costs and beer duty, added to both sides of the account.

2 Gross revenue *includes* £207,852 or £69,284 p.a. transferred from reserves to income for repairs, etc.

3 Gross revenue *includes* £105,000 or £26,250 p.a. transferred from reserves to income for repairs, etc. and £37,630 from subsidiary co. (Soames), £9,408 p.a. The net profit data differ from those quoted elsewhere because the Soames results are not taken properly into account in the ledger.

4 Gross revenue *includes* £20,000 (£6,667 p.a.) from reserves for repairs, £131,560 (£43,853 p.a.) from subsidiary co.

results include transfers from the Soames business which differ from the annual revenue generated by that business and shown in its published accounts. In contrast with the 1930's, when Steward & Patteson's gross revenue grew faster than costs in real terms (see Chapter 6, above), the period after 1936 witnessed costs outpacing revenue. On the new basis, costs rose by 77 per cent, while gross revenue increased by only 58 per cent, in 1939 values, from 1939 to 1946-9. The 'old basis' data show costs rising by 46 per cent in real terms, 1937/9-1953/5 [in 1937-9 values], and gross revenue up by only 30 per cent.[32] Why was this? Certainly, labour costs do not appear to have presented the problems which they did in the 1930's. These costs, including directors' fees and pensions, rose by only 14 per cent in real terms, 1939-46/9 [new basis data], while overall costs increased by 77 per cent; over the longer period to the mid-1950's, the less complete data show labour costs rising by only 26 per cent, 1937/9-1953/5, again much lower than costs as a whole.[33] Undoubtedly, the persistence of high raw material costs and taxation was the principal factor here, as already indicated. It was also difficult to raise revenue significantly in the post-war period, when demand began to fall off.

No action was taken to transform the brewery's tied house estate. Steward & Patteson's empire was made up of a mixture of some very good outlets and many small, decaying, rural outposts, vital perhaps for village social life but at best marginal in terms of profitability. The average annual supply to part of the estate in 1952 and 1953 is given in Table 42. For deliveries to about 420 houses (the Soames pubs and the Yarmouth and King's Lynn agencies are excluded), it reveals the unspectacular average of 132 barrels in 1952 and 128 barrels in 1953, or 2.5 barrels a week for each pub. And this statistic includes bottled beer. Furthermore, the contrast between high- and low-volume outlets remained as great as ever. In Norwich, for example, there were several pubs in the new, suburban housing areas selling over 300 barrels a year, but there were also many in the inner-city districts whose sales were barely a third of this figure. Thus, in 1954, the 'Larkman' in Dereham Road sold 484 barrels of draught beer and 4,904 dozen bottles, while the 'New Star' on Quayside sold a mere nine barrels of draught and 334 dozen bottles.[34] The position was worse in the county, where average sales barely topped the one hundred-barrel mark, compared with nearly 200 barrels in Norwich (Table 42). Here, no less than sixty-six of the 246 pubs were selling under twenty-six barrels of draught beer a year in 1954, or half a barrel a week. The only substantial sales were made in the larger towns such as Dereham, seaside resorts such as Sheringham, and the dormitory suburbs of Norwich still in the county (Hellesdon, Drayton, etc.). Some basic outlets survived on very low sales indeed: the 'Chequers' at Gressenhall with two barrels of draught beer in 1953 and four in 1954, the 'Lion' at Panxworth with nine and eight barrels.[35] All this should not be taken to imply that such pubs were merely being forgotten. The 'New Star' in Norwich, for example, was only half a mile from the brewery, could be supplied by horse and dray, and required little or no investment. City sites had a value which the brewery felt could be realised at leisure. In the county the policy was one of either keeping open 'the last pub in the village' or of holding on in a competitive position until a rival brewer closed *his* pub. Steward & Patteson displayed the relaxed,

TABLE 42

Annual Deliveries to Public Houses, 1952–3 (barrels per pub)

Year to November	**Norwich**		**Norfolk** *(excluding Ipswich area)*		**Total** *(including Ipswich area)*	
	draught	*draught & bottled*	*draught*	*draught & bottled*	*draught*	*draught & bottled*
1952	140.1	197.6	62.3	105.1	83.7	131.9
1953	134.6	194.0	58.7	102.7	78.9	128.3

Source: Steward & Patteson Estate Book, BR1/156, N.R.O.

Note: bottled beer estimated on the basis of 24 dozen pints being equivalent to one 36-gallon barrel.

complacent attitude of a leading company, secure in its regional market and unaware of the storm to come. A few pubs were closed in 1952-4 - one in Norwich, half a dozen in the county are shown in the delivery book. However, rationalisation was not something to be pursued with vigour by a company which prided itself on its contribution to village life. If it had been, the enterprise might have been in better shape to beat off the challenge of the merger boom of the early 1960's.

For Steward & Patteson, then, profits remained healthy despite the atmosphere of mild depression in brewing after the war. However, the company had responded by strengthening its hold on the low-volume rural outlets of East Anglia. This meant squeezed margins on a larger turnover, and the challenge of modernising a vast public house empire after war-time and austerity restrictions. There is certainly evidence that the company increased its spending in this area - expenditure on public house repairs increased from £25,000 per annum in 1939-45 to £80,000 per annum in 1946-9, and to £124,000 in 1950-5, for example - and the board minutes do contain references to the opening of new pubs, the most successful of which appear to have been 'The Grove', in North Earlham, Norwich (1938) and the 'Selkirk' in Ipswich (1956).[36] Spending on the brewery was again steady if unspectacular. Investments were made in bottling and mineral water production in 1950 and 1955, and several improvements were made in malting, including the introduction of oil-firing in the pneumatic maltings in 1955. A new refrigeration plant was installed in 1950-1, and distribution was assisted by the opening of a new brewery garage in 1939.[37] None of this suggests any radical changes in a business which was regionally secure, continued to hold the Royal Warrant (obtaining a Warrant to

19. Steward & Patteson dray at the Royal Norfolk Show, c. [*G.S. Rose/Riviere coll.*]

supply beers to H.M. Queen Elizabeth II in 1955), and won prizes at competitions organised by the *Brewing Trade Review*.[38] Marketing was similarly restrained. Advertising was extended by the hiring of seventy sites in Norfolk and Suffolk in 1944, but the range of beers remained much the same as in the 1930's, and the only significant change was the buying-in of lager from J. Peters of Hull.[39]

Of course, it is easy now, with the benefit of hindsight, to criticise the brewery for not combining a policy of aggressive rationalisation with retailing improvements. But resources were not limitless, the brewing world in the early 1950's was not that of a decade later, and Steward & Patteson remained a successful regional concern, dominated by families which retained a very traditional paternalist brewing image.

Ownership, Control and Business Strategy, 1936-56

After the re-registration of Steward & Patteson as a public limited company in 1936, and the sale of 150,000 £1 ordinary shares, the ownership of the company naturally became more diversified. The shareholders' register thereafter contains the names of small rentier investors, and of institutions - insurance companies, banks, nominee companies, and investment trusts. Nevertheless, the brewery was still dominated by the founding families and their relatives. The board of directors, membership of which was confined to the Morse and Steward/Finch families from 1915 to 1950, continued to hold large blocs of controlling ordinary shares. Table 43 shows that the directors held, in their own names, 21 per cent of the total in February 1939 and 16 per cent in February 1946. If we assume that they also controlled the proxies of shares which they held jointly as trustees or executors, and the shares of close relatives such as Geoffrey Morse, a former director, and Eirene Steward, Donald's mother, then their effective control extended to a majority stake in the business - 58 per cent in 1939, 51 per cent in 1946. And this surely underestimates the degree of control, since the calculation excludes the shares in the hands of sons, married daughters and their husbands, uncles, aunts, nephews and nieces, of Morse, Steward/Finch, and Patteson lineage. In fact, the institutional interest in the company was relatively limited for the first decade or so. In February 1946, for example, the largest of such shareholders was the Prudential Assurance Company, with only £16,900 in ordinary shares.[40]

TABLE 43

Ordinary share holdings in Steward & Patteson, 1939 and 1946

Date	*Ord. share capital held by directors in own name*		*Ord. share capital held in own name and jointly (as executors, trustees, etc.)**	
	£	%	£	%
22 Feb. 1939	128,905	21.5	346,795	57.8
28 Feb. 1946	96,852	16.1	307,847	51.3

Source: Steward & Patteson Shareholders' lists, company files, Companies' House, London.

* Included here are the ordinary shareholdings of G.G. Morse and Eirene B. Steward.

Direct control diminished after the merger with Soames in 1949. Soames shareholders were allotted £147,360 in £1 ordinary shares, and Hugh M. Peacock of Peterborough, one of the directors, joined the Steward & Patteson board. The move did not lead to an instant dispersal of shareholding, since 96 per cent of the allotment went to only 10 persons: Phyllis and Constance Soames, Hugh and Constance Peacock, Leopold and Norman Harvey, Montague and Margeurite Fenwick, Charles MacLeod, and Helen Walwyn. But thereafter a gradual dispersal of ownership was evident, and more institutional investors appeared. By February 1957 the directors held only 5.6 per cent of the equity capital, and could probably count on the proxies of only another 30 per cent. About 10 per cent of the ordinary shares were now in the hands of insurance companies, such as the Prudential, Pearl and the Norwich Union, and nominee companies, such as Control Nominees and West Nominees.[41]

TABLE 44

Steward & Patteson Board of Directors, 1936–56

Director	*Born*	*Appointed*	*Chairman*	*Left*
Charles Hugh Finch	1866	1895	1931–45	Dec. 1952 Retd.
Arthur Francis Morse	1872	1904	1945–51	Feb. 1957 Retd.
Alfred Finch	1870	1905	—	May 1943 Died
Peter Charles Finch	1905	1933	—	June 1947 Resgd.
Francis John Morse	1897	1936	1951–*	*
Sydney Arthur Morse	1902	1936	—	*
Donald Charles Steward	1907	1936	—	*
Hugh Myddleton Peacock	1906	1949	—	*
Francis Cecil Hipwell	1888	1950	—	June 1953 fixed term
Michael Valentine Briton Riviere	1919	1951	—	*
Anthony Walter Fenwick	1928	1955	—	Oct. 1960 Resgd.

* Remained in office until Steward & Patteson Ltd. became a subsidiary company of Watney Mann Ltd. in 1963.

Public status initially made no difference at all to the composition of the board, though this also changed in the 1950's. For some time membership was confined to insiders, and for the first decade, 1936-45, the company continued to be led by Charles Hugh Finch as Chairman, a septuagenarian of failing strength. He was replaced by the equally elderly Colonel Arthur Francis Morse in December 1945, a man of seventy-three, and a director of forty-one years' standing. He served as Chairman until December 1951 and, like Finch, did not relinquish the post until shortly before his eightieth birthday. When these stalwarts of the old guard retired as directors in 1952 and 1957 respectively, they were voted pensions of £2,000 a year. They died in 1954 and 1959.[42] Both men gave the brewery long and sterling service, but by the late 1930's effective management lay elsewhere, with the younger directors, Peter Finch, Sydney Morse, and Donald Steward. In addition, there was Francis John Morse, who had joined the Board in November 1936 after the resignation of his brother Geoffrey. But as a successful solicitor in London he was not at first keen to take an active part in day-to-day management, although he had advised on the conversion of Steward & Patteson to public company status.

The coming of war presented something of a management crisis at Pockthorpe. Not only did the three younger directors join the armed forces, but two became long-term prisoners of war. Sydney Morse was captured in Crete in 1941, and Donald Steward in Singapore a year later.[43] The remaining directors were Charles Finch, Arthur Morse, and Alfred Finch; the latter died in May 1943 at the age of seventy-three. There was thus an urgent need for active management, and Francis John Morse agreed to work on a full-time basis, having moved to Norfolk with his family in the course of 1939. Born in 1897, John was educated at Winchester, and in 1915 entered the war, emerging with the rank of captain in the Royal Air Force and the Croix de Guerre. After taking some time to settle down to a career in the 1920's - like his father George he was a keen Alpine climber - he tried the law. The move was successful; he qualified as a solicitor in 1929 and in 1931 became a partner in the firm of Lawrence, Graham & Company. His elder brother Geoffrey had been earmarked for the brewery, it seems, but his resignation in 1936 had weakened the board. John had little alternative but to abandon his legal career for brewing. Once in Norwich, however, he threw himself wholeheartedly into the task of management, and also found time for public service. He was a local magistrate from 1943 to 1960, a City Councillor, 1941-6, and in 1950 joined the Norwich Diocesan Board of Finance, acting as Chairman from 1955 to 1960. At Pockthorpe he succeeded his uncle Arthur as Chairman in December 1951, by which time he was proving to be a worthy successor to George Morse, Chairman of the company from 1915 to 1931. He shared his father's capacity for hard work, managerial 'presence', and ability to handle people. By a slightly tortuous route, then, the management succession was secured.[44]

The ending of the war produced some tensions within the directorate. It was difficult to fit the three returning directors into suitable or acceptable roles. One of them, Peter Finch, soon left to concentrate on farming. He resigned in June 1947, and when his father Charles retired five years later, the Finch representation on the Board came to an end. Donald Steward was put in charge of the Yarmouth agency, and he quickly found his metier in the organisation of those sporting and social events which do so much to bind a local brewery to its community. Sydney Morse appears to have been the most successful of the three, being appointed Vice-Chairman of the company in July 1957. He also became a director of the Norwich Corn Exchange, and the Norwich Union (from 1956), and in 1967 served as High Sheriff of Norfolk. Nevertheless, it is fair to say that Steward & Patteson was a business very much led by the chairman. John Morse did appreciate the need for able lieutenants, however, and while he reserved strategic matters to himself, he consciously strengthened middle managment. Thomas Spencer succeeded W.J. Culley as company secretary in June 1946; Hipwell's successor as head brewer, James Heard, appointed in July 1950, was well-trained and his assistants were both diploma members of the Institute of Brewing; L.R. Canham was an able estates manager; and there were sound appointments to posts in mineral waters and the King's Lynn and Yarmouth agencies.[45]

By the late 1940's many brewers saw the need to revitalise management in the more difficult conditions of austerity. In Norwich, for example, the death in October 1949 of Francis W.W. Morgan, aged eighty-two, chairman of Morgans brewery since 1933 and a director since 1913, was followed by the appointment to the board of the company secretary (an accountant) and a solicitor. There were also board changes at Bullard's. When Ernest Bullard, a director since 1918, died in 1946 at the age of seventy-seven, he was replaced by Douglas Baker and William Thomson; after the death of the chairman, Edward Bullard, in 1950, following a forty-six-year stint on the board (twenty-two years as chairman), the new directors served as managing directors.[46] Another indication of change was the collaborative agreement between Bullard's and Youngs Crawshay Youngs in October 1941, which involved an exchange of shares and directors.[47] Clearly, brewery directors now required financial acumen, legal expertise, and skills in inter-company negotiation in addition to the past virtues of quality and cost control and tied house management. At the very least, youthful energy was needed in an industry noted for gerontocracy. At Steward & Patteson the Soames merger was once again the catalyst for change. The move brought Hugh Peacock onto the board as the first 'non-family' director, in August 1949. In the following year he was joined by Francis Hipwell, who retired as the company's head brewer. Hipwell's appointment was for a three-year term, lasting until his sixty-fifth birthday. However, it should not be assumed that this was merely a grace-and-favour appointment, since the ex-brewer had a wealth of knowledge concerning the production of beer, and had several contacts in the trade (he was a director of Phipps

& Company, the Northampton brewery later taken over by Watney Mann).[48]

The appointment of Peacock and Hipwell broke the mould of confining representation on the board to the founding families. A further departure from tradition was the introduction of two 'new blood' directors, Michael Riviere, in March 1951, and Anthony Fenwick, in January 1955. Both were young men on appointment - Riviere was thirty-two, Fenwick only twenty-seven. But it is difficult to say that they could offer instantly more then youthful vigour. Neither had received more than a brief provincial training or could apply to the company the management skills learned at business school or with a large-scale company. But this is not to say that their impact on Steward & Patteson was negligible. Michael Riviere, educated at Bradfield and Magdalen College Oxford, was a member of a well-known artistic family. However, his father, a doctor, was a director of the Norwich Union, and a firm link with the brewery came with the marriage in 1952 of Michael's younger brother, Daniel, to Kinbarra Joanna Morse, the only daughter of John Morse, newly-appointed Chairman of Steward & Patteson. Riviere had joined the brewery in February 1949

20. Michael Riviere, director from 1951, making presentation to James Heard, head brewer from 1950, in c.1960 [*H.G. Kimpton/Riviere coll.*]

after a pupillage with Flowers of Stratford and eighteen months at Morgans. He at first assisted Sydney Morse at King's Lynn, but quickly took an interest in brewing science and was given responsibility for production (he became production manager in November 1961). Under his guidance experiments on a commercial scale were carried out, in conjunction with the Institute of Brewing, in malting techniques and the use of new strains of barley. At the time of the merger in 1963 Riviere was Chairman of the Institute's Barley Advisory Committee. Anthony Fenwick's contribution appears to have been more limited. One of the Soames family appointments - he was a nephew of Hugh Peacock - he worked for a time at Spalding but was not a success. He left the board in October 1960.[49] Nevertheless, these appointments were a clear indication that Steward & Patteson accepted the need to strengthen its management team as its empire grew.

Mergers and Merged, 1957-63

It is almost a cliche to point out that the British brewing industry was in a highly volatile state in the late 1950's and early 1960's. Steward & Patteson was fully involved in a series of aggressive mergers which raised the level of concentration significantly. In terms of employment, the share of the top three brewers increased from 13 per cent in 1951 to 16 per cent in 1958, then more than doubled to 33 per cent in 1963. By this time, the leading five firms controlled 51 per cent of sales. At the same time, marketing was transformed by the introduction of keg beers and the increasing popularity of lager, which halted the long-term trend from draught to bottled beer.[50] No sizeable brewery was left untouched by these developments. For Steward & Patteson, the seven years from 1957 saw its continued regional growth. In January 1957 it bought sixty-six public houses in Lincolnshire for £175,000 from the Flowers Group (a merger of J.W. Green of Luton and Flowers of Stratford), and a further twenty-one houses for £41,000 in June 1958. These purchases were balanced by some sales to Flowers.[51] But the most important transaction of the period was undoubtedly the acquisition of East Anglian Breweries of Ely and Huntingdon in August 1957, which added 400 pubs to the Steward & Patteson empire, now totalling 1,250 houses. Then in 1961 Steward & Patteson and Bullard's each bought a half share in Morgans Brewery in Norwich. By this time Steward & Patteson was one of the largest non-

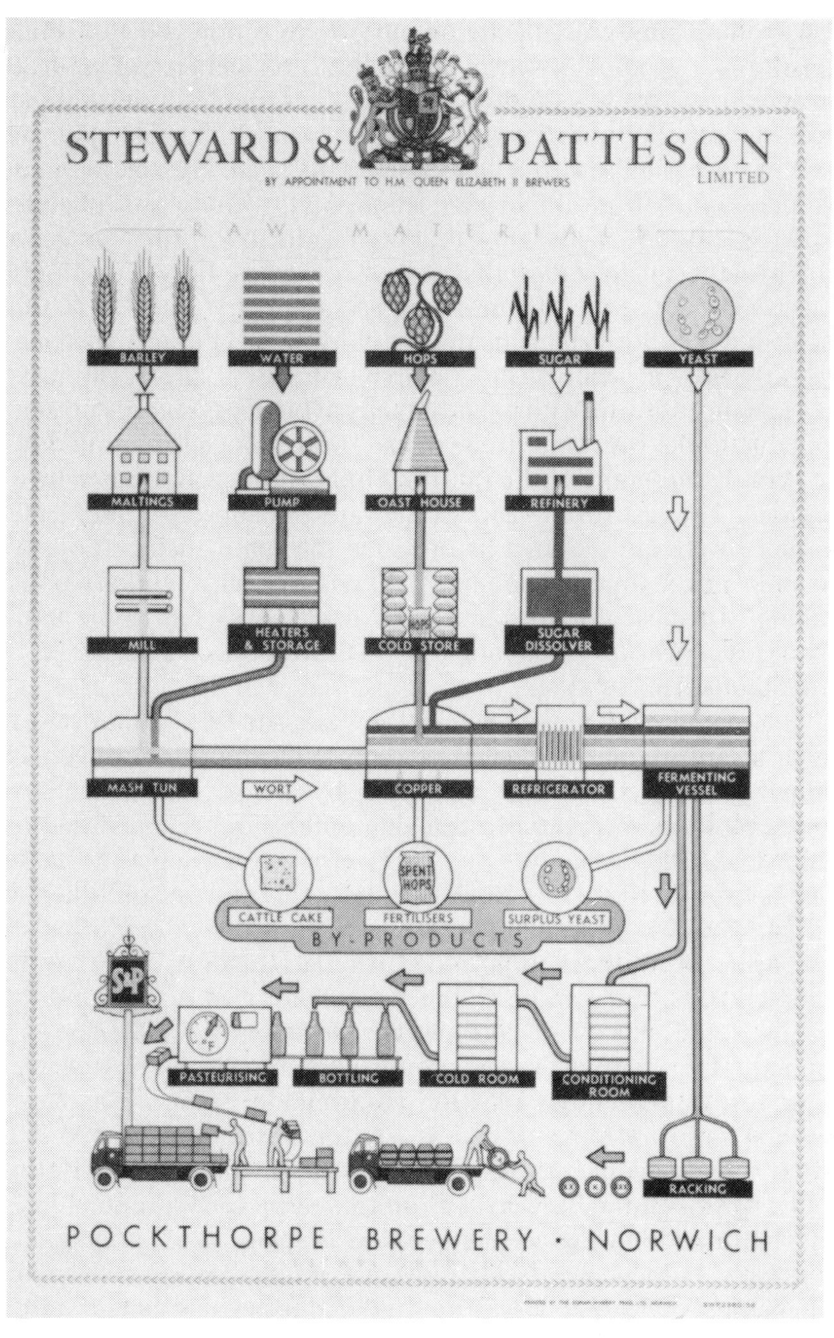

21. The brewing process, c.1958 [*Bridewell Mus.*]

metropolitan breweries in the country. Its position did not remain undisturbed for long, however, and within two years it was subject to an assault by Watney Mann. In November 1963 Watneys made a successful offer for both Steward & Patteson and Bullards, establishing itself in East Anglia with a vengeance. This is a controversial tale to tell, particularly from the present standpoint, with no brewing left in Norwich (July 1985), and now that the results of the 1963 merger are fully evident, in the rationalisation of breweries, brews, and public houses. The consequential monopoly position of Watneys in Norfolk has inspired public criticism, and the Norfolk 'Beer desert' was one of the early rallying cries of the Campaign for Real Ale.[52] The task is made all the more difficult by the paucity of business records presently available to the historian. In any case, events moved very quickly in the period, and many of the informal bids and negotiations were not recorded. The last seven years of Steward & Patteson's independent existence were quite unlike its previous 165 years' history, and were certainly not a time for mature deliberation, and cautious policy-making. In these circumstances, the historian is left to the tender mercies of oral history, dependent upon the imperfect memories of the participants who survive.

The merger with East Anglian Breweries in 1957 is an event for which a fair amount of documentation has survived, however. The company was a classic case of growth by merger, and indeed, was chosen by John Vaizey to illustrate the process in his contribution to Lesley Cook's book on the *Effects of Mergers*. Over the period 1907-30 three brewers in Ely - Hall, Harlock and Legge - and one in Littleport - William Cutlack - had merged to form Hall, Cutlack & Harlock. In 1938 Mills of Wisbech was added. In Huntingdon two brewers - Marshall Bros. and Jenkins & Jones -amalgamated in 1932 and then acquired Lindsell's Chatteris brewery to form Huntingdon Breweries Limited. Then in 1950 the two groups joined forces as East Anglian Breweries. In September 1954 the Huntingdon brewery was closed, and brewing was concentrated at Ely for distribution to 500 or so outlets.[53] The evidence suggests that the merger habit did not diminish in Ely. Although the brewery was quite well placed with pubs in Ely (26), Huntingdon (12), Littleport (15), Ramsey (15), Soham (12), Chatteris (15) and Lincoln (18), most of its empire lay in much smaller settlements, and the area was not one of spectacular consumption. Some of its best pubs were outside the region - in Peterborough and Newark.[54] Its chairman, Lt.-Col. Sir William Lindsell, had, while

22 and 23. Pockthorpe brewery, November 1959:
i] Cleaning the coolers
ii] The bottling line [*E.C.N./Colman & Rye Lib.*]

chairman of Huntingdon Breweries, approached Greene King of Bury St Edmunds in 1948 but without success, and there seems little doubt that the predatory policy of J.W. Green of Luton (later Flowers) caused anxiety. Greene King had itself bought Simpson's of Baldock in 1954.[55] It is not clear who made the first move in the negotiations, but in June 1957 Steward & Patteson made a formal offer to acquire the £300,000 ordinary capital of E.A.B. on the basis of 135 S. & P. shares for every 100 of E.A.B. After the bid succeeded in August, an allotment of £404,999 in ordinary shares was made to E.A.B. shareholders.* Of the issue 57 per cent was distributed to the five major shareholding families - Brooks, Cutlack, Goodliff, Hickley and Lindsell. The only large institutional shareholder was the Legal & General, with a 4 per cent stake. Four directors - Col. Lindsell, J.R. Brooks, Mrs E.E. Cutlack, and Anthony Hickley - resigned, leaving Col. William P. Cutlack and John J. Goodliff as Chairman & Managing Director and Assistant Managing Director respectively. In an exchange of directors, they joined the Steward & Patteson board, and at Ely were joined by John Morse and Michael Riviere. The two new directors owned, with their immediate families, 25 per cent of the Ely subsidiary's equity.[56]

The merger with East Anglian Breweries proved to be more valuable than that with Soames. Respectable levels of consumption were reported for 404 E.A.B. public houses in 1954-6 - much higher than for the Soames houses - and less than twenty had an annual sale below twenty-six barrels.[57] Furthermore, there was at first no question of a brewing rationalisation to match that carried out at Spalding in 1949. The Ely brewery continued to supply the E.A.B. estate with both draught and bottled beer until 1968, and production amounted to about 65,000 barrels a year in the period 1959-61. The amalgamation had the effect of increasing Steward & Patteson's ordinary paid-up capital from £0.75 million to £1.15 million and its total capital, including debenture stock, from £1.55 million to £1.95 million (Table 45). Further adjustments were made in 1960. In February an issue of £538,125 in 6 per cent cumulative preference shares was made to buy up E.A.B.'s preference share capital of £512,500; a further £14,948 in preference shares was issued by capitalising part of the share premium account, and the existing 5 per cent shares were converted to form a single class of 6 per cent. In August the ordinary shares were sub-divided into units of 5*s*. (25p) and in November the £280,000 in 4 per

*The final price, including preference shares was £958,072.

TABLE 45

Steward & Patteson Capital, Profits and Dividends, 1957–63

Year ending November	*Ordinary*	**Capital Paid-up [£]** *Pref.*	*Debenture*	*Total*	*Net Profits†* *[£]*	*Rate of Return* *%*	*Ordinary Dividend* *%*
1956	747,360	519,244	280,000	1,546,604	124,713	9.8	12.5
1957	1,152,360	519,244	280,000	1,951,604	246,234	—	14.0
1958	"	"	"	"	257,845	—	15.0
1959	"	"	"	"	355,884**	—	20.0
1960	1,152,360	1,072,317	"*	2,504,677	302,076	13.6	22.5
1961	"	"	1,000,000	3,224,677	362,422	16.3	22.5
1962	"	"	"	"	342,861	15.4	22.5
1963	"	"	"	"	327,437	14.7	22.5

Source: Steward & Patteson Annual Reports and Accounts, 1957–63, and see Appendix D, Table 6.

* Debenture stock redeemed on 1 November 1960.
† Net profits are net of debenture interest.
** Includes £60,757 from sale of surplus whisky stocks.

Note: no rates of return are shown for 1957–9 since E.A.B.'s pref. share capital was not purchased by the company.

cent debentures was redeemed (88 per cent was already in the company's hands). This left the company's paid-up capital at £2.2 million. But despite the increase in capital, the company's published accounts revealed a position which was stronger than before. The declared profits of the expanded group after tax increased over the period 1957-60 and ordinary dividends were raised from 12.5 per cent in 1956 to 22.5 per cent by 1960 (Table 45). The profits of E.A.B. (from 1961 Steward & Patteson Ely) averaged £97,276 per annum, 1957-62.[58]

In Norfolk, merger activity continued to reflect the hectic conditions in the trade as a whole. In 1957 Lacons of Yarmouth came under the Whitbread 'umbrella', with the latter taking a stake of about 20 per cent (full control was secured in 1965, and brewing ceased three years later). In Norwich, Youngs, Crawshay & Youngs merged with Bullard in 1958. Then in 1961 the Morgans brewery was acquired jointly by Steward & Patteson and Bullard. If Morgans' Chairman, Sir Robert Bignold, is to be believed, he had been trying for some time to bring the three breweries together to secure the independence of Norwich brewing. However, it is doubtful whether the eventual course taken was quite what he had in mind. In December 1960 the two breweries offered Morgans 105*s*. [£5.25] for each of its 270,000 £1 ordinary shares, and in the following month the bid was raised to 107/6 [£5.37½], valuing the shares at £1,451,250. This proved successful. The acquisition was valuable in that Morgans had much the most modern brewery in the city - it had been refurbished after wartime bombing - together with a tied estate of 400 pubs. However, despite assurances to the contrary at the time of the offer, the purchasers were only interested in the pubs. They were not prepared to split brewing into three locations while there were still opportunities for increased scale economies at Pockthorpe and Bullard's Anchor brewery. It was this stance which was soon to threaten their independent positions. The division of public houses proceeded amicably. As Bullard's chairman, Gerald Bullard, later recalled, 'these were shared out one morning between us, after John Morse and I had cut cards to see who should have the first pick'. Both sides got what they wanted. Steward & Patteson established a stronger base in Norwich, while Bullard's concentrated on the county areas. Julian Crawshay, a Bullard director, reported that 'the barralage [sic] has come out about 1,000 barrels in Steward & Patteson's favour but mostly at long range. We have established ourselves very strongly in Peterborough, King's Lynn, Sheringham, Cromer, Yarmouth and Lowestoft; Steward & Patteson went for Norwich which we did not mind as we are already dominant ... This is the situation for which we aimed and the tactics adopted were successful in getting the result we wanted. Steward & Patteson are also very satisfied.' S. & P. beer was then installed in their half-share from 1 October 1961, and a revision of the boundaries between their Norwich, King's Lynn, Spalding and Ely districts followed.[59]

The Norwich breweries' joint decision to sell the King Street brewery to Watney Mann in the same year, 1961, was quite another matter. It appears that the extended empire of the two concerns was too large for two units of production, but too small for three. Consequently, with the sale of Morgans brewery, Steward & Patteson and Bullard entered into a trading agreement with Watney's in which the latter undertook to supply their tied houses with certain of its proprietary lines such as the keg 'Red Barrel' and bottled Brown Ale. However, far from being a useful addition to the range of beers offered, Watney's products, which were promoted strongly by national advertising, quickly began to oust the Norwich beers in their own outlets. As early as July 1962, for example, Bullard's reported that

Watney's keg draught beers were responsible for no less than 51 per cent of the brewery's total bitter sales.[60] By this time, Steward & Patteson and Bullard had reached the cross-roads of their ambitions. Both were stretched financially by the purchase of Morgans, which necessitated a joint investment of about £1.8 million. Steward & Patteson's response was to issue £1 million in debentures carrying a fairly high interest rate - they were issued at 98 with interest of 6¾ per cent, secured by a floating charge on the company's assets. The existence of S. & P. as an independent brewer was thus threatened simultaneously by financial and marketing pressures.

There were certainly signs that the board was showing more dynamism in the wake of the Morgans purchase. In February 1962 it decided to abandon malting in Norwich in order to expand its bottling plant, and in July of the same year considered the first report of a joint committee with Bullard's set up to examine uneconomic public houses in villages. Here it was shown that Steward & Patteson had closed thirty-eight village pubs since April 1961 while Bullard's had closed thirty-two, and agreement had been reached about the closure of a further thirty-five and thirty-two houses respectively.[61] In addition new pubs were opened, including the 'Canary' in Norwich, at a cost of £38,000, and the historic 'Dolphin Inn' in the same city was restored.[62] But while production at Pockthorpe increased after 1956 and ordinary dividends were maintained, net profits faltered after 1961, and it is doubtful whether the directors (and the chairman in particular) had the appetite for the challenge of lager and keg beer. The company's stock book amply demonstrates the penetration of the 'national' breweries with their well-advertised brands. In March 1957 there are the first references to Whitbread's bottled Mackeson stout and to Carlsberg lager. In September 1961, following the trading agreement, the company was holding stocks of Watney's Red Barrel, the most successful of the early keg beers. In the following March there are entries for Harp Lager and Watney's Brown Ale.[63] The merger wave of 1959-63 was both defensive and aggressive; defensive for smaller breweries seeking to combine to retain independence and viable size; aggressive for larger companies such as Bass, Whitbread and Watney Mann (which had recently grown by absorbing Manns, Phipps, Ushers, and Wilson & Walker in 1958-60), which sought outlets to facilitate large-scale production and national distribution. In 1963 Steward & Patteson was on the receiving end of an aggressive merger bid.

24. Reopening of the 'Dolphin', Norwich, 21 September 1960 (left to right: Francis John Morse (Chairman, Steward & Patteson); Dr Launcelot Fleming, Lord Bishop of Norwich; James Fletcher-Watson (architect); Alfred E. Nicholls (Lord Mayor of Norwich) [*E.C.N./Colman & Rye Lib.*]

The purchase of Morgans brewery in Norwich and the lack of tied houses in East Anglia made a Watney bid likely. In the course of 1963 it became clear that Watney's were buying shares of both Steward & Patteson and Bullard in the open market. On the London stock exchange, S. & P. ordinary shares, which had stood at 38*s*. [£1.90] in early January 1963, had drifted down to 32*s*. [£1.60] by the end of the month; but in July the price began to jump, and a high point of 41/3 [£2.06] was reached at the end of August. Similar trends may be observed in the price of Bullard's ordinary shares.[64] The two breweries then took advice from the merchant bankers, Schroder Wagg. A confidential report prepared by Gordon Gunson (a Schroder director) in August examined the breweries' barrelages, before tax profits and yields over the period 1959-62 and concluded that a fair price for Steward & Patteson ordinary shares would be 39*s*. [£1.95], with 19*s* [£0.95] suggested for Bullard's. Given existing Watney Mann data (ordinary shares c.24*s*. [£1.20] and dividend 20 per cent), it promised to give S. & P. shareholders a 44 per cent increase in dividend income and a 2.6 per cent increase in capital value.[65] Following negotiations between the parties, which involved Baring's (for Watney Mann) and the Watney Mann chairman, Simon Combe, an informal offer was made in October. For Steward & Patteson this amounted to one 5*s*. [25p] Watney ordinary share plus 13/9 [69p] in cash for each S. & P. 5*s*. ordinary share, which valued S. & P. ordinary shares at 38/9 [£1.94] and promised a 38 per cent increase in dividend income but with no increase in capital value. By this time the shares had drifted down from their end-August high and were fetching about 38*s*. [£1.90] in the market. Gunson noted that the offers - for Bullard the suggested price was 18/6 [£0.92½] - were 'below the levels we had sought to obtain' but nevertheless considered them 'fair and reasonable'.[66] A formal offer was made in the following month, November 1963, on the same terms. For preference shareholders 100 Watney 6¼ per cent cumulative second preference were to be exchanged for every 100 S. & P. 6 per cent preference shares. It was also revealed that the London-based conglomerate already owned about 17 per cent of Steward & Patteson ordinary shares and 16 per cent of the Bullard equity. Both Norwich boards indicated their willingness to accept the bid, which was worth approximately £20 million, the Steward & Patteson element representing £9 million. In February 1967 the company's breweries and 1,064 licensed properties were finally sold to Watney Mann for £7,666,270.[67]

Why did Steward & Patteson accept the bid? According to Sir

Jeremy Morse, son of the Chairman, John Morse was far from 'confident that a regional brewery in a predominantly agricultural area would do as well as a national brewery, and he saw the advantage of giving the family shareholders large and small a more marketable asset'. The response of one Bullard shareholder was no doubt characteristic of many in both companies. 'When I think of that block of shares left to us', she told a director, 'what - 13 years ago - & what has happened since, it's quite incredible. I do think it's wonderful what you and Gerry [Gerald Bullard] have achieved in that time, & I am going to enjoy it enormously'.[68] But the younger directors of S. & P., joined by Anthony Morse, a son of the Vice-Chairman, in August 1963, were apparently hostile to the merger with Watney Mann, and the latter's assurances about the preservation of the business as a subsidiary company and the retention of the Pockthorpe and Anchor Breweries were no doubt judged to be as convincing as their own promises at the time of takeovers. Nationally, the beer market was picking up - production jumped from 23.8 million bulk barrels in 1958 to 29.0 million in 1963 - and there was no reason why the company could not have restructured its product-range, although its ability to finance fundamental changes may have been weakened by its own merger activity. The Watney offer was clearly financially attractive to the vendors.[69] Above all, of course, brewing management is about personalities. Elsewhere, as at Greene King, where the determination to remain independent was strong, independence was retained.[70] In Norwich, on the other hand, both the Morse and the Bullard interest had been diluted by capital expansions to fund mergers, and neither was prepared to sacrifice financial opportunity for sentimental appeals to the retention of local brewing. By March 1963 over 30 per cent of Steward & Patteson's ordinary shares were held by institutional investors such as Barclays Nominees, Lloyd's Bank Trustees, Control Nominees, Legal & General Assurance and Prudential Assurance. The largest shareholder was West Nominees, with 516,700 shares. The share register for 4 March 1964 charts the lack of determination to resist. Among the shareholders selling to Watney Mann before the formal offer was made were Lloyd's Bank, which disposed of 16,000 shares in March 1963, and Francis John Morse, the Chairman, who sold 44,500 in July.[71]

Perhaps the decision to sell was a wise one. The subsequent history of brewing in Norfolk is certainly depressing, though the full story will not emerge until the relevant business records become available. For a time Steward & Patteson and Bullard operated as quasi-independent subsidiaries of the Watney Mann Group, whose own Norwich concern, Watney Mann (Morgans), was re-named Watney Mann (East Anglia) in 1963 to reflect its status as a management company. Brewing was continued at four sites: Pockthorpe, Anchor Brewery, King Street, and Forehoe Brewery, Ely. John Morse and Gerald Bullard joined the main Watney Mann board, and one of the Watney Mann directors, Robin Combe, son of the chairman, joined the Steward & Patteson board. However, the pressure to rationalise both the brewing facilities and the tied estate soon built up, and although at the time of the bid Simon Combe had offered assurances that the two Norwich companies would continue to maintain an independent trading existence, he had also referred to the opportunities offered by the merger to streamline production and distribution.[72] Combe's personal involvement had done much to reassure the Norwich brewers about a future of fairly loose control by the parent company under the Watney umbrella. A brewer of the old school and chairman of Watney Mann since 1950, he had strong Norfolk connections. In 1932 he had married Silvia, elder daughter of the fourth Earl of Leicester, and had a house at Burnham Thorpe in the north of the county. But his death in April 1965 was to open the way for a less sympathetic response to brewing operations in East Anglia.[73]

After the merger renewed attention was paid to the rationalisation of the tied house estate in the region. At first, the pace was rather leisurely. Meetings of a joint Property Rationalisation Committee in the summer of 1964 produced the information that Steward & Patteson had closed twenty-five and Bullards fourteen of the competitive uneconomic houses earmarked for closure in 1962. In all, the two breweries had closed 203 pubs since October 1961, 122 of them belonging to Steward & Patteson. An analysis of the 1963 trade was then considered; it identified no less than 549 houses selling under 100 barrels a year (363 Steward & Patteson). However, the directors of the two breweries remained reluctant to take draconian steps. Attention was focussed upon the 256 pubs selling 70 barrels or less, then upon 172, and finally upon only 85 (52 Steward & Patteson). Some acceleration of the process of closure was evident in 1965, and in February 1966 it was reported that there were now 447 pubs trading at under 100 barrels, a reduction of 102 in about eighteen months. Of these, 309 belonged to Steward & Patteson, who had cut the number of their low barrelage houses by 15 per cent.[74] More radical action followed the formal acquisition by Watney Mann (East Anglia) of the assets of the two Norwich breweries in 1966-7. A major reorganisation of the tied estate in the west of the region in 1967 involved the transfer of some 330 pubs to Phipps, Watney's Northampton subsidiary. Two years later, a major review of the remaining houses was initiated.[75]

On the brewing side, the concentration of production in Norfolk was first contemplated when outline planning permission was sought for a new site at Hellesdon, outside Norwich, in 1966. However, the plans were quickly scrapped in the wake of the economic crisis of July, and attention was focussed upon Watney's existing assets. In September 1967 a feasibility study was commissioned to examine concentration at the former Morgans brewery in King Street, where a new £0.5 million fermenting block was completed in March 1968. By this time, the future of the other brewing sites was clear. In September 1968 production ceased at both Bullard's Anchor Brewery and the Ely Brewery (the latter closed altogether in February 1969). Pockthorpe followed suit shortly afterwards, the last brew being made in January 1970. A refurbished brewing complex in King Street included a £2.2 million investment in a new packaging-warehouse-distribution block and offices, which was announced in November 1969 and completed in 1973. In July 1970 the local beers were re-named 'Norwich Mild' (ex-Bullard) and 'Norwich Bitter' (ex-S. & P.); they were expected to compete with Watney's branded products, the premium 'Red Barrel', 'Starlight', a weak bitter, and 'Special Mild'. The management accounts in the last full year before brewing rationalisation, i.e. to 28 September 1968, reveal that Pockthorpe was the major producer, brewing 130,812 barrels at an average gravity of 1034.9°. At King Street production amounted to 79,098 (gravity: 1033.6°), at Bullard's 55,245 (1031.9°), and at Ely 41,389 (1034.7°).[76]

In the volatile world of brewing in the 1960's and early 1970's, it was not long before Watney Mann itself was the victim of a takeover bid. In June 1972 the company was swallowed up by Grand Metropolitan Hotels, who paid a (then) record price of £434 million. Demand for local beers was affected by the growing taste for lager and consumer lobbying for 'real ale'. The S. & P. logotype was used again in 1984 for a traditional, cask-conditioned bitter brewed at King Street, which for a time brewed 'real ales' for a number of Grand Metropolitan subsidiaries. However, this proved to be shortlived. In the summer of the following year, the King Street brewery was also closed down, and production of S. & P. Bitter, the last remnant of Steward & Patteson's

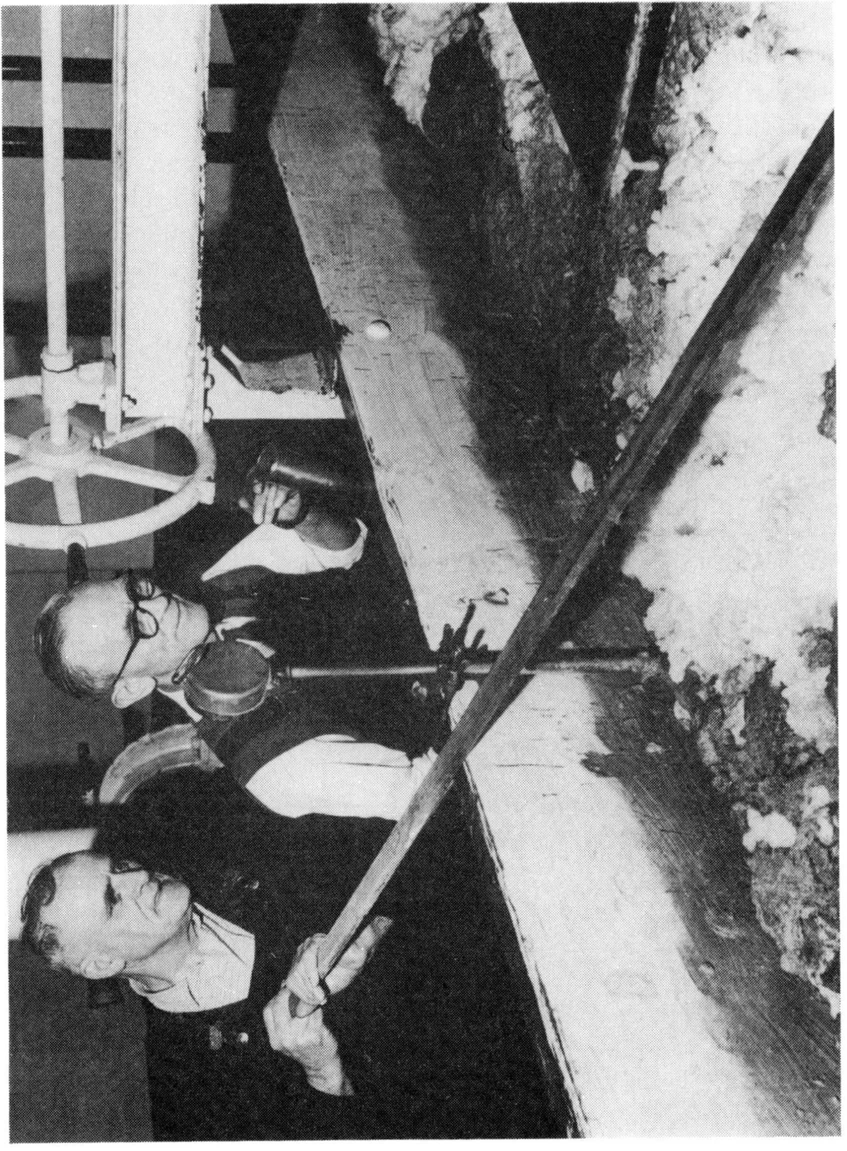

25. The last brew at Pockthorpe, 27 January 1970 [*E.C.N./Colman & Rye Lib.*]

presence in brewing, was transferred to the Group's Manchester brewery (Wilson's). It is currently [1986] manufactured for the Norwich Brewery Company (as Watney Mann (East Anglia) has been renamed) at Trowbridge (Ushers) in Wiltshire. For 170 years Steward & Patteson traded successfully while priding itself on the quality of its beers and its obligation to the City of Norwich, in which it had been established for so long, and to small rural communities throughout East Anglia. Its sale to Watney Mann appears to have been more a reflection of pessimism about operating in the future than a response to its current financial position, which remained sound. The sudden demise of an historic provincial business has not only induced a sense of loss in local consumers, aggravated by recent attempts to revive 'S. & P. Bitter' and 'Bullard's Mild', but has also caused regret in the community at large.

APPENDIX A

The Patteson Pedigree

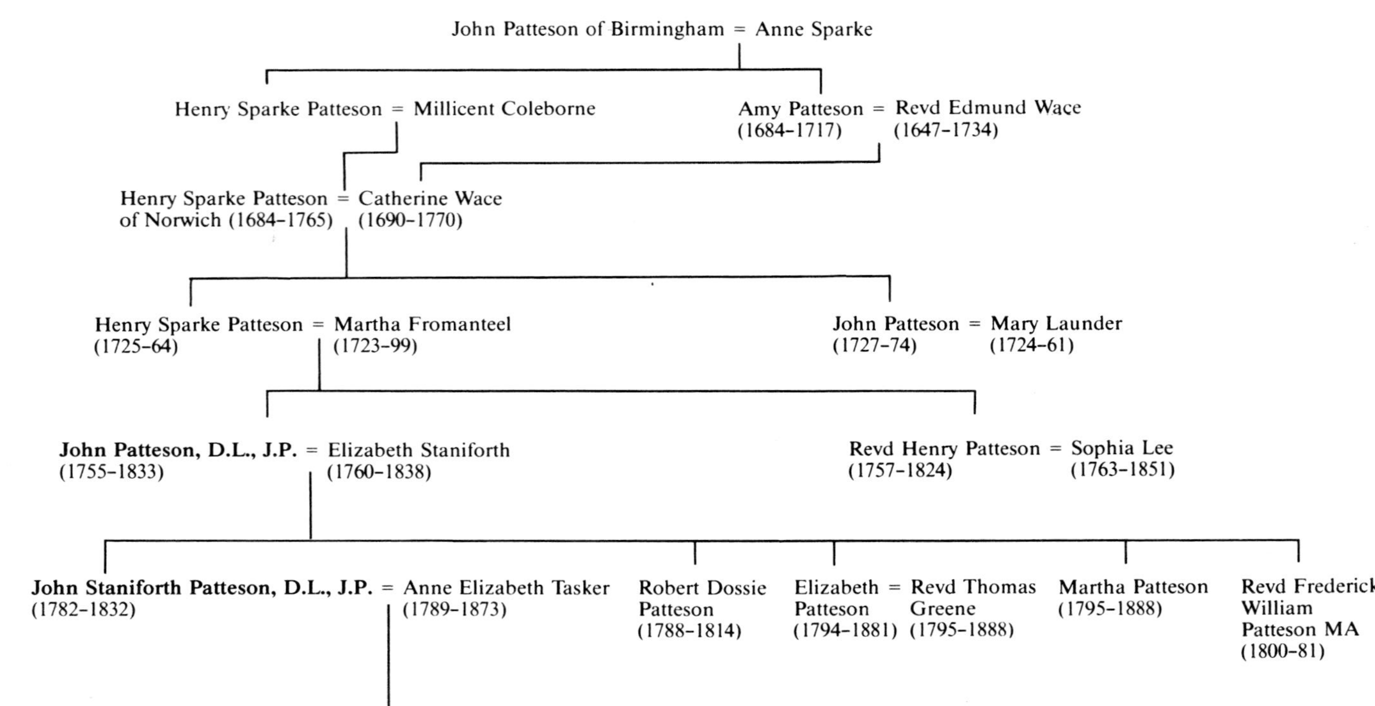

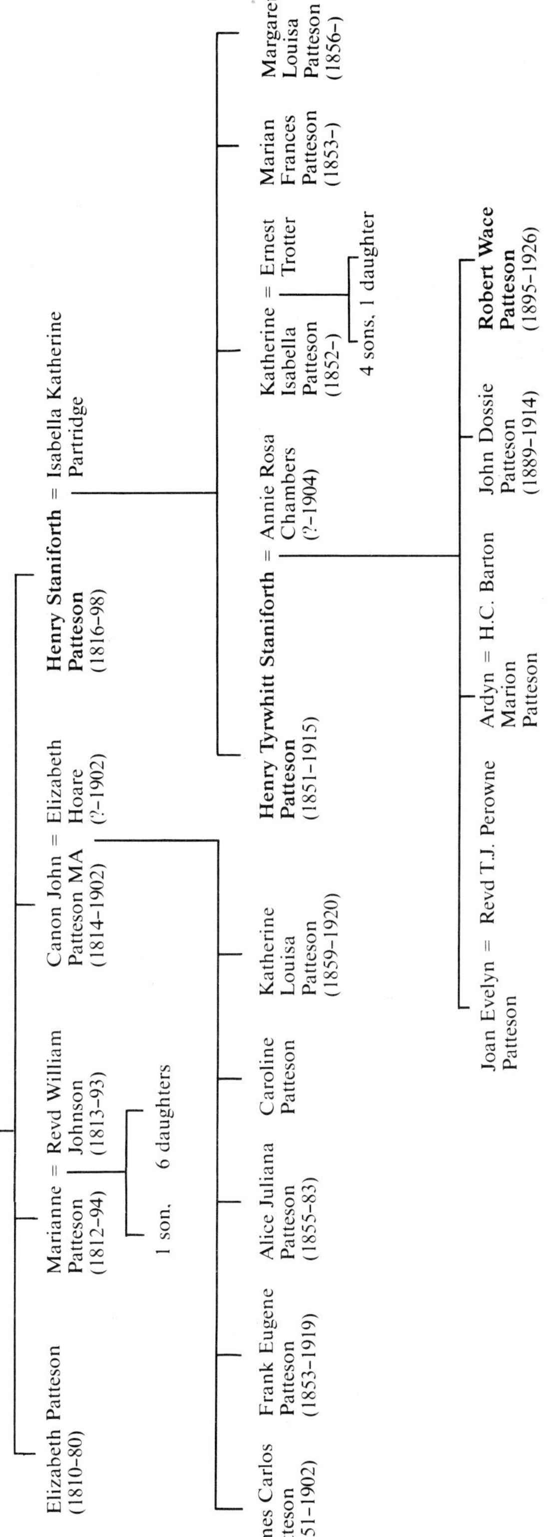
Elizabeth Patteson (1810–80)
Marianne Patteson (1812–94) = Revd William Johnson (1813–93)
1 son, 6 daughters
Canon John Patteson MA (1814–1902) = Elizabeth Hoare (?–1902)
Henry Staniforth Patteson (1816–98) = Isabella Katherine Partridge
James Carlos Patteson (1851–1902)
Frank Eugene Patteson (1853–1919)
Alice Juliana Patteson (1855–83)
Caroline Patteson
Katherine Louisa Patteson (1859–1920)
Henry Tyrwhitt Staniforth Patteson (1851–1915) = Annie Rosa Chambers (?–1904)
Katherine Isabella Patteson (1852–) = Ernest Trotter
4 sons, 1 daughter
Marian Frances Patteson (1853–)
Margaret Louisa Patteson (1856–)
Joan Evelyn Patteson = Revd T.J. Perowne
Ardyn Marion Patteson = H.C. Barton
John Dossie Patteson (1889–1914)
Robert Wace Patteson (1895–1926)

APPENDIX B

The Steward Pedigree

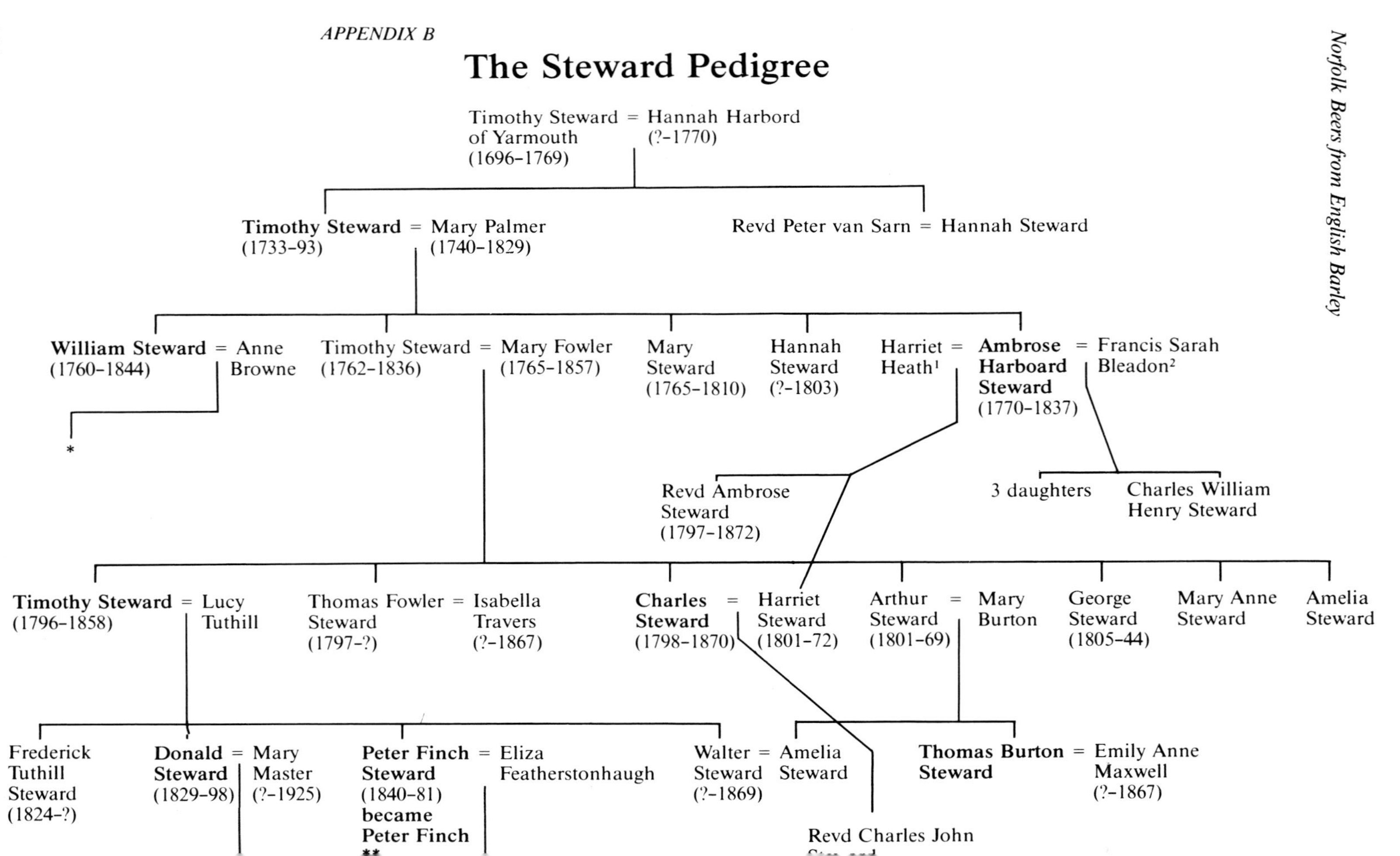

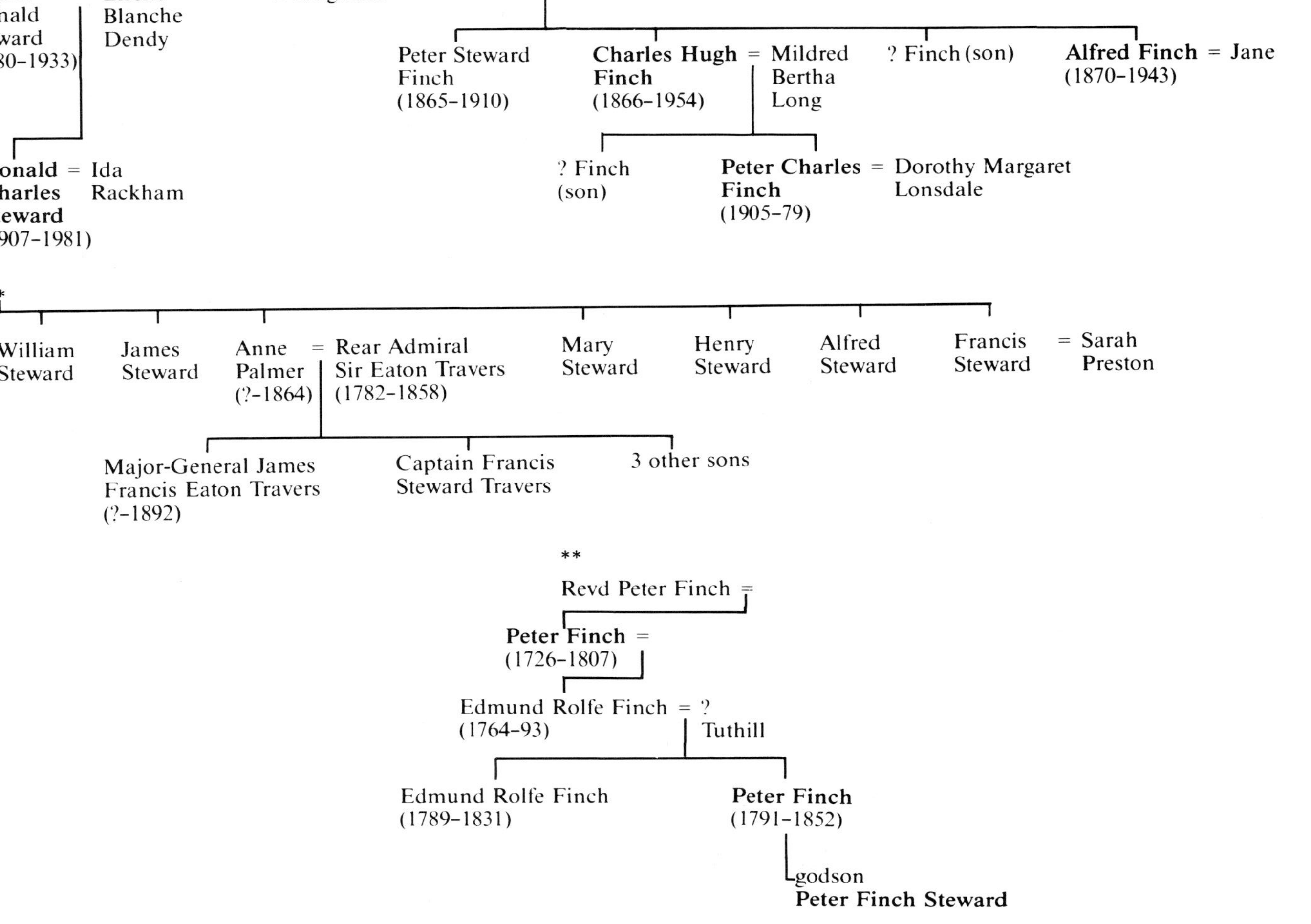
Rupert Donald Steward (1880–1933) = Eirene Blanche Dendy
2 daughters
Donald Charles Steward (1907–1981) = Ida Rackham
Peter Steward Finch (1865–1910)
Charles Hugh Finch (1866–1954) = Mildred Bertha Long
? Finch (son)
Alfred Finch (1870–1943) = Jane
? Finch (son)
Peter Charles Finch (1905–79) = Dorothy Margaret Lonsdale
*
William Steward
James Steward
Anne Palmer (?–1864) = Rear Admiral Sir Eaton Travers (1782–1858)
Mary Steward
Henry Steward
Alfred Steward
Francis Steward = Sarah Preston
Major-General James Francis Eaton Travers (?–1892)
Captain Francis Steward Travers
3 other sons
**
Revd Peter Finch =
Peter Finch (1726–1807) =
Edmund Rolfe Finch (1764–93) = ? Tuthill
Edmund Rolfe Finch (1789–1831)
Peter Finch (1791–1852)
godson
Peter Finch Steward

APPENDIX C

The Morse Pedigree

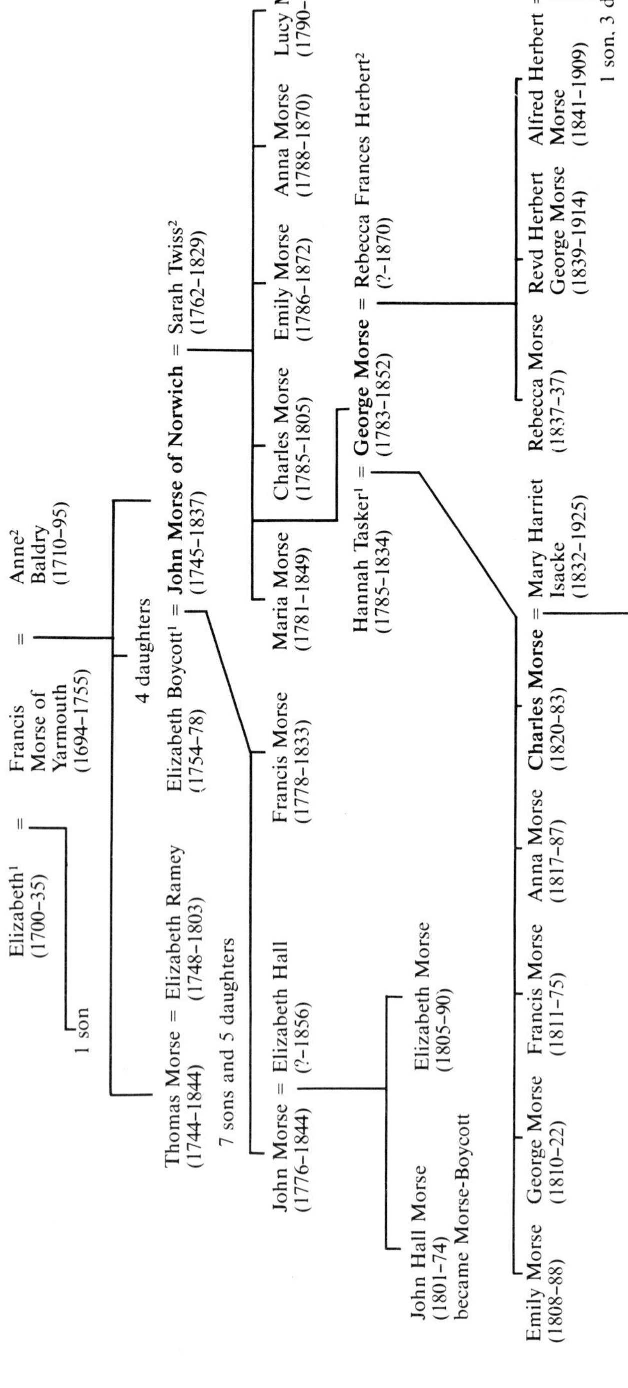

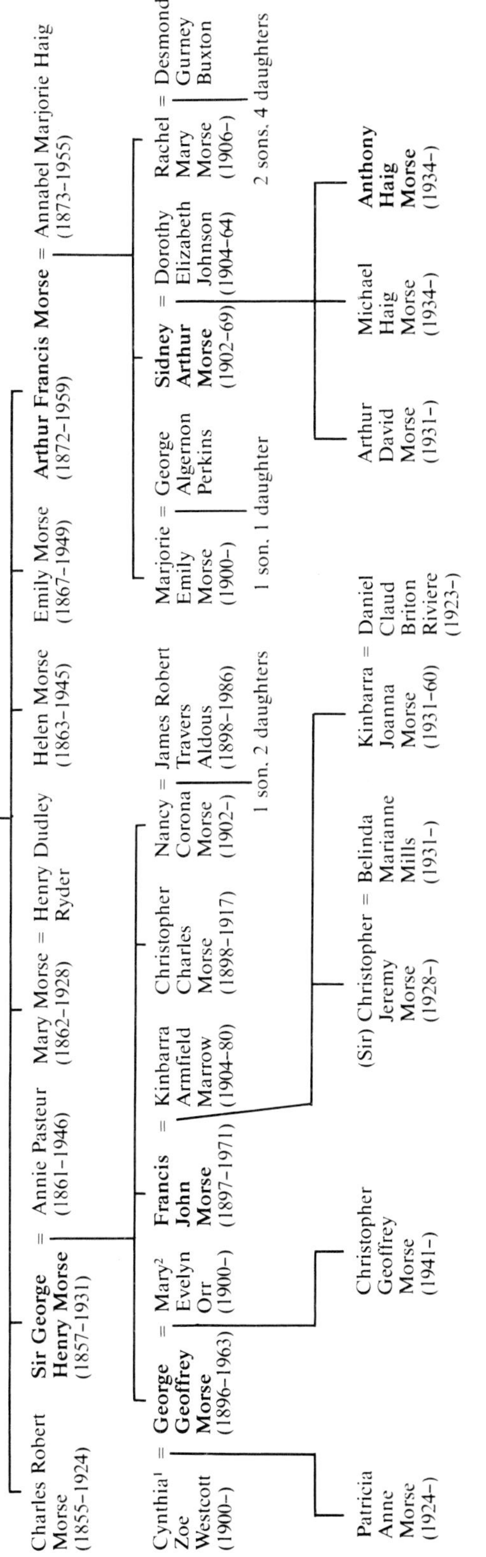

Note: the Pedigrees cited here are derived from several family trees and do not pretend to be complete.

APPENDIX D. STATISTICAL TABLES

Table 1. Beer Production of Norwich Common Brewers, 1792–1800 (numbers of 36-gallon barrels)

Year ending 5 July	*Greeves*	*Beevor*	*Postle*	*Day*	*Finch*	*Tompson*	*Weston*	*Latten*	*Seales*
				All beer (strong, table, small)					
1792	740	3,041	4,455	14,053	8,936	13,177	11,129	508	539
1793	1,519	3,231	4,416	13,157	11,005	13,610	11,639	927	—
				Strong beer only					
1792	477	2,402	3,626	10,801	?	11,796	8,222	?	327
1793	1,388	2,632	3,511	10,318	?	11,869	8,604	498	—
		Patteson		*Ganning*					
1795		7,277½		7,341½	8,353½	12,851¼	7,188	206¼	—
1797		16,139¼ [21,689¼]*		8,011		12,176½ [14,058½]*	7,696½ [9,470¼]*	230	—
				Morse					
1798		18,492		7,649	7,501	11,257	6,790	—	—
1800		20,019¼		6,843½	7,609¾	8,830¼	5,530	—	—

Source: Norfolk Chronicle, 1795–1800.

* All beer.

Table 2. Steward & Patteson Beer Production and Total Sales, 1886–1936 (in 36-gallon barrels)

Year ending November	*Production*	*Sales*	*Year ending November*	*Production*	*Sales*
1886	77,751	72,571	1912	111,846	108,194
1887	83,926	78,019	1913	112,985	109,993
1888	83,355	77,457	1914	122,852	118,827
1889	82,867	77,625	1915	99,325	96,856
1890	81,879	76,679	1916	110,060	109,312
1891	83,625	78,152	1917	72,922	72,500
1892	82,737	77,449	1918	67,351	66,272
1893	85,352	79,174	1919	102,352	100,871
1894	75,679	70,282	1920	117,935	118,048
1895	74,818	69,204	1021	101,732	101,038
1896	84,355	78,726	1922	81,546	80,996
1897	86,858	80,002	1923	83,382	82,186
1898	92,607	85,217	1924	84,622	83,365
1899	100,095	92,666	1925	88,483	88,228
1900	103,314	95,570	1926	84,466	83,538
1901	102,722	97,021	1927	81,858	81,772
1902	104,228	98,101	1928	84,687	83,959
1903	108,244	103,731	1929	84,363	83,288
1904	105,799	101,867	1930	90,304	88,817
1905	105,893	102,952	1931	85,851	84,658
1906	110,851	107,239	1932	68,972	68,932
1907	111,723	107,992	1933	76,482	76,092
1908	115,627	113,009	1934	86,103	86,263
1909	111,879	108,964	1935	94,309	93,662
1910	110,488	108,794	1936	95,949	97,355
1911	111,761	109,731			

Source: Steward & Patteson Account Books, BR1/101, 104, and 110, N.R.O.

Note: Sales include beer purchased from other breweries, and exclude 'Cage Beer' (consumed by brewery workers), and beer distributed to agencies for finings.

Table 3. Steward & Patteson Ltd. Profits, 1896-1914

Year ending November	*NET PROFITS Gross of debenture interest*	*Return on Isssued Capital £580,000*	*NET PROFITS Net of debenture interest*	*Return on Share Capital £300,000*	*Ordinary Share Dividend*
	£	%	£	%	%
1896	38,237	6.6	27,410	9.1	6.0
1897	38,157	6.6	27,330	9.1	6.0
1898	40,526	7.0	29,699	9.9	6.5
1899	45,284	7.8	34,457	11.5	6.5
1900	48,,352	8.3	37,630	12.5	7.0
1901	44,405	7.7	33,812	11.3	7.5
1902	45,408	7.8	34,885	11.6	8.0
1903	54,510	9.4	43,903	14.6	9.0
1904	55,679	9.6	45,016	15.0	10.0
1905	54,467	9.4	43,827†	14.6	10.0
1906	64,553	11.1	53,913	18.0	12.0
1907	67,931	11.6	57,291	19.1	12.0
1908	72,971	12.6	62,331	20.8	13.0
1909	65,311	11.3	54,718	18.2	13.0
1910	49,309	8.5	48,254	16.1	13.0 plus 10.0 bonus
1911	68,038	11.7	57,491	19.2	13.0
1912	58,512	10.1	47,965	16.0	13.0
1913	63,165	10.9	52,618	17.5	13.0 plus 12.0 bonus*
1914	78,626	13.6	68,103	22.7	12.0

Source: Steward & Patteson Account Books, BR1/101, 104, N.R.O.

* 12 per cent bonus transferred to Share Purchase Account
† As reported in accounts. Total income *minus* total working costs equals £43,467.

Table 4. Steward & Patteson Ltd. Profits, 1915-36

Year ending November	*NET PROFITS Gross of debenture interest* £	*Return on Issued Capital £580,000* %	*NET PROFITS Net of debenture interest* £	*Return on Share Capital £300,000* %	*Ordinary Share Dividend* %
1915	61,679	10.6	51,844	17.3	13.0 + 1.0*
1916	56,110	9.7	47,244	15.7	13.0 + 1.0*
1917	80,911	14.0	72,511	24.2	13.0
1918	74,719	12.9	66,646	22.2	15.0
		£880,000		*£600,000*	
1919	78,930	9.0	71,090	11.8	5.5
1920	73,646	8.4	65,806	11.0	5.5
1921	45,700	5.2	37,860	6.3	5.5
1922	44,563	5.1	36,397	6.1	5.5
1923	49,061	5.6	40,498	6.7	5.5
1924	58,831	6.7	50,151	8.4	5.5
1925	91,903	10.4	83,060	13.8	6.0
1926	61,688	7.0	52,728	8.8	6.0
1927	66,686	7.6	57,726	9.6	7.0
1928	70,855	8.1	61,895	10.3	7.0
1929	82,473	9.4	73,513	12.3	7.0
1930	92,854	10.6	84,174	14.0	7.0
1931	93,963	10.7	82,579	13.8	7.0
1932	73,248	8.3	62,110	10.4	7.0
1933	79,804	9.1	68,635	11.4	8.0
1934	106,095	12.1	94,926	15.8	8.0 + 2.0*
1935	116,475	13.2	105,306	17.6	8.0 + 4.0*
1936	111,398	12.7	100,045	16.7	8.0 + 4.5*

Source: Steward & Patteson Account Books, BR1/73, 101, N.R.O.

* Bonuses
Ordinary dividends paid free of income tax. The shareholder paid the tax to 1925, the company paid (therefore dividends are free of tax) from 1926.

Table 5. Steward & Patteson Beer Production and Total Sales, 1937–61 (in standard barrels)

Year ending November	*Production*	*Sales*
1937	99,623	99,960
1938	105,741	106,143
1939	112,296	112,315
1940	108,106	106,937
1941	110,302	110,395
1942	130,624	131,298*
1943	134,693	136,012*
1944	148,422	155,380*
1945	139,832	147,116*
1946	125,511	128,028
1947	123,802	124,985
1948	118,013	119,002
1949	108,123	109,672
1950	123,319	124,536
1951	119,112	115,186
1952	113,549	110,828
1953	111,492	107,415
1954	105,258	101,203
1955	102,399	99,362
1956	97,173	n.a.
1957	104,031†	n.a.
1958	107,026†	n.a.
1959	115,909†	n.a.
1960	110,613†	n.a.
1961	118,092†	n.a.

Source: Steward & Patteson Account Books, BR1/101, 102, 111, N.R.O.

* Includes beer brewed for Morgan's and Lacons.
† Pockthorpe only (excludes production at Ely).

Table 6. Steward & Patteson Ltd. Profits, 1937–63

Year ending November	*NET PROFITS Gross of debenture interest* £	*Return on Issued Capital*	*NET PROFITS Net of debenture interest* £	*Return on Share Capital*	*Ordinary Share Dividend* %
		£1,030,000 %		*£750,000* %	
1937	108,547	10.5	97,378	13.0	12.5
1938	111,723	10.8	100,554	13.4	12.5
1939	111,924	10.9	100,755	13.4	12.5
1940	92,172	8.9	81,003	10.8	12.5
1941	76,276	7.4	65,107	8.7	12.5
1942	79,605	7.7	68,436	9.1	12.5
1943	79,807	7.7	68,638	9.2	12.5
1944	88,872	8.6	77,731	10.4	12.5
1945	90,368	8.8	79,199	10.6	12.5
1946	95,896	9.3	84,727	11.3	12.5 + 2.5*
1947	118,405	11.5	107,236	14.3	12.5 + 2.5*
1948	117,576	11.4	106,253	14.2	12.5 + 2.5*
		£1,247,660		*£967,660*	
1949	114,663	9.2	103,494	10.7	12.5 + 2.5*
1950	116,125	9.3	104,956	10.8	12.5 + 2.5*
1951	110,089	8.8	98,920	10.2	12.5 + 2.5*
1952	124,784	10.0	113,615	11.7	12.5 + 2.5*
1953	126,047	10.1	114,878	11.9	12.5 + 5.5*
		£1,546,604		*£1,266,604*	
1954	113,307	7.3	102,138	8.1	12.5 + 1.5*
1955	123,571	8.0	112,402	8.9	12.5
1956	135,882	8.8	124,713	9.8	12.5
		£1,951,604		*£1,671,604*	
1957	257,403	—**	246,234	—**	14.0
1958	269,014	—	257,845	—	15.0
1959	367,053	—	355,884	—	20.0
		£2,504,677		*£2,224,677*	
1960	313,245	12.5	302,076	13.6	22.5
		£3,224,677		*£2,224,677*	
1961	374,547	—**	362,422	16.3	22.5
1962	410,361	12.7	342,861	15.4	22.5
1963	394,937	12.2	327,437	14.7	22.5

* Bonus
** RR not calculated as E.A.B. pref. capital not bought by S&P until 1960, and in 1961 interest on new debenture stock not paid for a full year.

Notes

CHAPTER 1

1. *Norfolk Chronicle*, 5 August 1893.
2. Henry Sparke Patteson III (1725-64) was the son of Henry Sparke Patteson II(1684-1765), Norwich ironmonger and banker, and Catherine Wace. Daniel Fromanteel (1678-1731), mayor of Norwich in 1725, came from a Walloon family. W. Rye, *Norfolk Families* (Norwich, 1913), p.654; B. Cozens-Hardy and A.E. Kent, *The Mayors of Norwich 1403-1835* (Norwich, 1938), pp.116, 141.
3. The first Pattesons appear to have been Birmingham inn-keepers: Rye, op. cit. p.654. See Appendix A for the Patteson Pedigree.
4. Elizabeth Staniforth's mother was Catherine Dossie of Sheffield. The summer residence of Norton Hall, near Bury St Edmunds, passed *jure uxoris* to Patteson on his marriage. After this Chapter was written, Trevor Fawcett included a full account of Patteson's journeys abroad in 1768-71 and 1778-9 in his 'Argonauts and Commercial Travellers: the Foreign Marketing of Norwich Stuffs in the later Eighteenth Century', *Textile History*, XVI (Autumn 1985), 151-81.
5. C.B. Jewson, *Jacobin City. A Portrait of Norwich in its Reaction to the French Revolution 1788-1802* (London, 1975), p.88.
6. Patteson Papers, Boxes 2 and 3, Q.171B, Norfolk Record Office (N.R.O.).
7. P. Browne, *The History of Norwich* (Norwich, 1814), p.65; Jewson, op. cit. p.78.
8. C. Mackie, *Norfolk Annals* (Norwich, 1901), I, p.9.
9. Oakes's Diaries, HA521/1-14, Suffolk Record Office (S.R.O.), entries for 24 July and 16 August 1792, 7-8 March, and 6-8 June 1793. My thanks to Jane Fiske and Dr Richard Wilson for these references.
10. Lease, William Quantrell to John Patteson, 24 October 1792, Patteson's Papers, Box 2, Q.171B, N.R.O. Patteson's father, Henry, had owned at least one public house, the 'Black Horse' in St Gregory's Norwich, acquired in 1760 and passed on to his son: Steward & Patteson Title Deeds, BR12/34, N.R.O.
11. For complete data see Appendix D, Table 1.
12. Ibid. Beevor won £20,000 in the State Lottery in 1794, *Norfolk Chronicle*, 5 April 1794.
13. Estimate based on William Steward's view that the country trade was about 105 barrels a house per annum, Steward's evidence, *Select Committee on the Retail Sale of Beer*, 22 March 1830, P.P.1830, X, p.93.
14. Yarmouth Rate-Book, 7 July 1795, L1/21, N.R.O. 'Stock' valuation assumed to be 4% of Stock value: see Norwich (Appeals to the Poor Rates), Q.S. vol.II, 1775 to 1809, N.R.O.
15. Oakes's Diary, 13-15 and 27-9 September, 1 October, and 13 November 1798, 21 January 1799, S.R.O. The joint capital appears to have been £10,000: Diary, 4 March 1799.
16. St Stephen's rate assessment, 3 March 1819 and 1820, N.R.O.; Isabella K. Patteson, *Henry Staniforth Patteson. A Memoir* (Norwich, 1899); Mackie, op. cit. I, p.172.
17. I am grateful to Dr Roger Ryan for this information. See his 'The Early Expansion of the Norwich Union Life Insurance Society, 1808-37', *Business History*, XXVII (July 1985), 166-96.
18. I.K. Patteson, op. cit.; J.R.T. Aldous, *Family Notebook*, II (Norwich, 1964), p.67. Tasker came to London in 1795, and died in 1798. His widow Susanna Allan was the daughter of Charles Allan, a leading English merchant in Rotterdam, who later moved to Norwich. I am grateful to Sir Jeremy Morse for this information.
19. Information from Roger Ryan. Both John (1806-7) and John Staniforth (1811-13) had been directors of the Norwich General.

CHAPTER 2

1. Steward & Patteson Title Deeds, BR12/13, BR12/34, N.R.O.; *Norfolk Chronicle*, 9 May 1795. Patteson also acquired the 'Black Swan' in Norwich in 1799.
2. Alfred Head estimated capital employed at about £8 a barrel, William Steward at £7-8, evidence to *S.C. on Retail Sale of Beer*, 22 March 1830, P.P.1830, X, pp.90-1. Charles Barclay referred in 1817 to a country brewery with an output of 3,000 barrels a year and a capital of £30,000, which suggests an estimate of £10 a barrel, P.P.1817, VII, p.238, cit. P. Mathias, *The Brewing Industry in England 1700-1830* (Cambridge, 1959), p.129. (Cambridge, 1959), p.129.
3. Ibid. p.142; Pockthorpe Brewery Plan, 1820, BR1/178, N.R.O.
4. Mathias, op. cit. pp.396, 546, 548.
5. Ibid. p.546.
6. Profits were 9% in year ending September 1799, 7% in 1800. The sale price was £25,500. Oakes's Diary, 10 November 1801, 30 January and 1 February 1804, S.R.O.
7. Steward & Patteson Title Deeds, BR12/34, N.R.O.
8. Courage Title Deeds, Q.198B/5/10, 11, N.R.O.
9. Cf. Mathias, op. cit. p.117ff.
10. Cf. advice in brewing manuals such as William Ford, *A Practical Treatise on Malting and Brewing* (1862 edition).
11. Steward pedigree book (kindly lent by the late Mr Donald Steward of New Buckenham); C.J. Palmer, *The Perlustration of Great Yarmouth*, 3 vols. (Great Yarmouth, 1872), *passim*. See Appendix B for the Steward pedigree.
12. J.D. Murphy, 'The Town and Trade of Great Yarmouth, 1740-1850', University of East Anglia Ph.D. Thesis, 1979, pp.117-57.
13. William Steward's evidence to *S.C. on Retail Sale of Beer*, P.P.1830, X, 22 March 1830, p.91.
14. Yarmouth Rate-Books, 6 July 1790 and 14 April 1801, L1/17, 28, N.R.O.
15. Yarmouth Rate-Books, October 1820, L1/44, N.R.O.
16. Palmer, op. cit. II, pp.102-3.
17. Yarmouth Rate-Books, 8 July 1800 and 14 April 1801, L1/25, 28, N.R.O.
18. Country Brewers' Society Minutes, 24 and 31 May, 10 and 14 June 1822, 26 April, 10 and 24 May 1824, 12 March 1830, Annual General Meeting Minutes, 15 April 1823, 28 April 1830, etc. Brewers' Society Library London. I am grateful to Michael Ripley of the Brewers' Society for this reference. Cf. also William Steward's evidence, 22 March 1830, loc. cit. p.93.
19. See, *inter alia*, Mackie, *Norfolk Annals*, op. cit. II, p.137. Steward became a Tory in later life.
20. Courage Title Deeds, Q.198B/6/6, 7, N.R.O.; Lease, 25 March 1824, in Steward & Patteson Ltd. Trust Deed, 30 July 1895, BR1/146, N.R.O.
21. Thomas Salmon's letter to *Norfolk Chronicle*, 24 July 1830; Mathias, op. cit. p.242.
22. Estate Book, 1831 (now destroyed), cit. in Aldous, *Family Notebook*, op. cit. p.136.
23. The total number of outlets was estimated to be 380-400. Cf. Pigot's *London and provincial commercial directory* (London, 1822), which lists 10 'inns' and 368 public houses, and the Norwich Poor Rate Books for June 1825 (250 public houses, etc. listed in 26 of the 42 parishes), N/T23/1, N.R.O.
24. Return, 27 February 1824, for year ending 5 April 1823, P.P. 1824, XVII.
25. Norwich Poor Rate Book, June 1825, N/T23/1, N.R.O.
26. Evidence, 22 March 1830, loc. cit. p.92.
27. Mathias, op. cit. p.546.

28. 11 Geo.IV and 1 Will.IV c.51 (beer duties), and 11 Geo.IV and 1 Will. IV c.64 (freeing of beer trade). The duty on malt was retained. See, for example, R.G. Wilson, *Greene King. A Family and Business History* (1983), pp.26-9.
29. Steward & Patteson Partnership Deeds, Indenture, 30 November 1863, BR11/8, N.R.O.
30. Aldous, op. cit. p.135.
31. See Appendix D, Table 1. When offered for sale in 1794 its capacity was estimated to be 15,000 barrels p.a.: *Norfolk Chronicle*, 11 October 1794.
32. Appendix D, Table 1, and *Norfolk Chronicle*, 11 October 1794 and 17 June 1797. The 1797 sale offered 32 public houses on freehold or long lease, and 20 on short lease.
34. W. Rye, *A History of the Parish of Heigham in the City of Norwich* (Norwich, 1917), p.183.
35. St Martin-at-Oak rate assessment, December 1797, August 1800, and June 1803, N.R.O., and Norwich Poor Rate Book, June 1825, N/T23/1, N.R.O.
36. This estimate assumes that the brewery sold beer to about 70-100 houses. Adams may have been James Adams, a founding director of the Norwich Union Fire Society (1797), who died in 1825.
37. W. Rye, *A History of the Parish of Catton in the City of Norwich* (Norwich, 1919), p.241.
38. *Norfolk Chronicle*, 12 December 1830. Later, Morse joined Timothy Steward (the younger) on the board of the Norwich Yarn Company, founded in 1833.
39. *Norfolk Chronicle*, 16 July 1831.
40. Aldous, op. cit. p.136. In 1819 Paget & Co. owned 52 Yarmouth houses and Sir Edmund Lacon & Co. 45, Yarmouth Sessions Papers, S10/1, N.R.O. Tied houses are not always a good indication of production levels, however. Lacon's expanded by 'exporting' beer to the London market.
41. Steward & Patteson Partnership Deeds, Indenture, 30 November 1863, BR11/8, N.R.O.
42. Ibid.
43. Ibid.
44. The brewery premises were occupied for a short period by J. Fellows: Norwich Poor Rate Books, March 1833 and 1834, N/T23/26, 29, N.R.O.
45. *Norfolk Chronicle*, 9 October 1830.
46. The figure includes 10 shops which sold beer as a sideline. The total number of outlets, including inns and taverns, was 528.
47. *Norfolk Chronicle*. 18 April 1829, 25 September 1830.
48. Ibid. 2 September 1840, cit. in Mackie, op. cit. I, p.401.

CHAPTER THREE

1. *Norwich Mercury*, 23 October 1852; St Mary's Coslany, Norwich Poor Rate Assessment, 1770-1822, N/T24, N.R.O. The Revd Peter Finch had Lancashire antecedents.
2. Appendix D, Table 1.
3. William Chase, *The Norwich Directory* ... (Norwich, 1783); *Norwich Mercury*, 23 October 1852; St Mary's Poor Rate, cit.
4. St Mary's Poor Rate, cit., and see also Table 5, above.
5. The brewery capital also included £1,200 for 'Howell's public houses' (brought into common ownership), mortgages, raw material stocks, horses, shares in the Norwich Corn Exchange and Yarn Company: Steward & Patteson Partnership Deeds, Indenture, 20 November 1838, BR11/8, N.R.O.

6. Charles Steward (1798-1870) was the third son of Timothy Steward the elder. He once commanded an East Indiaman: Palmer, *Perlustration*, op. cit. II, 155. Residing at Blundeston (Suffolk), he married Harriet, daughter of Ambrose Harbord Steward. Steward Pedigree, Appendix B.
7. Estimated by extrapolation from the lists in Steward & Patteson Limited Trust Deed, 30 July and Brewery Valuation, 3 July 1895, and index of Public Houses, 1895-1915, BR1/146-8, N.R.O.
8. Of the owners referred to in Table 8, only Robert Seaman, the wine and spirit merchant, was not a common brewer.
9. 1822-3: P.P.1824, XVII; 1830: P.P.1831, XVII; 1836-42: *H.L. Select Committee on the Operation of the Acts for the Sale of Beer,* P.P.1850, XVIII, Appendix to Minutes of Evidence, p.133.
10. E.M. Sigsworth, *The Brewing Trade During the Industrial Revolution. The Case of Yorkshire* (Borthwick Papers, No. 31, York, 1967), pp.3-6. Licensed Victuallers were brewing publicans selling beers, wines, and spirits; beer-house keepers who made beer sold it either 'on' or 'off' the premises.
11. In 1836-7, for example, common brewers in these districts had shares of 2 and 4 per cent respectively: P.P.1837, L. Shares were also low in Derby, Lichfield and Stourbridge.
12. In 1836-7 common brewers' shares were: 92% (Liverpool and Surrey), 91% (Rochester), 89% (Canterbury), and 87% (Sussex), P.P.1837, L. Proximity to either London or a major port may have been a factor determining dominance by common brewers, and the combination of malting and brewing functions may also have encouraged concentration.
13. G.B. Wilson, *Alcohol and the Nation* (1940), p.332. Stagnation in Norfolk is suggested by the excise returns on malt consumption which averaged 385,217 bushels in 1836-9 and 362,763 in 1846-9. P.P.1850, XVIII, and see also P.J. Corfield, 'The Social and Economic History of Norwich, 1650-1850: A Study in Urban Growth', London University Ph.D. Thesis, 1976, Table 62.
14. Steward and Patteson Partnership Deeds, Indenture, 20 November 1838, BR11/8, N.R.O. The partnership agreement of 1863 states that Henry Staniforth Patteson was admitted to the partnership in 1832, but no reference to any shares held by him is made before George Morse's death in 1852 (see above). However, Patteson signed the lease of the public houses belonging to Bell of Gorleston in 1845 (see above), where he is described as a partner. It is likely that he became a partner on his 25th birthday i.e. in 1841. See Indenture, 30 November 1863, BR11/8, N.R.O.
15. Steward, Patteson, Finch & Co. Out-letter Book, letter to Simon Silcock, 2 June 1843, BR1/44, N.R.O.
16. C.J. Allen, *The Great Eastern Railway* (1955), pp.24, 29.
17. Letter to Silcock, 2 June, and Silcock's reply, 19 June 1843, referred to in letter to Silcock, 28 June 1843, BR1/44, N.R.O.
18. Two barrels returned to Pockthorpe from London in September 1843 had been sent out on 19 December 1838 and 25 May 1840. Letters to Silcock, 2 September 1843 and 30 December 1845, BR1/44, N.R.O.
19. Letters to McKenzie, 16 January, 17 February, and 26 March 1846, and to William Morgan Jr., 26 March and 11 April 1846, BR1/44, N.R.O.
20. *Norfolk Chronicle,* 14 September 1841, cit. in Mackie, op. cit. I, p.411. The brewery had been owned by Robert Hawes, and some of his pubs, it seems, were later included in George Morse's property: Aldous, *Family Notebook*, op. cit. p.136.
21. John Sayers Bell (Gorleston), Lease to Steward, Patteson, Finch & Co., 4 April 1845, BR14/11, N.R.O.; Yarmouth Poor Rate Books, 24 January and 24 April 1845 (North Ward), and 23 January 1846 (all Wards), L1/70-1, 80-2, N.R.O. The mortgage of £28,000

is referred to in the Partnership Indenture of 30 November 1863, BR11/8, N.R.O.
22. Steward, Patteson, Finch & Co. Out-letter Book, letter to Silcock, 18 February 1847, BR1/44, N.R.O. There are references to the purchase of vats and pontoons in letters to W.W. Simpson, 18 February, J.W. & G. Stephens of Stowmarket, 6 and 12 March, Joseph Colyer & Co., 12 and 16 March and 7 April, and F. Wood, 20 April 1847, ibid.
23. Letter to Barclay Perkins & Co., 12 April 1846, and Mr Preston of Cromer, 8 April 1847, BR1/44, N.R.O.
24. Palmer, op. cit. I, 234; II, 287-8; Yarmouth Poor Rate Book, 28 June 1850, L1/83, N.R.O. Arthur Steward's agency is mentioned in the company's letter to Mrs McKenzie, 16 January 1846, BR1/44, N.R.O. He died on 11 January 1869; Probate, 22 September 1869, Will No. 365, N.R.O.
25. Steward & Patteson Partnership Deeds, Indenture, 30 November 1863, BR11/8, N.R.O.
26. Steward, Patteson, Finch & Co. Out-letter Book, letters to R. Roberts, 16 March, and John Pickford, 20 April 1847, BR1/44, N.R.O.
27. Steward & Patteson Partnership Deeds, Indenture, 30 November 1863, BR11/8, N.R.O.
28. Ibid. and Aldous, op. cit. p.138n.
29. Indenture, 30 November 1863, BR11/8, N.R.O. The document states that the sons took on half of Lucy Steward's share of a quarter of the partnership, although this conflicts with the shares determined in both 1838 and 1863 (see Tables 6 and 10).
30. Aldous, op. cit. pp.74-80, 85.
31. Indenture, 30 November 1863, BR11/8, N.R.O.
32. Ibid.
33. In 1850 Patteson married Isabella, daughter of Revd John Partridge, Rector of Baconsthorpe, Norfolk. See *Norfolk Chronicle*, 9 April 1898; Patteson Deposit, Box 5, Q171B, N.R.O.; Sir Robert Bignold, *Five Generations of the Bignold Family 1761-1947* (1948), p.xvii; I.K. Patteson, op. cit. pp.37-8, 48-9, 56-7; and Patteson Pedigree, Appendix A.
34. Steward's home at Catton Park had once belonged to George Morse. See *Norfolk Chronicle*, 29 January 1898; *Norwich Mercury*, 29 January 1898; *Brewing Trade Review*, 1 February 1898. Little is known about the activities of Donald's brother Walter. He married Amelia, the daughter of Arthur Steward (q.v.), and died on 23 May 1869: probate, 5 June 1869.
35. See, for example, W. Ford, *Practical Treatise on Malting* (1862 edition); E.M. Sigsworth, 'Science and the Brewing Industry, 1850-1900', *Economic History Review*, 2nd ser. XVII (1964), 536-50.
36. A.D. Bayne, *A Comprehensive History of Norwich* (1869 edition), p.616; Steward, Patteson, Finch & Co. Barley Book, 1865-1942, BR1/118, N.R.O. and cf. data in Appendix D, Table 2.
37. *Norfolk Chronicle*, 3 August 1878 (a similar advertisement appears in *East Anglian Handbook*, e.g. 1872); Anon., 'A Few Facts, Figures and Photos Relating to Pockthorpe Brewery, 1885-1945' (c.1945), presented to Charles Hugh Finch in commemoration of sixty years' service, John W. Stokes collection.
38. Steward, Patteson, Finch & Co. Wage Book, 1879-1916, BR1/134, N.R.O. Information on the company's houses in 1895 is contained in the Trust Deed, 30 July 1895, BR1/146, N.R.O.
39. G.B. Wilson, op. cit. pp.331-2.
40. Lucy Caroe, 'Urban Change in East Anglia in the Nineteenth Century', Cambridge University Ph.D. Thesis, 1965, pp.165-9. The population of Norfolk, 443,000 in 1851, increased to 445,000 in 1871 and 487,000 in 1881.

41. P.P.1856, LV; 1877, LXXVI. There are difficulties in using the local excise returns to establish the share of common brewers in total malt consumption. In the 1850's this appears to have been fairly static at c.80% but it drops sharply from 77% in 1859-60 to 28% in the following year (this is probably an error of transposition - the true figure may be 71%). After averaging c.30% 1860-6 the common brewers' share rises suddenly again to 59% in 1866-7, averaging c.60% until another sharp rise to 98% in 1871-2. Unexplained variations such as this raise doubts about the reliability of the series as a guide to the relative importance of brewers, licensed victuallers, and 'on' and 'off' retailers.
42. There is no direct evidence for the date of the Youngs and Crawshay amalgamation, but the firms were shown separately in the Poor Rate Book in Midsummer 1850, then appear as merged in *Mason's Norwich General and Commercial Directory and Handbook* (April 1852). For Weston's sale, see Mackie, op. cit. II, 137.
43. Steward & Patteson Trust Deed, 30 July 1895, BR1/146, N.R.O. One house was held on lease.
44. Ibid.
45. Steward, Patteson, Finch & Co., sale agreement with Bell's executors, 28 June 1865, BR14/12; documents relating to purchase of Bircham's Brewery, Reepham (title deeds, lots for auction, 8 June 1878), etc., BR15/1, N.R.O. See also auction notice in *Norfolk Chronicle*, 8 June 1878, which refers to '50 public houses' (49 have been traced in BR15/1). The purchase price appears in a solicitor's letter of 2 November 1878, BR15/1, N.R.O.
46. Mortgage Deeds and Reconveyances in BR11/3, 5, 7, etc. N.R.O. Note Henry Staniforth Patteson & Donald Steward (for the company) to Charles Morse and another, 27 November 1878, in BR11/7, N.R.O.

CHAPTER FOUR

1. Charles Morse, probate, 28 May 1883; Aldous, *Family Notebook*, op. cit. pp.85, 234. Whatever the nature of Charles II's illness, it did not prevent him from living to old age. Born in 1855, he died in 1924.
2. Bignold, *Five Generations*, op. cit. pp.xvii, 258.
3. Aldous, op. cit. pp.87-94, 231-41.
4. Lucy Steward, probate, 23 May 1877; Walter Steward, probate, 5 June 1869.
5. Charles Steward, probate, 30 July 1870, and Steward Pedigree, Appendix B.
6. Dame Anne Palmer Travers, probate, 28 November 1864.
7. Peter Finch, probate, 21 July 1882; *Norwich Evening Mercury*, 10 November 1919. His elder brother, Peter Steward Finch, born in 1865, died in 1910: probate, 17 November 1910.
8. Anne Elizabeth Patteson, probate, 19 January 1874, and Revd William Frederick Patteson, probate, 21 April 1882.
9. Steward & Patteson Partnership Deeds, Indenture, 25 October 1883, BR11/8, N.R.O.
10. Ibid. and 'A Few Facts, Figures and Photos Relating to Pockthorpe Brewery', op. cit.
11. Maj.-Gen. James F.E. Travers died in 1892, and his shares passed to his executors, F.S. Travers and the Revd Duncan Travers: probate, 21 April 1892.
12. H.T.S. Patteson, probate, 28 October 1915; Annie Patteson, daughter of E.J. Chambers of Eastwood Lodge, probate, 13 August 1904; John D. Patteson, probate, 29 December 1914; *Norfolk Chronicle*, 4 June and 5 November 1915. See also Patteson Pedigree, Appendix A.

13. C.F. Finch, probate, 14 June 1954; Peter Charles Finch, probate, 25 April 1979; *Eastern Daily Press*, 19 March 1954, 7 October 1935, 31 December 1952; Aldous, op. cit. p.79; information from Norwich Union (S.J. Thurston).
14. Data from G.B. Wilson, *Alcohol*, op. cit. pp.332-3, 364-70, summarised in K.H. Hawkins and C.L. Pass, *The Brewing Industry* (1979), p.17. See also T.R. Gourvish and R.G. Wilson, 'Profitability in the Brewing Industry, 1885-1914', *Business History*, XXVII (July 1985), 148, which gives consumption per head for the 15-64 age group.
15. Hawkins and Pass, op. cit. p.30; Steward & Patteson Brewing Materials Account, 1887-1962, BR1/110, N.R.O.; Table 16, below; *Country Brewers' Gazette*, 5 and 19 December 1883.
16. Wage and salary data from Steward & Patteson Account Books: Expenses and Charges on Trade, 1884-1957, BR1/107; earnings and numbers employed from Steward, Patteson, Finch & Co. Wage Book, 1879-1916, BR1/134, N.R.O.
17. Steward & Patteson Account Books: Quarterly Balances, 1886-1908, BR1/104, N.R.O.
18. Ibid.
19. Ibid.; R.G. Wilson, *Greene King*, op. cit. p.278.
20. Steward & Patteson Brewing Materials Account, 1887-1962, BR1/110, N.R.O. Data on gravities, expressed in brewers' pounds, were converted to specific gravities (divide by 0.36, add 1000).
21. G.B. Wilson, op. cit. p.58.
22. Steward & Patteson Account Books: Expenses and Charges on Trade, 1884-1957, BR1/107, N.R.O.
23. Steward & Patteson Account Books, BR1/104, 107, 110, N.R.O.
24. Ibid.
25. *Eastern Daily Press*, 7 October 1935; 'A Few Facts', op. cit.
26. Steward & Patteson Account Books, BR1/104, N.R.O. The company had bought Ferrier's Brewery in Yarmouth in 1884: *Norfolk Chronicle*, 25 October 1884.
27. Swaffham Brewery deeds, mortgages, etc., 1809-95, BR16/1, 3, 44 and 45, N.R.O. and Morse Pedigree, Appendix C. After Thomas Morse the Swaffham Brewery was managed by John Morse (1787-1830) and then by his son Arthur Morse (who died in 1856). Frederick was a cousin. The numerous transactions include the participation of London brewers, including John and Edward Courage, as mortgagees and trustees in the 1840's and 1850's.
28. Public house data from Norwich Rate Books, and information on Morgans and Bullard's from the company prospectuses, 14 March 1887 and 30 March 1895.

CHAPTER FIVE

1. Report and Valuation of Collins, Tootell & Co., 3 July 1895, BR1/147, N.R.O.
2. Revd C.J. Steward, probate, 5 February 1910, J.F.E. Travers, probate, 21 April 1892. It is not clear whether the adjustments concerning the Travers family were made in or prior to 1895.
3. Steward & Patteson Board Minutes, 4 and 16 July 1895, BR1/45; Debenture Stock Ledger, BR1/78, N.R.O.
4. Steward & Patteson E.G.M., 23 June 1898, BR1/82, N.R.O.
5. Steward & Patteson A.G.M., 28 January 1904, BR1/82; Register of Directors or Managers, 1918-1957, BR1/62; Reports & Accounts, 1949-51, BR1/100; Reports & Accounts, 1950-62, BR1/55, N.R.O.; *Eastern Daily Press*, 15 September 1948, 1 August 1955, 5 May 1959. In addition to his 400 shares, Morse held 308 shares jointly with Alfred Finch, Walter Long, and Arthur Robinson: Steward & Patteson Share Ledger, 1895-1920, BR1/71, N.R.O.

6. Ibid.; Steward & Patteson A.G.M., 2 February 1905, BR1/82, N.R.O.; *Eastern Daily Press*, 17 May 1943.
7. G.B. Wilson, *Alcohol,* op. cit. pp.48-9, 369-70.
8. Ibid. pp.107-13, and see Licensing Act, 1904, 4 Edw.VII c.23, and Act of 1910, 10 Edw.VII and 1 Geo.V c.24.
9. G.B. Wilson, op. cit. p.113.
10. Ibid. p.321; Finance (1909-10) Act, 1910, 10 Edw.VII c.8.
11. The growth rate of 2.3% p.a. was derived by regression analysis ($r^2 = 0.85$); the growth rate for sales was 2.79% ($r^2 = 0.92$).
12. Steward & Patteson Account Books, BR1/104, 101, N.R.O.
13. Table 21 above and Steward & Patteson Wage Book, 1879-1916, BR1/134, N.R.O.
14. Steward & Patteson Board Minutes, 19 January 1897, 23 June 1914, BR1/45, 48, N.R.O.
15. Steward & Patteson Estates Book, 1903-17, BR1/153; Steward & Patteson Norwich Public House Register, 1894-1947, BR1/157, N.R.O. The exceptions were the 'Lamb', Eaton (175 barrels p.a. 1906-8), and the 'Bird-in-Hand', Pockthorpe (149 p.a. 1906-8), both closed in 1909. Data on compensation from Public House Register, 1895-1915, BR1/148, N.R.O.
16. Agency losses: Swaffham £5,964, 1896-1914 [£314 p.a.]; King's Lynn £1,575, 1896-1914 [£93 p.a.]. Steward & Patteson Account Books, BR1/104, BR1/101, N.R.O.
17. Steward & Patteson Account Books, Quarterly Balances, BR1/104, 101, N.R.O. The references to Bass and Guinness can be found in Steward & Patteson Wine, Mineral Water, and Bottled Beer Accounts, 1902-21, BR1/124, and Account of Stock, Trade Alterations and Leaseholds, 1895-1945, BR1/129, N.R.O.
18. Steward & Patteson Norwich Public House Register, BR1/157, N.R.O.
19. Ibid.
20. Steward & Patteson Estates Book, 1903-17, BR1/153, N.R.O.
21. *Brewing Trade Review*, 1 August 1908. See also J. Brown, *Steeped in Tradition. The Malting Industry in England since the Railway Age* (Reading, 1983), pp.60-4. The brewery's technical changes were accompanied by relative instability in the brewing room. After the retirement of F.E. Doggett, Head Brewer, 1882-1902, there were three head brewers in post before 1914: H.W. Travers, 1902-5; G.D. Dahse, 1906-13; and W.B. Paterson, 1913-23. See 'A Few Facts ... Relating to Pockthorpe Brewery', presentation book to C.H. Finch.
22. See, for example, references to pensions in Steward & Patteson Pensions Registers, 1895-1946, BR1/143-4, and to housing in Trust Deed, BR1/146, N.R.O.
23. Yarmouth Agency Offences or Punishment Book, 1901-16. My thanks to Mr J. Strickland for supplying this reference.
24. C.H. Finch's Notes on Public Houses, 1896-8, BR1/162, N.R.O. The source also reveals Finch's attention to horses and drays.
25. Steward & Patteson Board Minutes, 1895-1914, BR1/45-8; Account of Stock, Trade Alterations and Leaseholds, 1895-1945, BR1/129, N.R.O. Average Price based on 95 purchases.
26. See, *inter alia*, Gourvish and Wilson, 'Profitability', loc. cit. 146-65; D.M. Knox, 'The Development of the Tied House System in London', *Oxford Economic Papers*, X (1968), 66-83; K.H. Hawkins, *A History of Bass Charrington* (Oxford, 1978), 36-65, and J.E. Vaizey, 'The Brewing Industry', in P.L. Cook (ed.), *Effects of Mergers* (1958), pp.403-11.

CHAPTER SIX

1. For U.K. Production (standard gravity barrels) see G.B. Wilson, *Alcohol,* op. cit. p.370.
2. Ibid. p.58.
3. U.K. hopping rate was c.1.5 lb. per bulk barrel (any gravity): ibid. p.71. Of today's premium bitter beers, Young's Special is 1046⁰ and Greene King's Abbot Ale is 1048⁰. Cf. CAMRA, *Good Beer Guide 1985* (St Albans, 1985), pp.43, 54.
4. Steward & Patteson E.G.M. Minutes, 31 July and 22 September 1919, BR1/48, N.R.O.
5. Transfers to reserves included £100,000 to General Reserve, £30,000 to Property Reserve, and £20,000 to Property Improvement Account, 1919-29: Steward & Patteson Profit & Loss Account Summary, 1895-1939, BR1/103, N.R.O.
6. Unit income in Steward & Patteson Account Books, Quarterly Balances, 1909-38, BR1/101, N.R.O., deflated by retail price index in C.F. Feinstein, *National Income, Expenditure and Output of the United Kingdom, 1855-1965* (Cambridge, 1972), T140.
7. See M.E. Rose, 'The Success of Social Reform? The Central Control Board (Liquor Traffic), 1915-1921', in M.R.D. Foot (ed.), *War and Society* (1973), pp.71-84, K.H. Hawkins, *Bass Charrington*, op. cit. pp.70-1, G.B.Wilson, op. cit. p.175, and G.P. Williams and G.T. Brake, *Drink in Great Britain 1900 to 1979* (1980), pp.106-12.
8. Hawkins, op. cit. pp.77-9, 85-6; G.B. Wilson, op. cit. pp.370; The Brewers' Society, *U.K. Statistical Handbook 1980*, pp.7, 88.
9. *Report of Committee (Chairman: Lord Southborough) on Disinterested Management of Public Houses*, 1927, P.P.1927, X, Cmd.2862, and *Report of Royal Commission on Licensing (England & Wales)*, 1932, P.P.1931-2, XI, Cmd.3988. For a synopsis of the reports and the brewers' response see G.B. Wilson, *Greene King*, op. cit. pp.113-15, 177-8, Hawkins, pp.79-84, and R.G. Wilson, op. cit. pp.199-203.
10. Steward & Patteson Board Minutes, 29 October 1917, 3 July 1922, 9 March 1925, BR1/48-9, N.R.O.; R.G. Wilson, op. cit. p.136. Deeds for six Dereham pubs are contained in BR18/1-5, N.R.O.
11. Public House summary table, in Steward & Patteson Account Books, BR1/101, N.R.O.
12. Steward & Patteson Board Minutes, 8 August and 7 November 1927, BR1/49, N.R.O.
13. For the Bagge family see, *inter alia*, Rye, *Norfolk Families*, op. cit. pp.19-20, Clement Ingleby, *A Supplement to Blomefield's Norfolk* (London, 1929), pp.175-7, and family tree, and Bagge family press cuttings, in Bradfer-Lawrence Collection, Bagge family IIId, N.R.O.
14. *Lynn News and County Press*, 26 February 1929, *Eastern Daily Press*, 10 August 1933. Another Lynn brewery, Hogge and Seppings, had been bought by Bullard's of Norwich in 1928.
15. Bagge Brewery Ledger Books, 1920-9, Bradfer-Lawrence coll. Bagge family XIIe, N.R.O. H.L. Bradfer-Lawrence was a land agent who also took an interest in breweries. As managing director of Hammond's Bradford Brewery from 1935 he revived the company's fortunes, principally by a policy of acquisition. See Hawkins, op. cit. pp.99-100.
16. Steward & Patteson Public House Register, 1916-32, BR1/149, N.R.O.
17. Cf. the tied estate of other breweries: Greene King, 482 (May 1929); Mitchells & Butlers, c.1,300 (early 1920's). R.G. Wilson, op. cit. p.270, Hawkins, op. cit. p.83.
18. Steward & Patteson Board Minutes, 26 August, 9 September and 12 October 1929, BR1/49; Balance Sheets, November 1928-9, in Annual Summaries of Share Capital, lists of directors, 1927-9, BR1/76, N.R.O.

19. Bullard's bought Elijah Eyre, and Bidwell's of Thetford, in 1924, and Hogge & Seppings (Wormegay), already mentioned, in 1928. Steward & Patteson also acquired Smith & Carman's brewery in 1927: Board Minutes, 19 April 1927, BR1/49, N.R.O.
20. Steward & Patteson Board Minutes, 26 October 1925, BR1/49, N.R.O. For the piecemeal improvement policy of Greene King see R.G. Wilson, op. cit. pp.195-6.
21. Steward & Patteson Board Minutes, 13 February 1928, BR1/49, N.R.O. and 'A Few Facts ... Relating to Pockthorpe Brewery', presentation book to C.H. Finch.
22. Hawkins, op. cit. p.83.
23. R.G. Wilson, op. cit. pp.201-2. Barrelage estimated very roughly from barrels sold (81,427 in year to 31 May 1929) and number of tied houses (482): ibid. pp.270, 273.
24. B. Oliver, *The Renaissance of the English Public House* (1947), cit. in R.G. Wilson, op. cit. pp.201, 319.
25. Steward & Patteson Accounts of Stock, Trade Alterations and Leaseholds, 1895-1945, BR1/129, N.R.O.
26. 'A Few Facts, ...', op. cit.; File of correspondence, 1931, John W. Stokes Collection.
27. At standard (1055^{0}) gravity, production fell from 19.6 to 15.7 million barrels. See G.B. Wilson, op. cit. p.370, and *U.K. Statistical Handbook 1980*, p.7 (data for year to 31 March, taken as calendar year of previous year).
28. *Statistical Handbook*, ibid. p.54.
29. Ibid. pp.7, 54.
30. Ibid. p.64.
31. Cf. Hawkins and Pass, *Brewing Industry*, op. cit. pp.50-1.
32. Steward & Patteson Register of Debenture Stock Transfers, 1895-1946, BR1/80; 'Strictly Confidential' statement of Steward & Patteson's position, 31 January 1936, in Auditors' statement and correspondence on company becoming public, 1936, BR1/66, N.R.O.
33. Steward & Patteson Account Books, BR1/101, N.R.O.
34. Steward & Patteson Board Minutes, 14 September 1931, 1 May 1933, BR1/50, N.R.O.
35. Steward & Patteson Account Books, BR1/101, N.R.O.
36. Steward & Patteson Board Minutes, 25 April 1932, 2 July 1934, BR1/50; Account Books, BR1/107, N.R.O.
37. Steward & Patteson Board Minutes, 11 July 1932, 8 April, 23 September and 28 October 1935, BR1/50; 'Estate Book' [Deliveries to Public Houses], 1930-40, BR1/154; Register of Norwich Public Houses, 1894-1947, BR1/157, N.R.O.
38. Steward & Patteson Board Minutes, 7 April 1931, 22 August 1932, 12 and 26 November 1934, 6 August 1935, BR1/50, supplemented by details in BR1/154, N.R.O.
39. Steward & Patteson Board Minutes, 25 July 1932, 2 December 1935; 24 November 1931, 21 October 1935, BR1/50, N.R.O.
40. Note the references to Managed houses from 1929, e.g. under 'stocks in hand', in Steward & Patteson Profit & Loss Account Summary, 1895-1939, BR1/103, N.R.O. The 'Morrison Arms', Norwich, opened on 18 October 1935, was managed for a year prior to finding a tenant: Norwich Register, BR1/157, N.R.O.
41. Steward & Patteson Accounts of Stock, etc., BR1/129, N.R.O. In 1930-6 over £40,000 was added to the £50,000 transferred to Property and Property Improvement Accounts by 1929.
42. Steward & Patteson Estate Book, BR1/154, N.R.O.
43. Ibid.
44. Steward & Patteson Board Minutes, 4 August 1931, BR1/50, and Account Books, BR1/101, N.R.O.

45. Steward & Patteson Board Minutes, 31 July 1933, 20 January 1934, BR1/50, N.R.O.; *Brewing Trade Review*, 1 January 1934.
46. Ibid. 16 November 1931, 16 October 1933.
47. Ibid. 26 August 1935.
48. Ibid. 25 July and 28 December 1932, 5 November 1934, 23 September 1935. The company also bought a bottle washing machine for the mineral water factory: ibid. 4 March 1935.
49. Steward & Patteson Share Ledger, 1895-1920, BR1/71, and Annual Summary of Share Capital and Lists of Directors and Shareholders, 1908-36, BR1/74-7, N.R.O. Company shares were priced by Collins, Tootell & Co., brewery valuers and accountants, the company's auditors. There is a suggestion in the correspondence with the company for 1896-1917 that the shares were being underpriced, for example when shares were transferred on H.T.S. Patteson's death in 1915. See Collins, Tootell-G.H. Morse, 24 January 1916, and W.C. Friend-G.H. Morse, 27 January 1917, BR1/83, N.R.O.
50. Annual Summary, etc. February 1920, BR1/75, N.R.O.
51. Ibid. February 1914, February 1936, BR1/74, 77, N.R.O. The calculations are as follows. 1914: 33.2% + 18.5% + 18.0% + 12.1% in Table 33 = 81.8%, plus the small individual holdings of C.H. and A. Finch, 3.8%. 1936: 14.1% + 9.7% + 8.1% + 5.8% + 6.9% in Table 33 = 44.6%, plus half of R.W. Patteson estate (A. Finch and others), 4.1%, A.F. Morse's individual holding, 3.8%, and other jointly-held shares, 7.5%.
52. *Eastern Daily Press*, 2 April 1931, and see also Aldous, *Family Notebook*, op. cit. pp.231-41.
53. Steward & Patteson Salaries Account Book, 1919-45, BR1/141, N.R.O.; *Eastern Daily Press*, 3 September 1926; Steward & Patteson Annual Summary, 1926-9, BR1/76, N.R.O.; Robert Wace Patteson, probate, 9 November 1926.
54. Steward & Patteson Board Minutes, 31 January 1927, 27 April and 27 July 1936, BR1/49-50, N.R.O.; *Norfolk Chronicle*, 3 August 1917; Aldous, op. cit. p.93. Geoffrey Morse married Cynthia Zoe Westcott (born 1900) of London in 1920 (one daughter). The marriage was dissolved in 1937, whereupon Geoffrey married Mary Evelyn Orr (born 1900) of Newry, N. Ireland. See Morse Pedigree, Appendix C.
55. Steward & Patteson Board Minutes, 6 February 1933, 30 November 1936, BR1/50, Salaries Book, BR1/141, N.R.O.; *Eastern Daily Press*, 6 May 1981; Rupert Donald Steward, probate, 1 December 1933.
56. Steward & Patteson Board Minutes, 30 November 1936, BR1/50, Salaries Book, BR1/141, N.R.O.; *Eastern Daily Press*, 21 April 1969.
57. Steward & Patteson Board Minutes, 18 January 1932, BR1/50, N.R.O.
58. Letter to Brewing Department, 7 October 1932, in C.H. Finch's Director's Notebook, 1932-3, BR1/172, N.R.O.
59. C.H. Finch, note, 17 October 1932, ibid.
6O. Steward & Patteson Board Minutes, 11 July 1932, BR1/50, Salaries Book, BR1/141, N.R.O.
61. C.H. Finch, note, 7 March 1933, Notebook, BR1/172, N.R.O.
62. B.G.C. Wetherall-C.H. Finch, 3 April 1933, Wetherall-Steward & Patteson Directors, same date, Finch, note, 11 April 1933, ibid.; Steward & Patteson Board Minutes, 8 and 15 May 1933, BR1/50, N.R.O. W.B. Paterson was Head Brewer, 1913-23. F.C. Hipwell, a pupil of Green's Brewery, Luton, was bottling manager, 1926-33, and Head Brewer, 1933-50. He joined the Board on 3 July 1950, at the age of 71. He retired on 27 June 1953. *Brewing Trade Review*, May 1969; Register of Directors or Managers, 1918-57, BR1/62, N.R.O.
63. Steward & Patteson Board Minutes, 4 May 1925, BR1/49, N.R.O.
64. Steward & Patteson Salaries Book, BR1/141; Board Minutes, 30 December 1918, 24

June 1946, 21 June 1950, BR1/48, 52, N.R.O.
65. 'A Few Facts ...', op. cit.
66. Cf. draft letters of reinstatement, May 1926, of Steward & Patteson and Bullard & Sons, J.W. Stokes collection. There is no reference to the General Strike in the Board Minutes.
67. Steward & Patteson Board Minutes, 4 July 1927, 2 April 1928, BR1/49 N.R.O.
68. Ibid. 4 May and 27 July 1931, BR1/50, N.R.O.
69. Ibid. 30 May 1932, 22 May and 3 July 1933, 25 March 1935, 4 July 1938, BR1/50-1, N.R.O.; Steward & Patteson Sick Pay for Workmen: Rules, 7 May 1909, J.W. Stokes collection; recollections of Hilda Hardingham, 11 April 1977, Stanley Thompson, 2 April 1977, and L.H. Moy, no date, J.W. Stokes collection.

CHAPTER SEVEN

1. C.H. Finch, 'strictly confidential' typescript, with Finch-W.W. Collins, 31 January 1936, BR1/66, N.R.O.
2. *Investors' Chronicle*, 4 April 1936, *Brewing Trade Review*, 1 May 1936.
3. Cf. Hawkins, *Bass Charrington*, op. cit. p.97, R.G. Wilson, *Greene King*, op. cit. p.207. Data from *Brewers' Almanack*, 1964, p.48 (Year to 31 March here counted as calendar year of previous year).
4. Hawkins, op. cit. pp.97-8.
5. The duty was actually raised in November 1947 and April 1948. Brewers' Society, *U.K. Statistical Handbook* (1980), p.54.
6. Steward & Patteson Board Minutes, 4 September 1939, BR1/51, N.R.O.
7. Brewers' Society, *Annual Reports*, 1940-4; R.J. Hammond, *Food*. Vol.III (1962), pp.576-7 (official war history).
8. Brewers' Society, *Annual Reports*, 1940-2; Steward & Patteson Board Minutes, 2 February 1942, BR1/51, N.R.O.
9. Brewers' Society, *Annual Reports*, 1940, 1943-4; Hawkins, op. cit. p.98. The government was sensitive to the brewing lobby. In 1943, for instance, the malt price was fixed at a level 21 per cent lower than the 1942 price, and when the 15 per cent cut in gravity was ordered in 1942, an exception was made of brewers already producing below 1030^{0}.
10. Steward & Patteson Annual Reports and Accounts, 1937-45, Guildhall Library, London; Steward & Patteson Account Books, BR1/102, N.R.O.
11. Company Reports and Accounts, Guildhall Library, London.
12. Steward & Patteson Board Minutes, 4 May, 8 June, 6 July, 4 August 1942, 17 May and 7 June 1943; 'Summary of War Damage to Licensed Houses As At 1.8.1943', Minutes, 16 August 1943, BR1/51; Statement of 'Licenced Premises damaged by Enemy Action. 30 April 1945', BR1/164, N.R.O.
13. Ibid. 21 June 1943.
14. Ibid. 1 February 1943.
15. Steward & Patteson Account Books, BR1/101, 102, N.R.O.
16. Ibid. The general price level increased by only 26 per cent, 1939-43: Feinstein, op. cit. T19-20.
17. Steward & Patteson Account Books, BR1/111, 117, N.R.O.
18. Steward & Patteson Annual Reports and Accounts, 1938-45, cit.
19. Brewers' Society, *Annual Reports*, 1946-51.
20. Brewers' Society, *U.K. Statistical Handbook* (1980), p.7, *Brewers' Almanack*, 1964, p.48.
21. Steward & Patteson Board Minutes, 15 April 1940, 20 and 27 January 1947, BR1/51, 52, N.R.O. The Ipswich 'agency' was retained as an organisational arm of the company.

22. Soames & Company Board Minutes, 10 February 1949, and see also 18 November 1948, 30 March 1949, BR1/36, N.R.O.
23. Steward & Patteson Annual Report and Accounts, 1949, and Chairman's statement, 27 January 1950, Guildhall Library, London; Steward & Patteson Annual Reports and Accounts, 1950 et seq., BR1/55, and Soames & Co. Annual Reports and Accounts, 1950-4, BR1/37, N.R.O.
24. *Lynn News and Advertiser*, 30 August 1949. Steward & Patteson sales were c.16,500 barrels p.a. higher than Bullard, 1950-5: Appendix D, Table 5 and Edward Moore & Sons (Chartered Accountants), 'Report to Bullard directors for year ended 30 September 1955', 25 November 1955, Correspondence files of Sir Edward Bullard (Director, 1951-68), BR138/2, N.R.O.
25. 12,996 barrels were supplied to Soames in 1953-5. An inventory in November 1955 revealed 224 freehold and 17 leasehold pubs and 6 off-licences: 'Steward & Patteson Ltd. Norwich. Licensed Houses - 6th November 1955', J.W. Stokes collection.
26. In 1936 95,949 barrels were brewed and the number of tied houses was 643. Assuming no free trade, this amounts to 2.87 barrels a week per pub. Data from pp.105, 115, 179.
27. Steward & Patteson Account Books, BR1/102; Green & Wright Reports and Accounts, 1955-65, BR1/57, N.R.O.
28. Steward & Patteson Board Minutes, 5 November 1955, BR1/53; Green & Wright Reports and Accounts, 1957-62, BR1/57, N.R.O. Steward & Patteson acquired all the ordinary share capital (1,500 x £5) and 2,713 of the 3,000 £5 6% pref. shares for a price of £33 per ord. and £5.25 per pref. share.
29. Cider income also rose, from under £1,000 p.a. in 1937-9 to £4,500 p.a. in 1953-4. Steward & Patteson Account Books, BR1/102, N.R.O.
30. Dawson's Mineral Water Co. Board Minutes, 30 September 1949, 13 and 23 March, 18 April and 13 December 1950, and E.G.M. Minutes, 1 May 1950, BR1/26; Steward & Patteson Board Minutes, 8 December 1950, 29 January and 26 February 1951, BR1/52, N.R.O.
31. Dawson's Mineral Water Co. Reports and Accounts, 1952, 1955-6, BR1/32, N.R.O.
32. New basis data: gross revenue £627,914 (1939), £995,144 (1946-9), costs £527,159 (1939), £935,196 (1946-9), in 1939 values. Old basis data: gross revenue £559,272 (1937-9), £726,788 (1953-5), costs £459,709 (1937-9), £672,247 (1953-5), in 1937-9 values. Data from Table 40, deflated by Feinstein's index of retail prices, op. cit. T140-1.
33. New basis data: labour costs £61,259 (1939), £113,985 (1946-9) or £70,076 in 1939 values. Old basis data: £48,403 (1937-9), £141,989 (1953-5), or £61,154 in 1937-9 values. Calculated from Steward & Patteson Account Books, BR1/101, 102, 107, N.R.O.
34. Steward & Patteson Estate Book (Norwich), BR1/158, N.R.O.
35. Steward & Patteson Estate Book (Norwich, Norfolk and Ipswich areas), BR1/156, N.R.O.
36. Steward & Patteson Account Book (inserted typescripts), BR1/102; Steward & Patteson Board Minutes, 8 November 1937, 13 February 1956, BR1/51, 53, N.R.O.
37. Steward & Patteson Board Minutes, 14 March and 9 May 1938, 5 January 1948, 17 January 1955 (malting); 2 January 1956 (mineral water machinery); 8 August 1938 (garage), BR1/51-3, N.R.O.; Steward & Patteson Annual Reports and Accounts, 1949, 1950, Chairman's statement, 27 January 1950 and 9 January 1951 (refrigeration, bottling).
38. The company won second prizes for bottled nips and bottled stout in the Brewing Trade Review's 1937 competition: Steward & Patteson Board Minutes, 11 October 1937, BR1/51, N.R.O. The Royal Warrant to the Queen was secured in 1955: Steward &

Patteson Annual Report and Accounts, 1955, Chairman's statement, 5 January 1956, BR1/55, N.R.O.

39. Steward & Patteson Stock Book, 1954-64, account for 31 March 1954, BR1/24, N.R.O.

40. Steward & Patteson Shareholders' lists, 22 February 1939 and 28 February 1946, Companies' House, London. Other small institutional investors included Norwich Union, Guardian Assurance, British Linen Bank, Pearl Assurance, National Provident Trust, and Bishopgate Nominees.

41. Ibid. 28 February 1957. Both nominee companies were based at 41, Lothbury, and were subsidiaries of Westminster Bank. The allotment to Soames shareholders in 1949 can also be found in the Companies' House files, but the details, recorded at a special meeting held at Spalding on 25 August 1949, are reproduced in the Steward & Patteson Board Minutes, 1949, BR1/52, N.R.O.

42. Steward & Patteson Board Minutes, 31 December 1945, 17 December 1951, 22 December 1952, 17 December 1956, BR1/52, 53, N.R.O.; *Eastern Daily Press*, 19 March 1954, 5 May 1959.

43. *Eastern Daily Press*, 30 March 1967, 6 May 1981.

44. *Eastern Evening News*, 12 March 1971; Sir C.J. Morse, 'Francis John Morse 1897-1971', typescript.

45. The Mineral Waters Manager was S.F. Baker, and the agents were H.A. Chesson (who had succeeded A.E. Massingham at King's Lynn in 1948) and H. Sayers (appointed in 1936) at Yarmouth. The assistant brewers were John Broad and John Strickland. Steward & Patteson Reports and Accounts, 1947-8, Chairman's statements, January 1948 and 17 January 1949, Guildhall Library; Steward & Patteson Board Minutes, 24 June 1946, 28 April 1947, 26 June 1950, 1 July 1957, BR1/52, 53; Register of Directors and Managers, BR1/62; Salary Books, BR1/137-40, N.R.O.; *Eastern Daily Press*, 30 March 1967.

46. At Morgans W.G. de Jonge, company secretary, and J.G. Swift, partner in Halsey Lightly and Helmsley, the company's solicitors, were appointed as directors. Morgans Reports and Accounts, 1949, Guildhall Library, and *Eastern Daily Press*, 31 October 1949. The information on Bullard comes from Bullard & Sons Board Minutes, 29 November 1946, 10 November 1950, and printed Report and Accounts, 1953, BR1/7, N.R.O., and *Eastern Daily Press*, 25 November 1946, 8 November 1950. Gerald H. Bullard, who trained at the College of Brewing, Birmingham and the Huntingdon Breweries, became chairman in 1952.

47. See the companies' reports and accounts for 1941, Guildhall Library.

48. Hipwell's connection with Phipps owed its origin to Hipwell & Co. of Olney, acquired by Phipps in 1920. Steward & Patteson Board Minutes, 21 June 1950, 29 June 1953, BR1/52, 53, N.R.O.

49. Riviere quickly established a reputation as a poet. See M. Riviere, *Notes on the Huguenot Family of Riviere in England* (1965); *Burke's Landed Gentry*, I (1965), entries for Morse and Riviere; Steward and Patteson Board Minutes, 26 February 1951, 13 December 1954, BR1/52, 53; Steward & Patteson Report and Accounts, 1960, BR1/55, N.R.O.; M.V.B. Riviere, 'Practical Application of Resteeping in a Pneumatic Drum Malting', *Journal of the Institute of Brewing*, LXVII (1961), 55-7.

50. P.E. Hart, M.A. Utton and G. Walshe, *Mergers and Concentration in British Industry* (Cambridge, 1973), pp.58-62.

51. Steward & Patteson Board Minutes, 28 January 1957, 11 June 1958, BR1/53, N.R.O.

52. Cf. CAMRA, *Good Beer Guide 1978* (St Albans, 1978), p.193 and Gerald Crompton, 'The Making of a Beer Desert', in Nigel Thompson (ed.), *Real Beer in Norfolk* (1980).

53. Vaizey, 'The Brewing Industry', in Cook, *Mergers*, op. cit. pp.410-11.
54. Typescript table of barrelages in E.A.B. pubs, 1954-6, inserted in Steward & Patteson Estate Book, BR1/156, N.R.O. The 'Cobden' in Peterborough sold 512 barrels in 1955, 522 in 1956, the 'White Hart' in Newark 396 and 452.
55. R.G. Wilson, *Greene King*, op. cit. pp.223-4, 228-30.
56. Steward & Patteson share allotment, 13 September 1957, Companies' House. A further £1 was subsequently added to ordinary paid-up capital, making £1,152,360 in all. Col. Cutlack (born 1881) had joined his father's Littleport brewery in 1904. Goodliff was younger (he was born in 1899). See Steward & Patteson Board Minutes, 25 June, 2 August and 23 September 1957, BR1/53, N.R.O.; *Brewing Trade Review*, August 1957, p.547; *Wisbech Standard*, 2 August 1957; *Cambridgeshire Times*, 16 August 1957.
57. Barrelages, BR1/156, N.R.O. Note: it is not clear whether bottled beer is included in the annual totals for each public house.
58. Steward & Patteson Agenda Book 1959-65, entries for 21 January, 25 February and 13 July 1960, BR1/59; East Anglian Breweries (from 1961 Steward & Patteson (Ely)) Reports and Accounts, 1957-62, BR1/56, N.R.O.
59. Steward & Patteson Agenda Book, 19 December 1960; Deed of agreement between Baring Bros., Bullard's and Steward & Patteson, 15 February 1961, BR1/176; W.B.J. Crawshay-Sir Edward Bullard, 26 May 1961, BR138/8; Steward & Patteson Annual Reports and Accounts, 1960-1, Chairman's statement, 18 January 1961, 17 January 1962, BR1/55, N.R.O.; *Eastern Daily Press*, 17 December 1960, 1 November 1974; *Eastern Evening News*, 21 December 1960.
60. Deed of agreement between Steward & Patteson, Bullard and Watney Mann, 8 March 1961, BR1/176; W.B.J. Crawshay, Reports on 'Advertising and Watney's Trade', 24 May 1962 and 'Advertising', July 1962, BR138/9, N.R.O.; *Eastern Evening News*, 10 March 1961. Watney Mann also aquired Morgan's subsidiary, Coca Cola Eastern Bottlers Ltd.
61. Steward & Patteson Agenda Book, 26 July 1961, 26 February and 11 July 1962, BR1/59; 'First Report of Joint Committee of Steward & Patteson and Bullard on Survey of their Uneconomic Public Houses', 12 June 1962, BR138/9, N.R.O.
62. Steward & Patteson Agenda Book, 12 October 1960, BR1/59; Steward & Patteson Annual Report and Accounts, 1960, BR1/55, N.R.O.
63 Steward & Patteson Stock Book, 31 March 1957, 30 September 1961, 31 March 1962, BR1/24, N.R.O.
64. London Stock Exchange Daily List, 1963, Guildhall Library.
65. Gordon H. Gunson-F. John Morse, 13 August 1963, enclosing 'Relative Values for B. and S.', BR138/10, N.R.O.
66. Gunson-Morse, 7 October 1963, in ibid.; Stock Exchange Daily List, 1963, cit.
67. *Investors' Guardian*, 8 November 1963; Conveyance, 21 February 1967, J.W. Stokes Collection.
68. C.J. Morse, op. cit. pp.11-12; Betty [Mrs B. Thomson]-Teddy [Sir Edward Bullard], 11 November 1963, BR138/10, N.R.O.
69. Brewers' Society, *U.K. Statistical Handbook* (1980), p.7. Two new directors joined the board in 1963, shortly before the merger with Watney Mann was completed. Anthony Morse, son of Sydney Morse and educated at Clifton and Trinity College, Oxford, was appointed on 5 August 1963. He took an interest in retailing and public house management but scarcely had time, by 1964, for much achievement. He is currently chairman of Everards brewery. A second director, B.E. Dillon, joined the Board in November 1963. Steward & Patteson Agenda Book, 22 July and 12 November 1963, BR1/59, N.R.O.
70. R.G. Wilson, op. cit. p.222ff.

71. Steward & Patteson Shareholders list, 6 March 1963 and 4 March 1964, Companies' House.
72. *Investors' Guardian*, 8 November 1963.
73. *Who Was Who*; Tom Corran and Christine Shaw, 'Simon Harvey Combe', in David J. Jeremy (ed.), *Dictionary of Business Biography*, I (1984), pp.759-63.
74. Property Rationalisation Committee Minutes, 9 June, 22 July and 29 October 1964, 27 January 1965, 2 February 1966, John W. Stokes Collection.
75. Watney Mann (East Anglia), List of Houses to be Transferred to Northampton, n.d., Stokes Collection; Watney Mann (East Anglia), Surveys of public houses in Norfolk, Suffolk and Cambridgeshire, May-June 1969, BR1/177, N.R.O.; *Brewing Trade Review*, February 1967.
76. Watney Mann (East Anglia), Management Accounts for the twelve months ended 28 September 1968, Stokes Collection; *Eastern Daily Press*, 4 August 1966, 29 March 1968, 1 November 1969; *Eastern Evening News*, 11 July 1968; *Norwich Mercury*, 7 November 1969; *Brewing Trade Review*, December 1969, July 1970.

Index